The Guinness Guide to
Coarse Fishing

Michael Prichard
and
Michael Shepley

GUINNESS SUPERLATIVES LIMITED
2 CECIL COURT, LONDON ROAD, ENFIELD, MIDDLESEX

Editor: Beatrice Frei

© Michael Prichard, Michael Shepley and Guinness Superlatives Ltd, 1982

ISBN : 0-85112-244-2

British Library Cataloguing in Publication Data
Prichard, Michael
The Guinness guide to coarse fishing
·1. Fishing
I. Title II. Shepley, Michael
799.1′2   SH439

Published by Guinness Superlatives Limited,
2 Cecil Court, London Road,
Enfield, Middlesex

Design and layout : Michael Prichard and Forth Design Associates

Typeset in 10 on 12pt Baskerville by Sprint, Beckenham, Kent
Printed and bound by Arnoldo Mondadori Company Limited, Toledo, Spain,
Colour origination by Colour Workshop

D.L. TO: 113-1982

Contents

Contents continued

Acknowledgements

Very few angling writers can succeed in their chosen profession without the help of many people. Young and old, the fishermen and women of Europe have given freely of their time, knowledge and assistance to both of us. We are particularly indebted to the Tourist organisations of Denmark, Scotland, Spain, Manitoba, Saskatchewan, Holland and Ireland for their advice and the way in which they smoothed the complicated journeyings of two avid anglers!

We gratefully acknowledge the help given by O. Mustad with illustrations on pages 12 and 55. Morris, Nicholson and Cartwright for pictures on pages 12 and 162. Hamish Campbell's photograph on page 20 and the colour picture on page 128 by Michael W. Richards of the Royal Society for the Protection of Birds. We are indebted to Rodney Coldron for his pictures on pages 26, 58, 64, 68, 69, 184 and 185, for Jens Ploug Hansen's photographs on pages 71 and 166 and to Bill Howes for pictures appearing on pages 31 and 134. We also thank Allen Edwards for the picture on page 167.

The photographs of Lelystad fish farm are published by courtesy of the Dutch organisation of Inland Fisheries. Our thanks are due to the British Record (rod-caught) Fish Committee of the National Anglers' Council for the British fish list and to the Scottish Coarse Fishing Federation for their record fish list.

Inevitably, travelling over such a vast geographical area involved us in complicated arrangements with both aircraft and sea ferries. We could not have covered the necessary ground without the assistance of Air Canada, Iberia, SAS, Sealink, B & I and DFDS seaways who carried us, our tackle and unmentionable bait.

Finally, we would like to thank Cathie Richardson and Debbie Prichard and our editor Beatrice Frei who retained their sense of humour whilst typing manuscripts that were always subject to doubtful timekeeping . . . the last cast always taking an hour or more!

Michael Prichard and Michael Shepley

Preface

You have to live with someone, they say, before you can really claim to know them. There is merit enough in the proposition but time shared in the comfort of homes, hotels and fishing lodges will only yield a certain sum of knowledge. It is time spent in the field which completes the picture and this applies particularly in angling circles. It has been my privilege to share many hours of fishing and subsequent conversation with both Michael Prichard and Michael Shepley. It is a fact that discussions, some might call them arguments, begun following a day's fishing on the Ansager river in Denmark, have been carried on in Scotland, Iceland and back and forwards across beautiful Ireland.

Angling talk is so often supported by untested theories. This, however, is not the case with the two Michaels whose knowledge is based upon experience. Michael Prichard, for example, has represented England many times in international sea fishing competitions. Michael Shepley has represented Scotland. Both are experts in the arts required for successful game fishing and both Michaels have garnered the experiences of others. It is rare for any discussion to reach the stage where there is full agreement and this certainly applies in angling. I think it to the benefit of angling that the two Mikes have collected their ideas up to form a distinct point of view. This has resulted in a volume covering subjects as diverse as fishery developments, tackle trends and competition fishing. Different species of fish have differing levels of intelligence which, at its simplest, means that some are rarely caught easily more than once. In the case of the carp this has meant more and more study on the part of specialist anglers into a constantly changing arsenal of baits. Mixes high in protein are part of this sporting research and are discussed by the authors. The angler's tackle plays a major part in this book. This reflects Michael Prichard's contribution to angling as a fishing tackle designer and his experiences derived from field testing of rods, reels and rigs.

No angler is complete without a deep love of nature and this is borne out by most of the superb illustrations, of which there are more than two hundred in this volume. To this is added the visual value of line drawings which illustrate knots, tackles and rigs in a manner which is easy to follow.

The last survey into angling showed that in Britain alone there are more than two million and twentyeight thousand participants. More significant, however, is the fact that of this vast army of anglers, fifty per cent are below the age of twentyfive. This represents a huge reservoir of enthusiasm but only a narrow channel of angling experience. *The Guinness Guide to Coarse Fishing* will prove to be an invaluable source of reference. Distilled, as it is, from the collective experience of the authors.

The book is also a complete entertainment.

Allen Edwards

Man . . . the angler

Alone with Nature and his sport

As old as time: this fossilised fish shows perfectly, in stone, the intricate structure of the bones and powerful tail.

Man is an instinctive hunter, and from the beginning of history has been engaged in catching fish. At what stage the necessity of capture for food evolved into angling for pleasure is difficult to assess, but today the sporting angler no doubt feels a similar sense of achievement . . . of competing against a completely wild fish, presenting a hook bait to the quarry in a natural manner, and fooling the particular species into taking his lure. It matters little that instead of knocking the fish over the head and taking the catch home to feed the family, the catch is more often returned to the water.

Sport fishing in European countries largely originates from techniques developed in the British Isles. Even in America, anglers merely copied methods evolved here, although much of the new material technology of the last decade has come from abroad, notably Germany, America and Japan.

Hook power

The development of the fish hook from the days of the caveman to present times, has with modern innovation become a sophisticated exercise, dealing with such things as corrosion, temper, colour, composition and shape. The Norwegian company of O. Mustad and Son must rate as one of the most famous manufac-

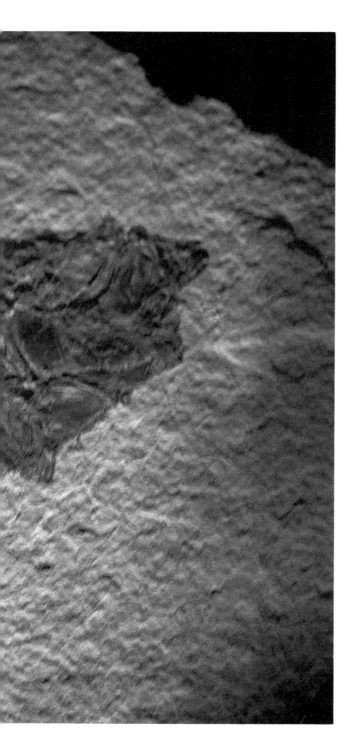

Catch . . . then release your fish.

But other materials are even more perishable, and there is no doubt that wood was also used extensively as a material for making hooks. Less than two hundred years ago, Lapp fishermen were still using wooden hooks made from tough juniper, and hawthorn with its pointed thorns has also been improvised to form a very efficient hooking device . . . in fact barbless hooks!

Nowadays, many anglers are reverting back to barbless hooks, and finding that this doesn't necessarily mean an increase in fish lost. Indeed, there would appear to be little difference, other than fish can be released much quicker, and suffer less potential damage and excessive handling than if they were hooked on barbed patterns. So impressed with the conservation aspects of barbless hooks have the Canadian Province of Manitoba become, that they have promoted a 'Go Barbless' scheme, complete with certificates and awards for conservation-minded anglers, who safely return their catch alive back to the water.

At Bohuslän in Sweden there are rock carvings dating from the Nordic Bronze Age, the earliest known pictorial art in Scandinavia — etchings depicting what life was like in those early days of civilisation. One such illustration shows two men fishing at anchor in a boat. One figure in the prow of the boat is using some kind of rod with line and hook attached, while the other, towards the stern, is either fishing with a hand line or shorter rod. Even if their fishing was necessary to provide food, it must have been one of the more pleasant occupations of this community even in those times. Methods were no doubt primitive, indeed coarse, but our use of the term coarse fishing today has a different connotation.

turers in the world. As angling interests developed, so the Mustad sales force journeyed across the world, searching for business and researching the multitude of fishing applications they found, with a keenness matched only by the hooks their labours produced. The Mustad factory in the little town of Gjøvik in Southern Norway is little more than a hundred years old, but hooks are known which date from the Stone Age. Almost all surviving examples are made of bone, and some are at least five thousand years old. Bone and horn deteriorate with age, and so we have few examples left, and practically all hooks from the Stone Age are to be found in museums.

Left: Dating from the late Stone Age, about 1800-1500 BC, this fish hook is carefully hewn from flint. Found at Rogaland in Norway, the hook measures 4.4 cm and has a broad top for attaching the fishing line.

Far left: 7.4 cm long, and strong enough for a fjord cod. This sturdy fish hook is made of bone and came from Skipshelleren Cave, Nordhordland in Norway. Like the flint hook, this too is from the Stone Age, and has an eye as well as a sharp, barbed point.

These iron fish hooks (left) date from the Viking Age around AD 800-1030, and were found together with other belongings and tools in the grave of their owner.

This eyed fish hook is made of bronze, and was found in a rich man's grave at Fagerheim, Sande in Vestfold, and is the oldest bronze fish hook found so far in Norway, dating from about AD 150; actual length is 8.4 cm.

Unbeaten for more than fifty years — the King of Fish — proudly displayed by its captor, Miss G W Ballantyne of Caputh. This magnificent salmon was hooked on the Lower Murthly Beat, River Tay.

One of the earliest metal hooks, made of bronze, was found in Norway at Fagerheim, Sande in Vestfold, and dates from about AD 150. Iron hooks from the Viking Age (AD 800-1030) have been found, and later eyed bronze hooks were found dating from the Middle Ages AD 1030-1536) on the site of an ancient market town adjacent to Lake Mjøsa. Bone continued to be used by the Lapps in the northern part of Norway, and examples more than fifteen hundred years old have been found.

We seemingly have to wait until a great deal later before much is written about the art of making fish hooks in English angling literature. As interest grew in fishing as a sport, rather than as a necessary means of catching food, so the flood gates opened nearly five hundred years ago.

Dame Julians Berners wrote *The Boke of St. Albans*, printed in Westminster in 1496. She was in all probability a prioress, and within that book, *The Treatyse of Fyshinge wyth an Angle*, deals in part with the making of hooks . . . darning needles for small fish, embroidery needles for larger fish, and tailor's or shoemaker's needles for the largest specimens . . . and tells how the angler can make the steel pliable, how to shape and temper it, and how to make the barb. There is evidence to suggest that the thesis dates from even earlier, but it is interesting how history has repeated itself down through the ages, and how often the fairer sex has shown male anglers the way. In 1922, Miss G W Ballantyne caught the British Record salmon of 64 lb within yards of her home at Caputh on the River Tay. Apart from the tunny record (851 lb), the heaviest saltwater claim was for a mako shark weighing 500 lb, also taken by a lady angler, Mrs J M Yallop, off the Eddystone Light in 1971. It's surprising, therefore, that the gentle art of coarse fishing hasn't produced more response from the lady anglers.

The classic among early angling books, of course, is Isaac Walton's *The Compleat Angler*, first published in 1653, and read ever since. On hooks his advice is not so practical as Dame Berners' who advocated making your own, but Walton recommended that one go to an experienced hookmaker. England's best of the day, according to Walton, lived in London, a Charles Kirby of Harp Alley, Shoe Lane . . . 'the most exact and best hook-maker this nation affords'.

The holiday angler

In those days, and for a long time to come, travel was an arduous business. However, with the Industrial Revolution and the building of the railways, even remote areas of the country became accessible, and as yet on a small scale, leisure time and travel slowly developed, and with them, the sport of angling and angling tourism.

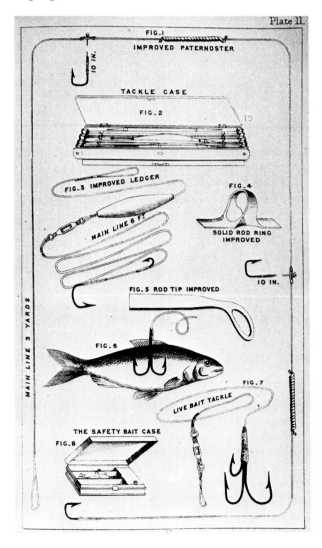

One of Walton's critics, a contemporary named Robert Franck, had little patience with the unpractical digressions of *The Compleat Angler*, complaining in his own tome *Northern Memoirs* that Walton 'stuffs his book with morals from Dubravius and others, not giving us one precedent of his own practical experiments'. Franck must have been one of the first angling tourists to chronicle his fishing journeys. The fishing tour which Franck describes actually took place during the 1650s. Following the publication of *Northern Memoirs*, some forty years later, a second, smaller edition of Franck's book, edited by Sir Walter Scott, was published in 1821.

It was more than a century after Franck's celebrated jaunt, before Colonel Thornton's epic piscatorial travels around 1780, which are recorded in an illustrated account published in 1804. Although sceptics have questioned some of his 'Walter Mitty' exploits, and fishery managers today would surely question some of his methods, he was undoubtedly a keen angler with some splendid fish to his credit. The colonel was accompanied on his tour by an artist. Since anglers neither had cameras, nor the facility of deep-freezing their specimens in those days, why should we doubt Reinagle's painting of Colonel Thornton's Loch Petulich pike which weighed in at a creditable 49¼ lb?

There were other coarse angling visitors to Scotland. G L Ashley-Dodd relates in *A Fisherman's Log* of how he and his daughter landed 19 pike to 28½ lb in a day from a Wigtownshire loch. Much more recently, in 1967, Fred Buller, whose book *Pike* has become a classic on specimen hunting, hooked and subsequently lost a probable fifty pounder from Loch Lomond.

Many of the Scottish coarse fish, such as carp and bream, were introduced by the monks and 'farmed' for the table. They must have enjoyed the sporting possibilities as much as the table fare. In recent years, many more waters have been stocked by English anglers; in some cases, visitors who have stayed and developed their own coarse fisheries, such as that at Hightae near Lochmaben. But even some of the rarer Scottish coarse fish, such as rudd, are not all recent introductions. In Thomas Tod Stoddart's book *An Angler's Rambles and Angling Songs* in the latter part of the 19th century, reference is made to a collection of fish from Castle Loch, Lochmaben. This includes the rudd, as well as other more widely distributed coarse species, and the silvery vendace, prized both by men and pike for their gourmet qualities.

David Foster's The Scientific Angler *was published exactly 100 years ago. Born at Burton-on-Trent in 1815, he was both naturalist and fisherman. Like Walton, Foster was enthralled with the River Dove and spent many hundreds of hours in the study and pursuit of its fish. Floats, plummets, line winders, leger rigs; they are all in his book.*

Paul Young plays F D Barker in the film 'Return to Paradise', set in Co Clare.

The man-made fishery

While man has assisted Nature in stocking many rivers, lakes and canals, other 'artificial' fisheries have been developed, sometimes from old gravel workings, other times by physically digging the pools out of the ground in suitable locations. Not only have these activities resulted in more coarse angling availability, but the variety of species found in stillwaters has been dramatically increased to include those fish we would, not so long ago, have considered only as river species. Many stillwater fisheries now contain chub, dace and the like. On the banks of the Trent at Newark, Walter Bower, inventor and innovator, has created one such splendid mixed fishery.

The angling word spreads

Wales and Ireland, compared to England and Scotland, were comparatively late developers in the fishing scene. Wales, as the smallest of the four countries, has little angling literature dating much before Samuel Taylor's book of 1800, *Angling in all its branches*. Much is written of the Wye and naturally, as with Scotland, most is connected more with game fishing than coarse.

It is surprising that Ireland, with its wealth of waters and huge variety of species, was relatively late in angling development. Certainly, there must have been many who enjoyed the angling . . . perhaps they preferred to keep quiet about their sport. The printed record does not tell us anything about those early days. Colonel Robert Venables, in *The experienc'd angler* published in 1662, only makes passing reference to the five years he served — and fished — in Ireland. It is not until the mid-19th century, with Maxwell's book, *Wild sports of the west*, which describes a long fishing, hunting and shooting holiday in County Mayo, that we learn much about the Irish angle. One suspects, however, that perhaps the fishing was so good in Ireland that anyone already there or just visiting, was not prepared to pass on the good word. Certainly, in F D Barker's memorable book, *An Angler's Paradise*, he kept his pike haunts secret. The maps showing his sporting territory in Co. Clare were disguised with fictitious place names, red herrings, eventually unravelled in 1976 with the making of a film revealing the exact locations. The fish were still there, although the once famous pike loch at Corofin has become a trout fishery — with man's assistance. Such is the price of progress!

The organiser — the competitor

Fortunately, most of us who fish share in our favourite sport those special moments and places which hold personal memories. Angling can be a solitary sport, but it becomes doubly rewarding when shared with a companion . . . or a club. The angling club is a convenient *vehicle* for a whole variety of reasons. Travel to and from the fishing can be shared; the organisation, the preparation of tackle, choosing the venue . . . and the après fish, even if it is little more than a chinwag over a pint in the riverside local, all contribute to the flavour of an angling day. Once you get a few anglers together, on or off the bankside, it is only a matter of time before the competitive element creeps in. Not only is it fun to compete against the instincts of the wily fish, but why not at the same time do better than your neighbour? Even when pleasure fishing with friends, this competitive element is never very far away.

The match angle — the specimen hunter

Organised competition, even with the big money prizes available today, does not necessarily invoke a purely commercial attitude amongst the participating match anglers. For the chap who likes to be organised by others, it is an easy way to go fishing. The venue is chosen for him, even the exact peg where he is to fish is an objective exercise. He will gain his pleasure not just from the fish, which may well be small, but by beating the others fishing alongside. Match fishing is expensive, and even those at the top are unlikely to make much more than the financial input expended to ensure they go fishing. It is no coincidence that match fishing is at its greatest in the industrialised, heavily populated areas of the country; the anglers are there in numbers, but the fish tend to be small or extremely shy, or both. The skills thus developed, and the excitement of the competition, make up for the quality of the sport. There are, of course, the *oases*, and there are tempting reasons why some of the major competitions have gone overseas to Ireland and Denmark, where the coarse fishing is still relatively untapped. The same could also be said of Scotland, except that there is a potential clash with game fishing interests.

The correct method for carefully weighing a specimen — in this case a hefty tench — safely in a landing net

For the specimen hunter, Scotland, Ireland and Denmark aren't far away; and there are always the huge carp, pike and other monsters lurking in the private fisheries of England. Private does not always mean unavailable. There are still the loners, the *F D Barkers*, who prefer to keep their secrets — and the fishing — to themselves. In spite of pollution, industrialisation and water abstraction, we still have our angling, and with new developments, the future could well be bright. Certainly, the world is getting smaller, and anglers, as the travelling adventurers they have always been, will find plenty of scope here and abroad for many years to come.

At the end of a difficult day, the winning catch is registered by officials in a Trent club match.

The freshwater enviro

Clean gra

ment . . .
nbling oxygenated streams.

Left: Trout are likely to turn up in almost any zone, including the estuarial reaches, and three browns are in this net of dace and roach.

The picture below of a rainbow trout rising to surface flies typifies the Grayling Zone. Clean, streamy water and good weed growth.

Where water comes from

The warmth of the sun out over the Atlantic Ocean causes evaporation which travels towards Europe on the south-westerly prevailing winds. Precipitation occurs as rain discharged over the cooler landmass during most of the year and as snow in winter in the British Isles and across the colder continental countries in the north-east. For this reason, rainfall tends to be greater in the west, while the highland topography of the west coast also gives rise to shorter spate rivers, having a tendency to rise and fall quickly in response to rainfall in the catchment area. Rivers draining into the eastern seaboard of the British Isles, on average are longer, less swift flowing, and respond more slowly to heavy rainfall. Afforestation and modern irrigation methods, however, do tend to accelerate water run-off from adjacent land. This has the double effect of draining rainwater quickly, together with soil debris, into the river systems with resultant increased flow and high colouration, neither of them immediately conducive to good fishing. However, as with seasonal changes, the angler can benefit from the rise and fall of rivers, and the colouration when a river is in spate, and these are dealt with under fishing techniques.

Water also comes, of course, from snow-melt. A good winter fall of snow, especially on high ground where it is likely to lie for some time, will, together with a gradual increase in air temperatures in the spring months, ensure a steady flow in the rivers. A sudden rise in air temperatures will produce an immediate and devastating snow-melt which will cause flooding, and possibly ruin the angler's chances of a good steady river flow through the spring, unless there is sufficient rain to top up the supply.

Man-made catchments, such as hydro-electric and water supply reservoirs, can and do control river levels downstream of the dams; but discharge is gauged automatically, not by the angler's requirements, but by the demand on the grid for electricity, or water supply needs for towns and cities, homes and industry. Even when man interferes with Nature, it seems as if the natural environment compensates in some constructive way. The power stations, so necessary to industry and commerce, often sited on our rivers, produce in turn a super-heated environment where fish and their food grow to 'larger than life' proportions, and we will deal with these rather special situations in due course.

The quality of the water

Some species are more tolerant towards impurities and acidity than others. Certain levels of pollution will in fact encourage rather than detract from the growth of certain cyprinids, such as the bream and roach.

Food

Coarse fish graze the river bed, moving as a family or in larger shoals. Bigger groups of fish tend to swim with other fish of their own size. The weed that forms the food, or harbours it, can only grow in the slower waters below the Grayling Zone, and the relatively shallower margins in this zone also help promote weed growth through the action and warmth of the sun.

Breeding behaviour

Game species, such as salmon and brown trout, make definitive redds in which to lay and fertilise their eggs, and therefore need gravelly habitats, and clean, well oxygenated water in which to spawn. While other zones on certain rivers can give these characteristics, which explains why salmon will often be found on certain rivers such as the Tweed, making redds in the lower reaches, the requirements tend to be satisfied only in the upper reaches of most streams.

Coarse fish spawn haphazardly and do not necessarily require the gravelly habitat in quite the same way. While all the zones, bar the esturial area, are defined scientifically by fish species, these are indicative only of the types of fish most likely to be found in these particular reaches.

Species found in the Grayling Zone and above for rivers in the British Isles include grayling, salmon, brown trout, stone loach, minnow and Miller's Thumb. From the coarse angler's point of view, the Barbel Zone is the most prolific as a habitat and breeding area for quality fish and the predators that feed on them. Here the barbel, chub, dace, gudgeon, perch, pike, burbot (on the Continent), ide and nase are found. There is, of course, an inter-relation between zones, and the predators such as the pike will move upstream to feed on fish of the Grayling Zone, and likewise, brown trout will often drop downstream to feed on the richer bottom food of the Barbel Zone. The dace, on the other hand, is just as likely to nose upstream into the faster, streamy water to feed as much on surface flies as in amongst the gravel.

Within any zone, water flow is bound to vary tremendously from river to river due to seasonal trends and weather. Within the relatively shallow Barbel Zone, storms and annual snow-melt will cause rapid flushing, and due to the gradient of the river bed, oxygenation is almost as high as in the Trout and Grayling Zones. As a river falls over a defined gradient there is a rapid, regular intake of oxygen.

The Bream Zone

Here, as the rivers widen and deepen in the lowlands, several changes take place. As oxygen availability drops and the water current lessens, aquatic plants can gain a more secure root hold, and consequently the vegetation grows more lush. These conditions suit the cyprinids. Bream, tench, carp, rudd, roach, pike, perch, chub, dace, gudgeon, bleak, zander, ruffe and burbot all live here. Food quantity and quality is

Worcester — the urban environment. Here, the middle reaches of the Severn are broad with a smooth but powerful current.

HOW THE ENVIRON

All rivers, whether highland or lowland, have
clearly defined scientific zones, environmental
areas where oxygenation and/or gradient determine which species can live there. These specific
sections can be defined and identified, from source

HIGHLA

highest, and water temperature throughout the year is
higher and more constant than elsewhere on the river
system. For geographical reasons and proximity to the
coast, this zone on our larger rivers is most likely to be
affected by pollution through industrial growth and
urbanisation. Examples in England include the
Thames, the River Trent, lower Severn; in Ireland,
the lower Liffey; Scotland, the Clyde and in Europe
the Seine and Rhine. Pollution is less likely in the
Trout and Grayling Zones, but it is here that water
abstraction can be at its worst, for domestic and industrial supply and for hydro-electrical uses.

BREAM

OXBOW LAKE

TIDAL INFLUENCE

ESTUARIAL

to saltwater. From their headwaters to the sea, rivers have the following scientific zonation. Fish establish themselves according to species requirements which are:

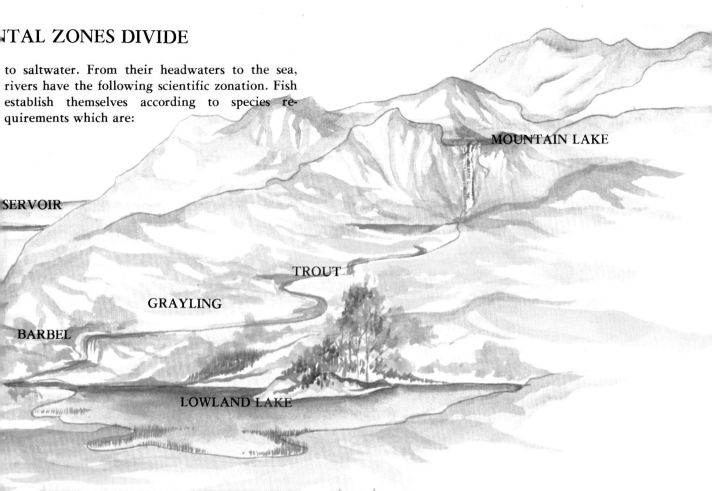

MOUNTAIN LAKE

RESERVOIR

TROUT

GRAYLING

BARBEL

LOWLAND LAKE

Estuarial Zone

The water tends to be brackish, but can be all fresh then all salt, depending on the gradient and the tidal phase. Fish species tend to move back and forwards with the tide. Coarse fish, such as bream and roach, can exist in such an environment, sharing the estuarial waters with shad, smelt, mullet, flounder and slob trout. Migratory fish, like eels, sea trout and salmon, remain for defined periods, often related to height of the river, and therefore freshwater flow, and the season. In times of low water in the river, salmon will tend to move in and out of the estuary with the tide. From late August, however, pressures of spawning will often encourage salmon to run through the Estuarial Zone even in times of low water. Sea trout, on the other hand, are less governed by lack of water but are equally sensitive to temperature. Unlike the salmon, sea trout *do* feed in freshwater, and will often hold for longer periods in the Estuarial Zone if the feeding is rich enough. The shads and smelt are also seasonal visitors, whereas the flounder and mullet will often be found throughout the year, and on a large estuary, surprisingly far upstream.

There is one other running water habitat — the canal. The canal can be described as a hybrid waterway, man-made and slow moving, dictated by the passage of boats and the related levelling of water as required to keep the canal navigable. Due to the lower levels of oxygen, species tend to be as in the Bream Zone, although random stocking on some waterways has increased the list of species beyond those normally associated with such an environment.

Fishing a canal is always subject to temperature variations far more critically than those found in the lowland river or on a stillwater particularly on infrequently used canals, which have shallowed and become silted up through neglect. Low oxygen content is the result of the even depth, relative shallowness, 4 ft is usual, and the diminished level of flow. Plants are relied on to boost the oxygen cycle, together with wind action on the surface of the canal. However, in regularly used canals, boat traffic tends to keep weed growth to a minimum which denies fish both food and oxygen. One result of an environment such as a canal, where fish species are closely confined and water flow is slack, is hybridisation. Both the Canal and Bream

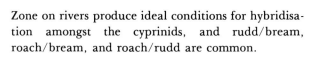
Zone on rivers produce ideal conditions for hybridisation amongst the cyprinids, and rudd/bream, roach/bream, and roach/rudd are common.

In the Barbel Zone, chub do spawn among roach and dace, but the production of hybrids is lessened where fish are able to adjust their spawning behaviour chronologically with the suitable environment assisting paired relationships rather than crowded shoaling.

Stillwaters

As with rivers, stillwaters are also divided into highland and lowland habitats. The mountain lochan, frequently the result of early glacial action, carries relatively few fish because of the constantly low temperature and oxygen availability. Trout, and occasionally introduced pike, live badly in this environment. The water tends to be highly acidic with a low pH, due to the peaty nature of the soil, with little water vegetation. The other species found in the mountain lochan is the char. This Arctic salmonid is far more adaptable to its chosen environment and survives well, supplementing its normal daytime diet of aquatic insects by surface feeding in the evenings. A vertical migration occurs on suitable nights, when char will be found rising to surface flies over the deepest parts of the lake.

The highland lake

Depicted by Loch Lomond and a number of similar situations in Ireland and Norway, the highland lake is deep in places, cold and lacking in dense vegetation except around the margins and islands. An ideal environment for predatory coarse fish feeding on the salmonids. Pike and perch are common here, with some fodder species, usually roach, which are more adaptable than rudd, bream, tench or carp. Loch Lomond, being relatively low lying and set amongst rich agricultural land and afforestation could also be described as coming within the next category:

The large lowland lake or reservoir

Usually rich in plant growth where the water isn't too deep for sunlight to penetrate, oxygenation varies markedly from summer to winter, and with large areas of shallows, water temperatures can also alter dramatically from season to season. The lake fishes well in the warmer months for all cyprinids and into the winter months for the predators and those shoal fish that can tolerate the cold such as roach, and to a lesser extent, bream. The thermocline plays an important part in how these fisheries produce.

Vertical migration

Fishing many years ago in early spring for the run of salmon through Loch Maree in Wester Ross, which precedes the more famous sea-trout shoals, my companion and I were returning back across the loch after a fruitless day's sport, which had resulted in only one sea trout kelt. Halfway across to our moorings, we noticed fish rising in the mild, calm conditions, right in the middle of the loch, above 80 or more feet of water . . . obviously not trout. They were in fact char, a shoal of perhaps 50 fish, grazing along the oily slicks, sucking in surface flies. Although our own tackle was over-heavy, 10-foot fly rods, wet sea-trout flies, and sinking lines, I took a brace of char in quick succession before the fish stopped feeding.

A hill lochan at the south end of Loch Maree near Kinlochewe is also the furthest north I have taken pike in the British Isles, from a shallow, weedy water which could be comfortably fished round in a day. The pike ran between six and twelve pounds, and took anything and everything thrown at them, including bucktail salmon flies fished on the fly rod. Some of the male fish bore scars which could have been the result of larger hen fish during early spawning activity.

Holme Pierrepont; sharing a man-made lake.

Match practice at Edgbaston Reservoir.

The village or farm pond

These habitats can be highly fertile, but are liable to agricultural pollution by effluents and pesticides washed into them from the surrounding land. Pig slurry is a major problem, and efficient and improved drainage and afforestation techniques can 'sour' the water, producing excessively low pH levels. Being located usually in rural surroundings, they are seldom affected by industrial pollution and extraction which has spoiled so much of our fishing on the lower reaches of major rivers. Seldom deep, the pond fishery tends to produce summer sport in the warm months only and will be adversely affected by a poor summer. Conversely, during periods of extreme high temperatures, surface and shallow margins will become devoid of fish life, with all species taking refuge in the deeper parts of the pond. Oxygen starvation is the hallmark of the pond, and only the more sluggish cyprinids such as carp, including crucians, and the tench survive.

The park lake

Often ornamental, the park lake can vary in size and depth, and if it is of an artificial nature, its introduced species can come as a surprise. The park lake is a worthwhile fishing habitat, often situated within a city or densely populated region, but supervised and maintained by the local council to keep environmental conditions at an optimum. Among the problems on such a fishery are over-fertilisation from waterfowl droppings and pollution from excessive food flung to the birds, both contaminating the bottom. Leaves also pose a problem on those ponds and park lakes surrounded by landscaped shrubs and trees. Dead leaves foul the bottom and prevent proper aquatic weed growth. Planted trees, albeit cultivated and positioned for environmental effect, may be excellent from a landscape point of view, but are rarely suitable for maintaining a clean aquatic environment.

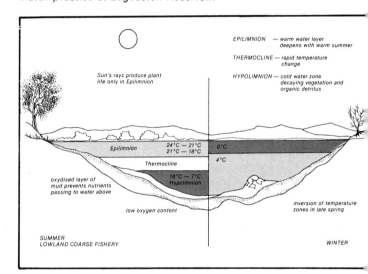

EPILIMNION — warm water layer deepens with warm summer

THERMOCLINE — rapid temperature change

HYPOLIMNION — cold water zone decaying vegetation and organic detritus

Sun's rays produce plant life only in Epilimnion

Epilimnion 24°C — 21°C / 21°C — 18°C 0°C

Thermocline 4°C

oxydised layer of mud prevents nutrients passing to water above

18°C — 7°C Hypolimnion

low oxygen content

inversion of temperature zones in late spring

SUMMER LOWLAND COARSE FISHERY

WINTER

The effect of temperature on a lake.

The Grand Canal at Prosperous.

23

The handsome perch parade in striped waistcoats.

The fish species

Fish are an important part of the development of our world's living creatures. They appeared on the earth long before birds, reptiles or mammals. The very earliest fish developed during the Palaeozoic period, during the Devonian and Silurian eras, at least 400 million years ago. These fish were primitive in the sense that they had no mouth with moving jaws. They sucked their food by attaching themselves to the prey, using a muscular disc to hang on and extract sustenance. The lamprey is probably the best known survivor of these primitive forms. Sharks and rays came next and have existed almost unchanged since their appearance. Their body shapes and perfect living function have seen few adaptations from the fossil examples that exist as evidence of the early sharks and their life in the seas. The bony fishes *Osteichthys* were the last group of fishes to arrive throughout the fresh and saltwaters of the globe. They have emerged as the most successful fish, forming an immense family over 20 000 species strong. As sportfishers, we concern ourselves with relatively few fish in the freshwater environment. Only 20, or so, different species are regularly fished for with rod and line. These sport fish have emerged because they either grow to large sizes or are famed for their ability to fight on the tackle used by the angler.

To be successful as an angler we need to understand something of the life style of our quarry, where they live, how they see, hear and feed. Because fish are found in an alien environment to our own, man has difficulty in understanding how his activities fit in to the fish's mode of life. Hunters can tell you of the behaviour of land animals and the birds that form the sporting prey, after all we have good vision that establishes behavioural characteristics through constant observation of the hunted. In considering fish, we find ourselves with the fundamental difficulty of not seeing clearly what *does* form behaviour!

Anglers need to study the water, to analyse each fishing trip in terms of what happened and how it came about in terms of what they were doing. Each species has a different habitat requirement that is fairly easy to learn about. The problems arise when fishing activities cause fish to alter their behaviour to avoid us. The senses of fish are slightly different from ours. They hear well, having both ears and a system for detecting vibrations through the water. Sound is transmitted far better in water than through air which means that the careless footfall, or any other form of indiscriminate noise, is heard by fish and they react accordingly by swimming away or going off the feed. Reaction to vibrations is more noticeable from fish in a stillwater situation where there are few underwater noises. But, in a river there will always be a certain amount of ambient water noise, created by the river's bulk movement of water which will mask some of the noise made when floats or leger bombs are cast into the stream.

Fish have reasonably good vision within a defined window above their heads. They see anglers sitting on the bank because of the refraction of light rays bent when penetrating the surface. We need to sit or move in such a way that our profile is broken up by the bankside trees and bushes. On an open riverside one can only hope that keeping perfectly still, while using every inch of vegetation as cover, will gradually lull the fish into forgetting our arrival and presence. The most important aspect of a fish's vision is how well they see one another and our baits. Some species, notably the

shoal fish like bream and roach, have good forward vision and a diminished ability to see things clearly alongside them. They rely on the other members of the shoal to give adequate warning of the arrival of a predatory species. On the other hand, the pike has its eyes facing forward and on the top of its head, indicating perfect vision in those directions. In fact the pike is one of the few freshwater fish that possesses binocular vision, enabling it to *rangefind*, a handy facility when moving in to pounce on a prey species in sudden ambush!

Fish taste and smell in a way that is hard for us to understand. They can take a bait into their mouths or taste it at distance, for the water acts as a carrier of odour; hence the value of groundbaiting which pulls fish into a defined feeding area. Obviously, there must be some vision influence with groundbaiting as particles travel downstream, but the addition of strong-smelling additives appears to attract fish more efficiently than a feed that has no additive. Just how acute a fish's smell-taste sense is has considerable importance to the angler who smokes, where taint from tobacco may ensure that he catches less than a non-smoking companion. Lake fishermen would be well advised to remove all traces of outboard engine fuel from their hands before baiting a hook! Probably the best way to avoid any tainting influence is to mask the smell by introducing another that is more acceptable to fish, such as rubbing the hands through groundbait or the hookbaits before fishing.

The freshwater fish

All fish found in freshwater have bony skeletons and are covered in scales that are embedded, partially, into the outer body skin covering. Most species are covered in a layer of slime which serves to further protect the fish against waterborne diseases absorbed into the body. The number of fins (limbs) and their position on the body varies somewhat and serves to establish the species to which the fish belongs. Scales also tell us a great deal about the species. The number of scales at different positions on the body will also identify the fish when there is difficulty as a result of hybridisation. This can happen when shoal fish spawn in the same area on a haphazard basis. Body shape and colour are the other features that establish the particular species to which a fish belongs. Some fish possess external organs of taste and feel, called 'barbules'. These appendages are placed around the fish's mouth, vary in number and position and also help in the accurate identification of the catch.

Barbel *Barbus barbus*

A long, muscular fish with clean, hard scales and large fins. The barbel is a running water species that hugs the river bed, searching among the debris for its food. The fish's belly is almost flat, allowing it to lie motionless while the power of the current sweeps over its back. The four barbules, two at the top of the upper jaw and one at each corner of the mouth, droop around a tube-like snout that is used rather like a vacuum cleaner to suck in masses of particles as they are swept toward the fish. The shape of the mouth and rooting behaviour suggests that we should present a bait by legered means that would simulate what the barbel expects to find.

Barbel exhibit some colour variation from river to river. As with most fish, there is a juvenile colouring which is slightly muted until the fish comes to sexual maturity and a possible variation in the depth of scale hue brought about by environmental conditions. Basically, the fish is dark olive green on the back, shading to a rich cream colour below the pectoral fins.

The silver bream, not widely distributed but still confused with immature bronze.

Left: A near six-pound barbel from the River Severn, taken during a match. Barbel are powerful, streamlined fish worthy of any angler's attention.

Top left: Pearly and pretty, the diminutive bleak often saves the day for the match fisherman when other species won't bite.

Above: This superb rudd-bream hybrid fell to float-fished maggot at Sallins on the Grand Canal.

Left and below: A bronze slab of bream, all eight pounds of it from a Midlands fishery. In the Bream Zone on rivers and the stillwater environment of the canal, hybridisation is common, between rudd and bream as this net shows.

The barbel demands clean water in which to live. Found just below the trout habitat, the species seeks out hard gravelly riverbeds with prolific weedbeds that form a larder of insect larvae and other small creatures to support the appetite of this big eater! The presence of barbel, in any river, is a measure of the pollution-free quality of the water. There was a time when barbel had all but disappeared from the River Trent, but with the considerable efforts made by the Water Authority barbel have again re-established themselves in a number of stretches.

Bleak *Alburnus alburnus*

This is not a species for anglers to rave about. It is one of the smaller denizens of slow-flowing rivers where it gathers in immense shoals. While not popular as a worthwhile sporting species, the bleak can add weight for the matchman on hard-fished waters as well as providing pike anglers with a useful hook bait. The bleak has a dark green back, shading through silver sides to a white belly. The minute scales have a pearl-like quality and the fish were caught in their thousands at one time so that the scales could be stripped and used within the artificial pearl industry. Bleak frequent open water, swimming in the upper layers where they feed on plankton creatures although they have the ability to grab quite large baits.

Silver bream *Blicca bjoernka*

The silver bream is less widespread than the bronze bream in Britain, as it is confined to the Fenland drains and rivers of East Anglia. The species, however, is widely distributed on the Continent but does not grow very large, rarely exceeding 12 oz. With bright silvery scales along the flanks, this fish is frequently confused with the young of the bronze bream. Claims for specimen silver bream often prove to be immature common bream. There are distinct differences between the two species. For instance, the pelvic, anal and pectoral fins of the silver bream are a pale orange colour with a fine grey band to the fringes. There is no pronounced hump behind the head as the body rises toward the dorsal fin. The eyes in a silver bream of comparative size will be much larger. This fish cannot be placed among the quality fighters found in freshwater, giving even less sport than a small bronze bream would display.

Bronze or common bream *Abramis brama*

Truly a fish of slow-flowing rivers and stillwaters, the bronze bream is sought after by many European coarse fishermen. It is a fish that grows to huge weights, sometimes reaching 15 lb or more where the quality of the water provides enough food to support the shoal. Bream feed and move around as a compact shoal made up of fish of similar size. It is not hard to imagine the daily food requirement of a shoal composed of large fish!

The bream is a deep-bodied fish, compressed across its width. The fins are large and the caudal fin is deeply forked. The bream has very small scales covered in thick slime. Colour varies with habitat and age; old fish are a dark black on the body that shades to a mahogany brown on the flanks. Juvenile fish are silvery, although they gradually grow darker after three years or so. Bream taken from peat-stained waters in Ireland are almost black all over, whereas bream from Danish rivers can be a light sepia brown.

Bream are able to extend the mouth into a tube-like projection that syphons up quantities of the mud to extract the bloodworm and other minute creatures that form part of the fish's natural diet. This liking for extremely small food animals dictates how we should approach the choice of hookbaits. Nothing is too small for the bream. The fish can be a finicky feeder, that often shows particular preferences for baits and then suddenly changes its mind in favour of a type of food that the angler cannot put onto a hook. Experience has shown that the bream's attention has to be held. This is done by introducing large quantities of groundbait into the chosen swim so that the fish get their heads down onto the feed. The hookbaits, cast within the groundbaited area, are then more readily accepted. Apart from keeping the bronze bream within fishing range, we first of all have to find them. On a massive lake this can be quite a problem. One major clue to the presence of feeding bream is the colour of the water. Any patch of discoloured water could mean that the fish are rooting in the bottom detritus. A stream of tiny bubbles, rising through the muddy water, is a definite indication that a shoal is at work.

This species hybridises with both rudd and roach when the different species are confined within a habitat. The resultant offspring can be superb fighters, displaying bodily characteristics of both parents. It seems that hybrids have the power to fight far better than either of the parent fish; perhaps this could be something to do with substituting the energy expended in annual spawning by a display of extra strength and aggression?

A nice catch of bream averaging 5 lb from the Shannon.

Carp *Cyprinus carpio*

The carp has undergone massive changes in appearance since being brought from Asia in the 11th century. How it arrived in Europe or who brought the first fish will never be explained. All we know is that the religious travellers of early Christianity brought the fish into their monastery farms as a food source.

There are four main types of carp in still and running waters. The 'Wildie' is a fully scaled, lean and muscular river carp that rarely grows to weights over 10 lb. Then we have three fish of the same deep-bodied conformation. The common carp is fully-scaled, with a dark, purple-black back shading to golden flanks and a rich creamy-white belly. The mirror carp has less scales, usually with a number spaced along the lateral line. These scales are much bigger than those found on the fully-scaled fish. The third carp variety has no scales, or perhaps a few minor ones near the tail. This fish has the name tag leather carp.

All three large carp are manufactured varieties, meaning that they have been produced as a result of selective breeding over a span of many years. Fast growing qualities were important to farmers that bred them for food in European countries. Angling has benefited from this activity by producing strains of fish that have made the carp our largest freshwater fish.

Carp are easily recognised. They have a single, large dorsal fin and a broad, deeply-cleft tail. There are four barbules around the mouth of the fish: two above the fleshy top lip and one drooping from each corner of the mouth. Carp are omnivorous feeders that possess, like most cyprinids, powerful crushing throat teeth on the pharyngeal bones that enable them to grind freshwater crustaceans and other shellfish that they find within the lakes and ponds. The species has a widely distributed introduction. They grow best in highly fertile lakes and ponds although there are some rivers, into which the carp has escaped, where they do well. The River Trent, below Nottingham, has a massive head of escapee carp that revel in the warm water from the Trent's numerous power stations, growing fast and providing the Midland anglers with unexpected sport.

The carp has been the subject of a lot of study by specimen groups. Its life style and work on new baiting tactics keep many anglers happily engaged. Very few other species, apart from perhaps pike, attract the serious attention that this proud fish seems to create.

Crucian carp *Carassius carassius*

Looking like a miniature carp but lacking any barbules, the crucian carp is known as a fish of the smaller lakes that possess a bottom composed of thick mud or silt. Crucians feed on the smaller creatures found among the bottom weed, bloodworm and daphnia being a regular part of their diet. In consequence, we have to fish extremely small baits for the species.

Crucian carp are not widespread in distribution, the South-East corner of England seemingly having most of the waters containing the fish. It is never, to our knowledge, taken in running water.

Left: A beautifully conditioned common carp displaying the powerful tail which gives this hard fighter the ponderous power of a prize catch.

Above: This slimmer version is a 'wildie' or river carp. Slimmer than the common, shape is built for speed.

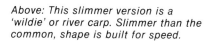

The baby of the family tops this trio of crucian carp, mirror (middle) and leather. The goldfish-like crucian has no barbules and seldom exceeds two pounds. Heavier tackle and skill are needed to land the other two.

Chub *Leuciscus cephalus*

The chub is a fish of running water, or so it was until people started to introduce it into stillwaters. They are powerful fish, with a thick, heavy-shouldered body suggesting a dour fighter . . . and that is just what the fish is!

Found in most northerly European countries, the fish is absent from Ireland, part of Wales and Scotland above the Forth-Clyde valley. This is a species that favours clean water, preferably a fastish river with variation in depth to provide deep holes and shallow gravelly runs. Shoaling when small, chub appear to lead quite a solitary life once they reach weights above 5 lb. They are fond of lying beneath over-hanging trees and under high banks where the current flow has gouged out favoured lies. The species is secretive and scary calling for a stealthy approach by anglers intent on stalking the larger specimens.

Chub are a dark green-black on the upper parts. The flanks are a golden colouration shading to a cream underside. The scales are large and hard-edged. Chub are sometimes confused, when small, with a near relative, the dace. The confusion can be easily overcome on a close inspection of both species. The chub has rounded edges to both dorsal and anal fins. The comparable fins on a dace are concave. A further identification feature is the difference in the size of the eyes. The chub's are relatively small whereas the dace has a brilliant, large eye.

Chub will take almost any bait offered and in a bold biting fashion, always providing he is not scared by seeing or hearing the angler. Float, leger and fly fishing methods will tempt him throughout the whole of the coarse fishing season.

Dace *Leuciscus leuciscus*

A finely made, delicate fish fond of gravel shallows and fast, clean water. Sometimes called the 'Dart', a name which truly describes a sight of the silvery fish as it flashes across the streamy water in search of tiny insects that have drifted down on the water's surface.

An early summer chub in superb condition. Generally a river fish, many of the new stillwater ticket fisheries are stocked with this blunt-headed tackle tester. They often feed close in to the bank, feeding on insects, worms and berries that drop off the banks and overhanging trees.

Dace never grow very large, a pound fish being highly praised, but they can give splendid sport on correctly chosen tackle. A maggot or minute redworm trotted with the current will be eagerly grabbed by dace.

Dace are found in similar situations as the chub. In addition it is also present in Ireland, having been introduced by English pike anglers. On the Continent we find the fish in most waters where it grows considerably larger than the fish of Britain.

Freshwater eel *Anguilla anguilla*

Like the marine conger eel, the eel of our rivers and lakes begins its existence deep in the South Atlantic Ocean. Spawned in the Sargasso Sea, it hatches and begins a journey to Europe that takes a full three years to accomplish. During the passage the tiny creature changes from a leaf-like shape to become a transparent, elongated fish just before arriving off our shores.

Ascending the rivers, the elver journeys into the smallest ponds and ditches to feed and grow. Upon reaching maturity, but not yet exhibiting any sexual development such as ripening gonads, the fish heads for the sea to undertake the journey back to where it began life.

Eels are easily identified as there is only one species present in our waters. There is a colour change during the time spent in freshwater. From a brilliant silver,

they become dark brown on the back with yellow underparts as they grow. Before returning to saltwater they again develop a silvery colouration on the belly. Eels are not popular with the mass of freshwater anglers, a dislike brought about by the fish's snakelike appearance no doubt but not a feeling shared by the sportsfishers of all nations! The Dutch Inland Fisheries Trust now has to import elvers from England and France to meet their eel stocking programme, such is the angling interest.

Two outstanding dace of over a pound.

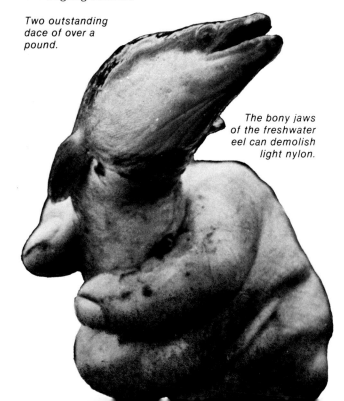

The bony jaws of the freshwater eel can demolish light nylon.

Grayling *Thymallus thymallus*

The grayling is a member of the Salmonoidei, so you might well ask why it appears within the pages of this book! The truth is that we, as fishers and lovers of this beautiful species, think that it is often misused by game fishermen who tend to measure it alongside the trout. They make an error of judgement if they assume that the grayling is in any way inferior in the fight!

Grayling occur in most parts of Britain but are absent from Ireland. Similar in habitat choice to the river trout, they seem to require slightly cleaner conditions and are therefore a monitor on the quality of the water. Nobody could mistake this fish as there is only one species in Britain. A huge sail-like dorsal fin extends high above the fish's back. The scales are small and hard to the touch. Like the trout, an adipose fin is present. Grayling can be taken on artificial flies, on worm and maggot baits. They will also at times take artificial minnows and small spoons.

The salmon and trout close seasons are not extended to the grayling so it becomes a legitimate coarse angler's quarry, something fit to grace the dinner table of any fisher, or to be returned carefully to the river.

Top: The beautiful slim shape of the grayling, a handsome and hard fighter.

Centre left: Grayling display a superb sail-like dorsal fin which they use against the current when hooked.

Bottom feeding gudgeon (left) have two barbules not four like the barbel — and they are much, much smaller!

Gudgeon *Gobio gobio*

The gudgeon is one of those little fishes that can be a bait-stealing pest on many rivers. Anglers catch them to use as live-baits for pike. The gudgeon has, on occasions, been identified as an immature barbel, a mistake brought about by a similarity in shape and the fact that this species does possess barbules . . . but only two, where the larger fish has four!

As an angling species, the gudgeon can hardly be called a fighter. It rarely weighs more than a couple of ounces at most. But, it is a free-biting little fish that can provide immense pleasure to youngsters taking up the sport. Incidentally, many a match angler has been glad of a few gudgeon among his catch when the going was tough.

Perch *Perca fluviatilis*

A flashy, colourful predator found all over the British Isles with the exception of the far North of Scotland. It is hard to mis-identify this species for it resembles nothing else other than the ruffe. There are two dorsal fins, the leading one with at least 12 sharp, spiny rays and a black colour patch at the base of the rear spines. The second dorsal is soft-rayed and gently rounded. Several black vertical bars colour the flanks of this hard-scaled species. Older specimens display a pronounced hump to the back, beginning just behind the fish's head. Bright red fins are a feature of the fish, particularly so during the breeding season which occurs in April in temperate waters.

Perch are present in just about every kind of fishery. On a fast river, the fish will favour slacks and eddies into which its main diet of small fish is swept. In slow-flowing rivers, the fish seeks out holes and undercut banks from which to ambush less fortunate species. Lakes seem to grow a profusion of small perch, fished for by small boys. Here perch use thick beds of reeds to provide the cover necessary to a predator.

The species can be fished for with maggots, but worms are the killing bait. Small blade spinners as well as small fish presented on paternostered tackles account for a number of the better fish.

Pike *Esox lucius*

The biggest of our predatory fish, pike are capable of growing to huge sizes in the larger lakes of the Northern Hemisphere where there are sufficient shoals of fodder fish to support their appetites. Pike are easily identified. A small dorsal fin, set far back on the body and matched by a similar anal fin suggests that the motive power is all in the tail. This is true of a fish that is made to dash forward, at great speed, over short distances. Pike have good forward vision, something needed by a killer! Fins trembling, it lies in wait like a cat that is about to pounce on an unsuspecting bird. Then, with a flick of the tail, the pike launches itself on its chosen meal. Often you will see a shoal of fish explode in fright above the surface of the water as a pike arrives among them.

The big specimens are female fish. Males rarely exceed 10 lb or so. They are extremely territorial in behaviour, selecting lies that give them the solitary existence that suits the hunter. Only at spawning time, around March depending on the water temperature and availability of flooded grasslands, do pike con-

What a magnificent fish the perch is with his bronze-green livery and a display of crimson fins and spiked dorsal.

Unmistakable. This predator isn't as big as some legendary pike.

gregate in numbers. Then one large female will receive the amorous attentions of a number of much smaller male fish. After all, her attentions are directed to breeding and not eating, for that she would surely do at any other time of the year. The appetite of the pike has become a grossly exaggerated legend (Falkus & Buller; *Freshwater Fishing*, 1975.). The cannibal brown trout is probably as great a predator.

What pike will do is clean up the environment for they are also scavengers. This trait is capitalised by anglers who offer deadbaits to the fish. The cleaning up instinct gains less acceptance when anglers witness the disappearance of baby ducklings, although nobody seems to mind the taking of a few water voles!

Roach *Rutilus rutilus*

The most popular coarse fish for British anglers, the roach can be found almost everywhere apart from the northernmost counties of Scotland. Fish found in Ireland originated in two river systems but are now spreading throughout the connected inland waterways. Such is the species' successful spread in Ireland that the two countries now enjoy the best of match fishing based on fantastic catches of this fighter.

Roach are green-black on the upper body with flashing, silvery scaled flanks and white bellies. The slightly concave dorsal fin begins at a point directly above the paired pelvic fins. The fins have a distinct

The slimmer roach is generally a bottom feeder.

pinky-orange tinge, especially noticeable at the breeding period which happens when the first warming days of spring arrive. At this time, the male fish grow spawning tubercles, looking like white pointed pimples, on their gillcases, head and foreparts. The fry are great survivors, eating anything in sight and frequently doing better than rudd when the two species are present in the same stillwater. There is hybridisation between the fish as well as with a number of other small cyprinids.

Roach are fast, delicate biters that demand sensitivity from anglers' tackle. Most baits are accepted but the humble maggot must reign supreme for this distinctive inhabitant of still and running water.

Rudd *Scardinius erythrophthalmus*

This proud fish often spends its life, from an angler's point of view, in the shadow of the roach. The tragedy is that it is too similar in appearance and size. Rudd are a fish of still or slow-running water. In that more favourable habitat, they seem to attain larger weights than the roach. They are golden scaled, deep in the body with brightly coloured red fins. A rudd's eyes are also brilliantly red-hued and the lower jaw extends beyond the top one, indicating that it feeds most often

above its head whereas the roach has the underslung jaw of a bottom feeder.

The dorsal fin's leading edge begins at a point midway above the fish's pelvic fins. The body of the fish is more angular than that of the roach, with a particularly sharp rise behind the vent, at the anal fin.

Most of the food of this species consists of tiny live water creatures, which tells the rudd angler that he should scale down his tackle and use small morsels as hookbait. The immature fish will always beat their larger shoal members to the feed so a rudd fishing expedition is often a lengthy affair, before the quality fish can be induced to take the bait.

Rudd favour weedy areas, where they can hide but let the sun warm their backs. Floating crusts will drop minute particles that lure the rudd from their cover and slow-sinking maggots, fished as singles on a 16 hook, will encourage them to feed avidly.

Take a careful look at your catch before releasing them back into the lake. Particular note should be taken of bream-shaped fish with large fins that have the large, golden scales associated with the rudd. Such a fish may well be a hybrid, for they are quite common when the two species live in the same environment.

Rudd tend to feed above their heads.

A quintet of specimen tench — our fish of summer.

Tench *Tinca tinca*

This is a thick-set olive-green fish with large, rounded fins and minute scales that almost seem to be lost within the fish's skin. Tench have small, pig-like eyes of a deep red hue. The mouth droops, is large and has one barbule at each corner. Slimy when held, the fish is found in stillwaters and very slow-running rivers of Britain and Ireland. It is associated with angling in the warm months of summer and for traditional reasons is regarded as the quarry on the opening day of the English coarse fish season.

Tench are powerful fighters, pound for pound more

able to test angler and tackle than equivalent sized bream or carp. They are fond of lobworms but will take maggots as a bunch and breadflake, which should be offered on a hook and breaking strain of line capable of handling the fish.

At the beginning of each season, tench fishermen prepare the chosen swim with exceptional care, raking to remove excessive bottom weed and stir up the lake bed. It is thought that the fish respond to this stirring of the bottom as well as the liberal helpings of ground-bait that are in addition to the preparation. The anglers watch intensely for signs of bubbling in the swim that indicates the presence of feeding fish. Certainly, the tench gives its position away to the watcher as streams of tiny bubbles and discolouration occur, spreading upwards from the depths of the lake.

In the late autumn the tench appears to cease feeding altogether. Unlike the carp, which does react to warm currents produced in some waters by industrial water usage, the tench apparently decides to relax for the colder months. Perhaps it needs to regain strength after the rigours of spawning, when an enormous number of eggs are shed by the gravid females; although there may be other factors that influence the hibernation of the tench.

Wels or catfish *Silurus glanis*

An introduction from Eastern Europe that does little for the sportfishing of the British Isles. Apart from size, the species can grow to huge weights, its only attribute is that it is said to make good eating. It is a slow-moving species given to scavenging over muddy bottoms. Existing in only a few lakes and connecting waterways, the wels is a fish for specimen hunters that are prepared to give the time necessary to hunt down this monster.

Catfish (top right) are strictly for specimen hunters.

Zander *Stizostedion lucioperca*

This is a fish that falls into the perch family, rather than being a hybrid between pike and perch as the specific name suggests. The fish was introduced into Britain from Eastern Europe and has been widely condemned as a pest that is ruining Fenland waters. It is a predator that favours discoloured water habitats. In this it is at variance with the pike, a fish that does not seem to do well in muddy, clouded waters.

The zander has two dorsal fins: the first which is spiked and the second soft-rayed. The tail is forked and all of the fins are considerably larger, size for size, than the pike. The back is dark green shading to muted, silver flanks and a pure white under-belly.

Although not wanted in Britain as a part of the sportfishing scene, zander enjoy considerable popularity in Europe where fish farms breed the species for stocking still and running waters.

The zander is unpopular in Britain but undeniably handsome.

Th

Everything from a No 22 upwards. Floats, fly-floss — and boots; hooks, disgorgers, plummets and keepnets; baskets, holdalls, bait-tins, gaffs — and more boots. Weights, waders and wellies. A tackle dealer specialising in coarse fishing has to carry a huge stock. When, as in this shop, the customers go after everything that swims from bleak to blue shark, even the biggest shop can get crowded.

oarse fisherman's tackle

The length and weight of a coarse fishing rod for general use is always a matter of personal choice. Where an angler might favour a 12-ft rod, another might choose an eleven or thirteen footer for the same swim or river situation. An angler might choose a fixed-spool reel to match his 12-ft float rod, while his neighbour, fishing the same rod, might prefer a closed-faced reel. Both reels have their merits, but it is again down to personal choice at the final analysis. What is important, however, is balance in choice of outfit. There is absolutely no point in having a rod or reel out of balance with the rest of the tackle, any more than it is practical to fish with gear either far too heavy or far too light for the intended species, no matter how correctly balanced the outfit appears.

While some advocate ultra-light tackle as a sporting method, it can lead to extremes, where there is far too much risk of broken lines, and fish left trailing hook and terminal rig; there is nothing to commend such thoughtless action.

At times, the angler has to fish fine, especially on heavily fished waters where the fish are tackle shy, but this should always be done in the knowledge that occasional large specimens might come along, requiring both additional skill from the angler, and heavier line to cope with the superior strength.

Rods for the coarse fisher

Coarse fishing is a sport involving many different species, waters and attitudes. Therefore we have to define the particular aspect of the sport when discussing rods and other tackle. In general our activities fall roughly into the following group areas:

Floatfishing

Float fishing can be undertaken in both still and running waters, using a variety of methods and tackle.

Trotting down for all river fish can be handled by rods specific to the fishing style or by the so-called match rod.

Trotting rods average 11-13 ft and weigh between 10 and 14 oz; usually constructed from hollow fibreglass, although carbon rods may well appear in the future. The important thing is that a trotting rod has an all-through action capable of picking up line and setting a hook at distance.

Match rods are 11-14 ft in length, weighing between 7 and 12 oz. The action varies tremendously from region to region. In some areas there will be a preference for a fast tip, whereas other regional fishing styles will demand a through action. The rod will be balanced to the individual style of the angler and the fish he expects to take from known waters. These rods can be made from hollow fibreglass tubes, but there is a tendency to move toward carbon fibre because it gives increased tip speeds for strike reaction and a much lighter rod in the hand.

Swimming the stream is a style where the float is cast to a position upstream of the angler to fish down and around. The style calls for constant casting and retrieval of the terminal tackle.

Laying-on and stret-pegging are two float fishing methods where the bait is fished on the riverbed while using a float as the bite indicator. Both styles can be fished with trotting or match rods. Recently, however, there has been a return to a fixed-line system called the 'roach pole' which does away with a reel and running line. A tight, fixed-length line is fished from a take-apart or telescopic pole which may incorporate an elastic shock absorber to overcome the more powerful movements of larger hooked fish. Poles generally measure 4-10 m, and the longer poles are constructed from carbon fibre to retain lightness.

Light tackle float fishing on near stillwaters, such as canals, is now almost entirely restricted to match rods and the pole.

Legering

Over the last few years there has been a considerable change in the methods and tackle used by the leger angler. At one time the general-purpose float rod and its match counterpart had a threaded tip ring into which the owner could screw swing or quivertips. These rods were intended for float fishing, casting the sort of weights involved with that style. This normally meant a float and its accompanying split shot. They could handle the leger weights but not the swim feeders that came into the angler's armoury. A new-function group of rods grew up that were shorter, stronger and capable of casting the loaded feeder that could weigh 2 oz or even more.

Conventional leger rods from 10 to 11 ft in length are used on running and stillwaters alike for a wide cross section of freshwater species. This style of rod fishes with delicacy for chub, barbel, roach, bream, tench and relatively small carp.

Feeder rods, usually 8-9½ ft in length, are made in a wide variety of strengths to cope with, for example, barbel in a fast water or roach in a delicate streamy situation. Both rods may well be used to cast a swimfeeder, but the line diameters and consequent breaking strain would differ greatly. Most feeder rods are still manufactured from fibreglass but, inevitably, carbon fibre will increasingly appear on the scene.

Carp rods are instruments of specific ability needed to cope with fish of all sizes and to cast the distances that this particular style of coarse fishing demands. Great attention is paid to action and the ring furnishing as the carp rod can be subjected to stiff punishment while balanced to comparatively fine lines.

Pike fishing rods, about 10 ft long, are used to cast fairly heavy baits for fish of unknown weight. The rods are used in both leger and float fishing fashion and can probably be allied to a *stepped-up* version of the carp rod.

Spinning rods

This is an area where rods vary from the ultra light single-handed instrument of 7 ft to the 10 ft double-handed rod that will kill salmon and pike alike. Species range from perch of a pound or so to pike over the 30 lb mark. The rods are related, in action and strength, to the weight of bait cast rather than the poundage of fish that are expected to be caught. Lines vary from 4 lb breaking strain to 14 lb or more, so one can expect a wide variation in spinning rods between manufacturers. Action is a word often seen in advertisements describing the advantages of particular rods. This important in-built factor can be achieved in a number of ways.

1. By the material from which the rod is made, such as fibreglass, carbon fibre, or a mixture of both. Split cane, although regarded as slightly old fashioned, will give an action hard to duplicate in the more modern materials.

2. The type of weave used when the glass cloth is woven. A fine weave will give more wraps for the same wall thickness and a denser blank than an open weave cloth.

3. The taper of the mandrel used to roll the hollow tube which can be fast, slow, medium, or a mixture of any of these.

4. Some rod construction systems, such as follow-on ferrules or glass to glass, as they are sometimes called, change the tapered strength at each junction. This can be an advantage and a disadvantage, depending upon the use made by the manufacturer of the *steps* in taper and wall thickness. The constant taper, spigoted rod generally has a better action and construction.

5. The pattern to which the glass cloth is cut to form the wall thickness. A stiffened shoulder section can be applied or a decrease in the fineness of the rod tip can be achieved without using a compound (varied tapered) mandrel.

Reels, the types and their uses

Open faced fixed-spool reels

The most popular coarse fishing reel must be the fixed-spool. It is easy to use, relatively inexpensive and problem free. As with all fishing tackle, you get what you pay for . . . so there are hundreds of makes and patterns varying tremendously in price. Aim for the best that you can afford looking for the following points as being necessary for perfect functioning:

1. Close-meshing gears that do not judder when pressure is applied to the handle.

2. A fairly wide and not too deep spool. Casting is far easier when line peels off from a wide spool. Long casts do not take the line down far on the spool which would create friction on a narrow spool.

3. The smoothest slipping clutch possible. It must not snatch under pressure when a running fish has to be given line to prevent a breakage.

4. A positive closure of the bale arm that does not need too much pressure on the reel handle to snap it closed. Modern reels have a finger pressure closing system as well as the conventional internally tripped bale arm.

5. A chenile-wired rim to a housed spool will prevent line from becoming trapped behind the spool when casting in windy conditions. Skirted spool reels, which form a large number on the market today, have overcome this problem by ensuring that the spool fits over, rather than inside, the bale arm housing.

6. Good service back-up by the manufacturer that offers spare parts and an annual servicing facility.

Open faced fixed-spool reels are used in all forms of freshwater angling. If they have a failing it is that a trotting style is difficult to control, as far as the run-off of line is concerned. Also one can experience difficulty in closing the bale arm after a strike has been made with the line having to be trapped momentarily by a finger while the bale arm is closed. It is at that split second that a lot of fish get slack line and succeed in throwing the angler's hook.

Closed faced reels

Many river anglers, matchmen particularly, now use a closed faced fixed-spool reel. This type of reel incorporates the spool within a closed housing. Line feeds out from an orifice in the front of a cone. To cast, the engaging pin which picks up the line rather like a bale arm is retracted by a half turn of the handle. Line

Reels are a major tackle item required by the angler, and more than one is generally used during a day's outing. From the top: the fixed-spool reel, the closed-faced and the skirted spool reel.

then peels off the narrow spool until the handle is wound forward. This action automatically engages the pin which picks up the line as it crosses the spool rim. Wind has little effect upon this type of reel and the slipping clutch mechanism is every bit as smooth as one could set on an open faced reel. Closed faced reels are intended for fine lines. Thick nylon cannot be accommodated on the relatively narrow spool and it gives far too much friction as it comes off the drum and through the narrow opening in the front of the spool housing. But, for line up to about 6 lb breaking strain they can be an extremely useful addition to the angler's tackle box.

Single-action reels

There aren't many examples of the famed centrepin reel around these days, although one manufacturer intends to re-introduce a very famous reel — The Allcocks Aerial — to satisfy a demand from the traditional trotting style anglers. Without doubt the centrepin gave the best trotting function of any form of freshwater reel. It had drawbacks; casting any distance was extremely difficult unless you were an expert and one did not have the benefit of the slipping clutch. Nevertheless, the centrepin reigned supreme until the appearance of the fixed-spool reel which could cast very light weights over long distances and provide an insurance factor with its slipping drag.

Many traditional anglers also enjoy the aesthetic appeal of playing larger fish by the centrepin where, instead of the slipping clutch, the fish takes line direct from the revolving reel.

Fishing lines

Many manufacturers have brought out different coloured lines for various forms of angling, coarse, sea, game, spinning, bait etc, but the colourful gimmickry is designed to catch the angler as much as the fish. Apart from a limited use of braided lines when spinning with a multiplier for instance, almost all line is nylon monofilament. Nylon should be supple without too much stretch, have a good wet strength, and be capable of accepting all major knots, without too much loss of breaking strain. Some lines will show excellent wet strengths on a straight test, but immediately fail at very low knot strengths.

The best criterion for choosing a line is to aim for the highest wet breaking strain that gives the minimum diameter. A good knot is vital as the finest line will break easily if a poorly tied knot is used in the tackle make-up. Use the least number of knots, of proven worth (see knot tying section). When hunting specimen fish, only one knot need be used, that which ties the hook direct to the reel line.

The top reel here is an Avon style centrepin, ideal for long trotting, with sensitive rim control and direct feel between angler and fish during playing. The closed-faced bait casting reel and multiplier fish above the rod.

A lot of emphasis is put on different line colours to suit different types of fishing, but, in general terms, the more neutral colours will make the line less noticeable to the fish. Some nylon lines are available for spinning finished with multicoloured dyes, the idea being that for long casting, the line will not show up as a continuous length in the water. This camouflaged effect can also be used to gauge the depth of water being fished, especially from a boat, as the colour changes throughout the line are generally at a regular predetermined interval. When assessing a line's suitability for a given situation, always remember that the fish will most often be viewing the line from below, with the sky or nearby trees as background. In most circumstances then, a neutral grey-blue-green combination seems the ideal.

Fluorescent yellow nylon originating from America is available in Britain and Europe, and is generally used for spinning at distance, and helps pinpoint the terminal tackle, especially in poor light conditions. Although successful enough when used on relatively unfished waters, the very characteristics which make it helpful for the angler to follow, result in the nylon being easily spotted by the fish, and as such, of little use for the specimen hunter, or when after species easy to frighten

Ensure that it is in the shape of a V. U-section cut shot require excessive force to close them and the shot can also slip on the nylon. The cut needs to be at least two thirds of the way through the shot and exactly centred.

Allied to the shooters' needs, split shot comes in various sizes. Because of the manufacturing system, the sizes must be approximate and correspond to this formula:

SSG = 2 AAA	1 oz of shot =	15
SG = 1½ AAA	1 oz of shot =	20
AAA = 2 BB	1 oz of shot =	35
BB = 2 No 4	1 oz of shot =	70
No 1	1 oz of shot =	100
No 2	1 oz of shot =	120
No 3	1 oz of shot =	140
No 4	1 oz of shot =	170
No 6	1 oz of shot =	270
No 8	1 oz of shot =	450
No 10	1 oz of shot =	670
No 12	1 oz of shot =	800

There are many floats, in the modern tackle shop, that have an indicated shot loading. At the waterside, this indication often proves to be unreliable because of two factors. The material, from which the float is made,

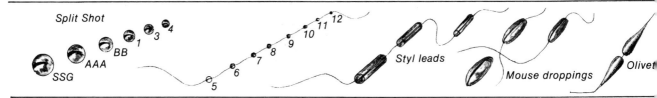

Lead weights

Probably the most important lead weights used in coarse fishing are split shot. They give us the necessary weight to cast the terminal tackle and are critical in balancing the particular float used to the water conditions. Split shot is not made specially for the fishing tackle trade but is a by-product of the cartridge industry. Anglers benefit from the shot dropped from the towers in that the sizes are variable and suit their purpose, but there is a snag! The shot required for shotguns is formed from hard lead that does not spoil the barrels of the guns. Anglers desperately need soft shot that can be pinched onto the line without bruising or cutting it. There will be many occasions, like getting an estimated shotting right, when we need to remove the shot. Now comes the problem as the lead shot is often far too hard!

There are a few manufacturers around the world, who specialise in making ultra-soft lead shot for fishermen. It is correct for angling use, but there is little money in making the shot as the requirements in annual tonnage must be fairly small. Good advice is to buy the softest shot available, taking a close look at the cut.

varies tremendously and the actual sizes of split shot are subject to variation. So, take the advertised shot loading as a guide only. Get to know each of your floats as it is possible to write on the loading with a fine mapping pen and white ink, that can then be varnished over to give the lettering permanence.

There are other types of split leads. The Styl lead is shaped like a sliced cylinder and is very useful when fishing hemp as a hookbait. Fish mistake conventional split shot, pinched on the line, as grains of hemp dropping through the water. They attack the shot giving line bites that can tempt the gullible angler into striking at nothing.

Mouse droppings are split leads of an unusual shape, that are generally made of very soft lead. Their shape partially avoids false bite indication but they do not follow the split shot scale of sizes.

The movement toward pole fishing necessitates using a more streamlined shape of lead sinker giving accurate loading to the sensitive floats used in this style of coarse fishing. Olivette leads, made in France, are bought threaded onto a piece of fine wire. This serves to keep the extremely fine hole clear of dirt. Line is threaded through the lead which is stopped at the required fishing position by the addition of the tiniest micro dust shot (size 12).

Legering weights

These leads fall into two categories: those that roll in a current and others that remain in a static position on the bed of the river. Another group exists for adding weight to a spinning cast. These leads are not part of the legering style of fishing.

Rolling leads

The most popular leger weight must be the 'Arlesey' bomb, named after a water in which Richard Walker achieved such important catches of large perch in the early sixties. Basically, it is a bomb weight into which a barrel swivel is moulded. Whether strung onto the reel line or fished on a separate link, this lead will roll across a current without tangling the line and terminal hook link. 'Arlesey' bombs are described in terms of their weight: ⅛, ¼, ⅜, ½, ¾, and 1 oz sizes. There

shape; it will hold the riverbed although it has one failing, due to being threaded onto the reel line. If it jams in the riverbed among stones or weed, the coffin lead is very difficult to break free . . . but this attribute is common to most leger weights, particularly when the tackle is not being constantly tended. At least two other styles of static weight come to us from the Continent: the Capta and Catherine leads are used for holding a fixed bait position. The leads are also designed to give a quick-change facility.

Spinning leads

Two main styles have survived from the early days of angling. The spiral Jardine lead is an easily changed weight around which the line is wrapped and trapped in a wire spiral set at each end of the lead. They are made in various lengths for both freshwater and sea anglers alike. In use, this type of weight can become unwound if the wire, spiralled ends, are not pinched closed to trap the reel line. The alternative is to secure the line either end with a double half-hitch, although this inevitably weakens the breaking strain of nylon.

The Wye spinning lead combines the function of adding casting weight and preventing line twist by ad-

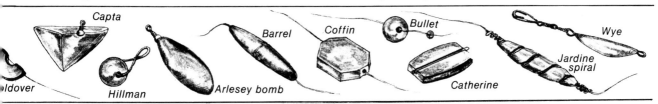

Capta Barrel Coffin Bullet Wye

ldover Hillman Arlesey bomb Catherine Jardine spiral

are bigger bombs, of this style, confined to the sport of shore-casting by the sea angler.

Drilled bullet weights, a perfectly round lead with a hole through the middle, can also be strung onto the reel line, but in dirty or weedy water they tend to jam as the drilled hole fills up with detritus, gravel and other silty deposits. Along with barrel weights, the bullet lead can be useful as a paternoster weight that balances the float but is fished clear of the bottom (see pike fishing).

The barrel lead, drilled to slide onto the reel line, will also function as a rolling leger weight. It is slightly more streamlined but has the same, unfortunate tendency to gather bottom debris in the drilled hole. Barrel leads are measured in terms of their length: ⅜, ½, ⅞, ¾, 1, 1½, and 2 in. The weight of each lead differs depending on manufacturer.

Static leads

These sinkers must stop where they are placed, subject to being of sufficient weight to stem the power of the current. The coffin lead's name is suggested by the

ding a barrel swivel to the wired body of the lead. The banana shape also gives an anti-kink quality to the lead. Wye leads are usually sized in terms of weight.

It is a tradition that the spiral and Wye leads should be painted green, to avoid them being struck at by predatory fish. We have had fish strike at spinning leads, from which the green paint had been removed after years of rattling around in the tackle box.

There are a number of lesser known leads for spinning, some of them providing anti-kink properties. Their use is a personal choice rather than a special function (see illustration).

The use and fixing of the various leads will be shown in illustrations concerned with particular rig construction throughout the chapters.

Leads used for spinning which don't possess an anti-kink arrangement are generally used in conjunction with swivels and separate plastic anti-kink vanes. Ball-bearing swivels are by far the most efficient for this type of work and help prevent line twist. The use of reversible baits also helps prevent kinking.

Bite indication

Bite indicators are critically important to the freshwater angler. It is rare for the modern angler to rely on sight and touch, of his rod tip or the line held in his fingers, to provide evidence of a bite.

Modern materials have been introduced into the art of float making, where at one time we were all concerned with the properties of Nature's own materials in our float making activities. But, when we look at the popularity of certain floats, we find that makers have looked outside our country for natural materials that can give better working properties or are cheaper substitutes for the Norfolk reeds, Elder pith and bird quills that satisfied our forebears!

Floats do three things for us: they suspend the bait in a defined position relative to the water and where we think the fish ought to be. Floats give us, by their movement from the norm, an indication of a bite from our quarry. Lastly, the float helps us to effectively control the way in which the tackle fishes, which may be concerned with where the float can be cast to by reason of its shape or in-built weight, or, the fashion in which it travels downstream in some types of current.

Floats divide into two clearly defined types: those that we use in a running water situation and floats for stillwaters. The basic difference is that the running water float has to act well in rivers of varied pressure and regularity. Not all rivers and streams flow at the same rate nor is there much uniformity of surface condition. A river like the Trent will have a tremendous variety of depths and flow patterns along its length, so we find families of floats emerging to cope with the varied conditions. These float patterns are then altered to suit waters of similar type.

Floats for fast-running water

In assessing any stretch of river or stream, we must consider the flow direction and its relationship to wind direction. The two factors are indivisible. In simple terms, the water strength and depth will determine what the float is made of while the wind and its direction will demand that the float has a particular shape. Fast-flowing water requires that the float should have good buoyancy, to defeat the turbulence, with the body placed high on the float together with a stabilising keel to steady the float. This can take the form of a wire or cane stem. Balsa wood is the common body material, although cork still has a place in the float box. There is one occasion when our river float might have a body placed at the base of the float. This is when a strong downstream wind combines with the current to defeat fishing with a traditional trotting float. The bodied float, fished bottom ring only,

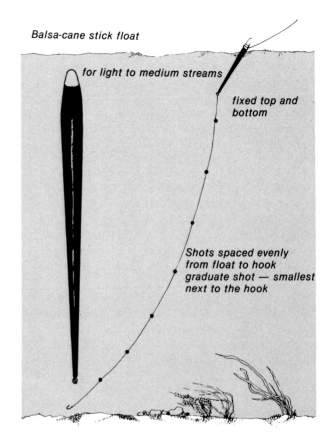

Balsa-cane stick float

for light to medium streams

fixed top and bottom

Shots spaced evenly from float to hook graduate shot — smallest next to the hook

allows the angler to bury the line below the water surface where it is unaffected by the strong wind. The fine reed or peacock quill antennae tip presents a smaller interference surface to the breezes that play across the surface.

The stick float

The stick float is probably used by more river fishermen than any other pattern. In various sizes the stick, usually made as a balsa body spliced onto a cane stem, can cope with streamy water where there is a constant speed of current. It is suitable for use in light winds that are blowing upstream or at right angles to the angler. Fix all stick floats with double rubbers or top rubber and thread your line through the bottom ring. A correct shot pattern is absolutely vital to ensure a good presentation. The shot should be attached down from float to hook like a string of beads. The heaviest shot are placed just under the float body with a gradual reduction in sizes nearing the bait.

Presupposing a shot load of about 2½ BB, these would be split to ensure a reduction of shot, placed at equally-spaced intervals, to sign off with a No 10 telltale shot at about 6 in from the hook. This light trotting rig cannot be easily cast with anything other than a side or underarm swing.

Overhead casts will give the tangle of all time! A major

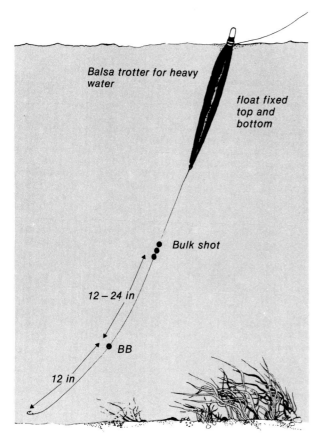

Balsa trotter for heavy water

float fixed top and bottom

Bulk shot

12 – 24 in

BB

12 in

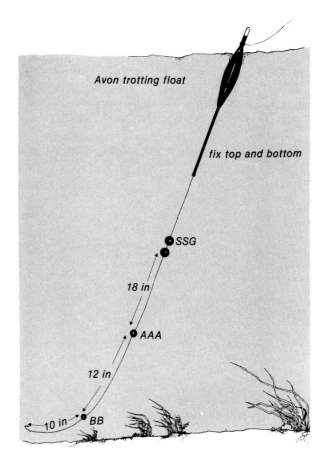

Avon trotting float

fix top and bottom

SSG

18 in

AAA

12 in

10 in

BB

advantage in the correctly shotted stick float rig is that it can be perfectly controlled through the swim. Start by casting the rig out with a progressive follow-through trying to extend the cast out onto the water. Hold the float back slightly to allow the shot and bait to get ahead of the float. This holding back should be repeated at intervals throughout the trot to cause the bait to lift slightly from its position just above the riverbed. Fish will be attracted to the lift of the ap-proaching bait. A halting of the float for a second or so at the end of the trot will let the fish become aware of the extent of the bait's movement. A repeated trot may well be met then with a solid bite. Stick float trot-ting should be accompanied by continuous loose feeding of hookbait that will sink and travel downstream at the pace of the trotted float. A little feed, positioned directly along the line of hookbait travel, ensures that the presentation appears to the fish as part of the loose feed.

The balsa float

There are times when stronger water conditions put the use of a stick float in trouble. A fast river with con-siderable turbulence requires more buoyancy in the float to counteract the increased flow that would bounce a stick float and also to carry the increased shot load necessary to get the bait down fast to fish in the streamy water.

Like the stick, balsas are fished double rubber in an upstream or right-angled wind condition. Neither type of float can be trotted from much beyond a rod length out. The shotting is similar to a stick pattern; all that changes is the amount of carrying capacity which can be 4 AAA or more. The balsa float needs to be carried in a variety of shot loadings. Having a range of floats enables us to cope with the subtleties of current varia-tion found on the turbulent stream. There is little need to extend the float's length, just an increase in diameter will meet the carrying ability. The larger, heavy shot carrying balsas are often referred to as chubbers as they are a favourite float for those anglers who specialise in pursuing that species in heavy water.

The 'Avon'

The most famous trotting float is the 'Avon', named after this famous south country river. Made as a balsa body through which a cane stem is passed, the 'Avon' has the ability to handle a stiff upstream wind that would hold a balsa completely still. The tip is fined down to cut into the wind but only to a point which keeps it easily seen at long distance. This float has ex-cellent stability, provided by the buoyant body and cane 'keel'. Shotting is loaded usually as a bunched pattern, giving early cocking, fast sinking of the lower rig and a reasonable casting quality for trotting down a centre line which may be several rod lengths out. Like the former trotting floats, the 'Avon' is fixed top and bottom.

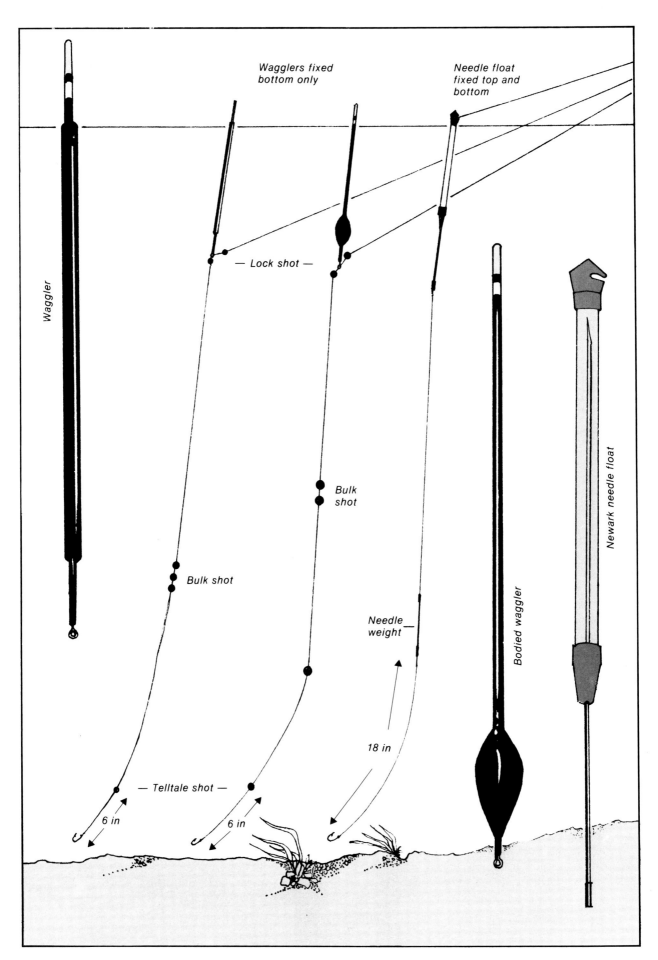

Waggler

Wagglers fixed bottom only

Needle float fixed top and bottom

— Lock shot —

Bulk shot

Bulk shot

Needle weight

18 in

Bodied waggler

Newark needle float

— Telltale shot —

6 in

6 in

The waggler

In a medium flow where there is a downstream wind, we alter our trotting tactics by introducing a float that is built rather like a stillwater indicator. Fished bottom ring only, the waggler allows us to sink the entire buoyancy below the surface, leaving just enough tip to give the angler a clear picture of what is happening. Straight wagglers can have a top finished at the same diameter as the peacock quill or sacandas reed from which they are made, or a small cane insert can be used at the tip to give a finer degree of float behaviour and bite indication. The straight waggler has an entirely different shotting pattern from the other running water floats. Bulk shot is added as a lock shot either side of the float ring. Then the rest of the shot loading is pinched on as groups of shot. Beginning at threequarters of the hook depth, one half of the rest of the loading is applied. Then at one-half of the depth the rest of the shot are attached, less a telltale shot which is pinched on at 6 in from the hook.

This delicate float system is ideal for catching 'on the drop' where fish in midwater take the bait before the whole of the shot loading has settled cocking the float at its optimum position.

The bodied waggler

Made of sacandas reed or peacock quill with a balsa body for greater carrying capacity and stability, the bodied waggler can be used in steady water flows with varying wind directions. These floats have a large shot capacity, something around 3 AAA or more and can be cast with an overhead style. Aim high to get the float and shot string to arc cleanly through the air. After casting, quickly arrest the float's trotting down movement while holding the rod tip below the water surface. This will sink the line to cut down the drag effect placed on the nylon by the wind. If used as a stillwater float, closing the bale arm then winding in a few turns will both sink the line and draw back the float after a slight overcast. This can be important for a heavy float and loading can frighten fish if allowed to drop with a splosh onto their heads.

Both styles of waggler float can be used effectively to monitor the movements of feeding fish at different levels in the swim. After casting, the float will ride high, cocked by the locking shot either side of the float ring. Then as the mid-water shot take effect, the float will sink and stabilise at a lower level. Finally, the lowest shot take effect. If you come to know the float's behaviour, any altered movement or delay in settling at the correct level could mean a fish has met the hookbait at an intermediate depth. So, be prepared!

The needle float

Similar in characteristics to a conventional 'Avon', this balsa and steel wire stem float settles more quickly into a stable trotting performance. The wire stem, together with another separate wire weight balanced to the float's carrying capacity, gives a streamlined presentation claimed by the maker, Walter Bower, to be far more efficient than equivalent split shot. The float sinks more rapidly and goes down further through the water, because there is a lot less friction to the float's movement. Another claim, and one in which there is considerable merit, is that this float and sinker system overcomes the challenge, by conservationists, that an angler's lead weights are responsible for the deaths of waterfowl . . . the Needle float relies on drawn stainless steel wire weights which cannot cause any poisoning problem.

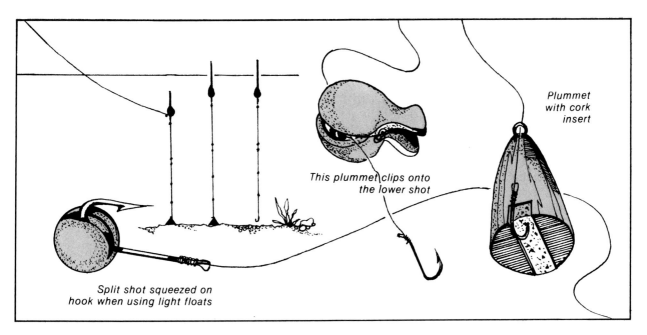

Split shot squeezed on hook when using light floats

This plummet clips onto the lower shot

Plummet with cork insert

Floats for slow-running rivers, canals or stillwaters

The zoomer

There are occasions when the float is needed to present a bait at distance in a slow-flowing river. If the wind is light, blowing from behind the angler or upstream, a zoomer will fill the bill. It has its limitations though. The depth at which it delivers the bait must never be more than about 9 ft. The zoomer is fished top and bottom with half the shot load, which could be a single swan, pinched on below the float ring. This shot stops the float from returning down the line under the powerful cast needed to get across to the far bank. The rest of the shot load is applied as bulk at half bait depth and one tiny telltale shot 6 in from the hook. You might wonder where the weight comes from to cast this specialist float; well it's in the base of the balsa body. A brass slug is glued in above a cane stub to which the float ring is whipped. The slug gives over half of the float's cocking requirement!

The float's fine cane stem can be a little difficult to see at distance, which causes concern because this is a sensitive float that will register the tiniest bites. Good eyesight is a must, because increasing the thickness of the stem would defeat the whole purpose of the float.

The dart

Like the zoomer, this float has an internal weight to give the necessary weight to cast while only needing the smallest shot to cock it to efficiency. Its use is on canals, slow-flowing waters and any stillwater where fish are sensitive to the weight of the angler's split shot.

The float body is of balsa into which a fine cane tip insert is fixed to give the delicacy of bite detection needed on hard-fished waters. The dart will beat the effect of light winds that scurry across the surface as only a mere trace of the antenna is visible after shotting. The float is locked at fishing depth with a tiny split shot either side of the ring. Further minute shotting is attached at two-thirds and one-third of the hook depth. A No 8 or 10 telltale shot should be pinched on 4-6 in from the hook. Grade the shot carefully as this float is the ultimate in sensitivity on a slow or stillwater.

The onion

This is another sensitive float for slow-running or stillwaters, especially useful when fishing at no more than two rod lengths out from your pitch. The low down balsa carries the bulk of the shot close under the float. Small split shot are attached in two groups, at

mid-water and halfway between that group and the hook. In this pattern lift and 'on the drop' bites can be detected from shy biting species. The lengthy antenna helps in establishing a bite that develops before the total shot loading has had time to take effect and will also beat all but the fiercest of surface breezes. Like the dart, the onion must be fished bottom only, with the line buried below the water, so that no above surface influences affect the behaviour of the float.

The insert waggler

Much finer in construction than the running water wagglers, this float is built for providing sensitivity in both slow and stillwaters. The sacandas reeds are spliced into each other in a diminishing diameter, toward the float tip, that decreases the amount of pull

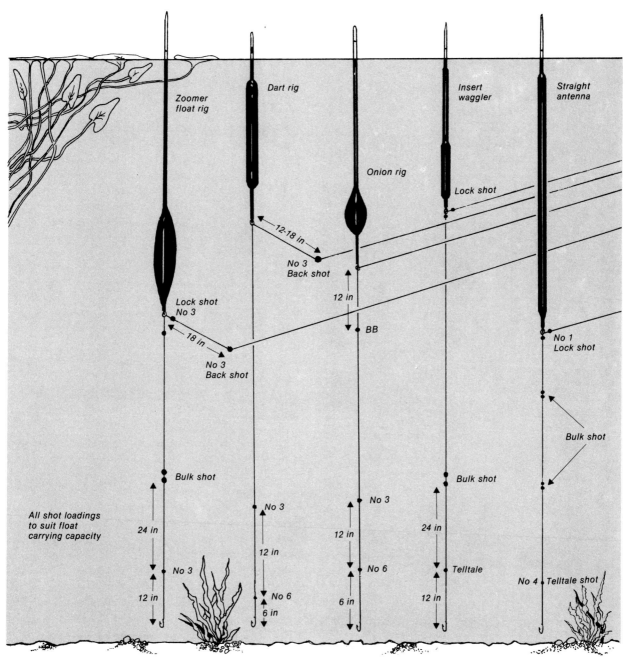

Zoomer float rig

Dart rig

Onion rig

Insert waggler

Straight antenna

Lock shot

12-18 in

No 3 Back shot

Lock shot No 3

18 in

No 3 Back shot

12 in

BB

No 1 Lock shot

Bulk shot

Bulk shot

24 in

All shot loadings to suit float carrying capacity

No 3

12 in

No 3

12 in

No 6

12 in

12 in

No 3

6 in

No 6

6 in

Bulk shot

24 in

Telltale

12 in

No 4 Telltale shot

necessary to sink the float as it is shotted progressively. This is a useful proposition where one may need to adjust the amount of float showing in order that good visibility is retained at distance.

If homemade, the insert waggler can be constructed in such a way as to give definite lift bite indication. One tiny shot, say No 8, is sufficient to sink the float from X to Z. Knowing this, the angler watches the float carefully after casting. If the settling down steps do not follow in a time established after the first few casts, something must be holding the float up? Or, when finally settled, with about ½ in of the ultra-fine tip above the water, there is an upward movement of the float that exposes the next body section, one can assume that a fish has lifted the bait off the bottom. Lifting the No 8 telltale shot will let the float shoot up above the water!

The straight antennae

Most antennae floats are built with a balsa body to carry the shot load necessary to cast more than two rod lengths. There are times, swimming the stream on slow rivers, when all we need is a sacandas or peacock body carrying a couple of medium shot. A fine cane insert tip is all that should be exposed above the water. The float can be locked either side of a float ring or attached with a single rubber to a cane stub. This may be preferable on a water where conditions of depth and distance require a regular change of float. Beating the wind and an increase in sensitivity of bite detection must be a requirement on water where we need to present a bait right on the bottom. Shotted down the line as a diminishing string, the split shot will give the float stability and get the bait down to fish fairly fast.

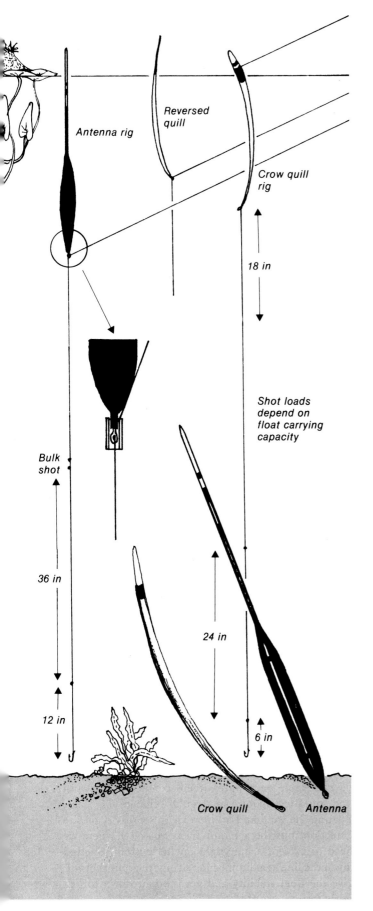

Antenna rig

Reversed quill

Crow quill rig

18 in

Shot loads depend on float carrying capacity

Bulk shot

36 in

24 in

12 in

6 in

Crow quill

Antenna

Floats for stillwater fishing

Quill floats

This is possibly the first float that anglers can remember using, which can still give perfect bite detection when used corrrectly. The quills of birds make the most sensitive floats as they are both delicate in fibre structure and have a large air space within the quill. Crow quills have been popular for years and one of our most famous exponents of the float fishing art, Billy Lane, was a great believer in using the crow quill in two ways. He suggested that used thick end up, this quill made a light float for swimming streamy water and when reversed, that is with the thin section forming the float tip, an ideal stillwater float for fishing under the rod tip.

A pattern of small shot, evenly spaced below the float, gives good control and provides the essential delicacy of presentation necessary for taking shy fish. Both float systems are fished double rubber and cannot be used in windy conditions or when the water is more than 6-8 ft deep.

Stillwater antennae

If anything curses efficient presentation of a bait on a lake or pond it is surface wind that swings the line in an arc, dragging the float across the water. A stillwater antenna, fished bottom only, will sink the balsa body deep, exposing only a small amount of finely tapered cane tip above the surface. With the reel line sunk, wind will have little effect on a float fished at up to three rod lengths out. There are limitations of depth, so the antenna can only be fished in water of about four-fifths of the rod length. Any setting beyond that makes casting nearly impossible. In general use, the float is shotted with the bulk of weights locking the float to depth. The remainder of the shot loading is spaced at equal distances down the line with a minute telltale shot at 6 in from the hook where it gives the bait an anchoring point should there be a slight surface drift or underwater current. Many stillwaters will exhibit a bottom movement where water is continually shifting under the influence of convecting currents.

When a stillwater is too deep to fish with a normal antenna, we turn to the sliding float technique. Here the reel line runs freely through two float rings to be stopped at the plumbed depth by a stop knot tied into the line. The shape of the float does not vary, only the method of attachment to the line.

When fishing at extreme distance the angler has two choices of float: either a massive antenna capable of carrying a heavy shot load to improve the casting ability or to buy a specialised antenna float called the 'Missile'. This float, as the name implies, is intended to

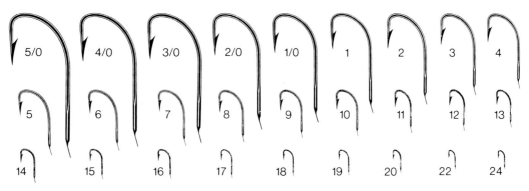

Forged, flatted, bronzed, short shank Mustad crystal hooks shown actual size.

cast long distances and carry a reasonable shot loading. Part of the weight necessary to achieve distance and cock the float is added as a brass insert at the base of the balsa body. The stem, which could be peacock quill or sacandas reed, has to be of sufficient thickness to be visible. Shot the missile at two-thirds of the plumbed depth with all the weights needed to cast and sink it to the correct depth. A telltale No 6 is placed between the hook and bulk shot; at about 12 in would be right.

Some anglers fit their missile style floats with extra-small diameter float rings at the base in order that they can be used as long distance sliders.

Hooks

There must be more controversy over the right type of hook to use than any other part of an angler's terminal rig. With thousands of patterns to choose from, anyone could be forgiven for not quite understanding the subject.

We ask three things of any hook: it must hold bait in a perfect mode of presentation, penetrate well on the strike and hold securely throughout a sustained fight. Quite a lot to ask from a frail piece of metal that costs just a few pence! Possibly, because they are small items and fairly cheap, anglers rarely give adequate thought to buying the correct kind, and having bought them, tend to keep and carry them in poorly constructed boxes. Hooks need to be stored in a way that prevents them rattling around when the angler is trudging along the river bank. The points and barbs can easily be turned which will mean a lost fish. Inspect the hook carefully before tying it to the nylon. A good idea is to give the point a slight pull away from the hook shank. This will indicate the temper of the particular iron. Too much temper when the hook is made makes them brittle, snapping off at the point below the barb where the metal is sliced. Not enough temper produces a hook that will open up and straighten under the kind of pressure that a good fish can sustain.

There are three types of hook. Two come as loose packeted hooks. The most popular has an eye to which

the nylon is tied. Then there is a variety called spade-ends. These hooks have a flattened end to the shank that swells out providing a shoulder against which a whipping knot jams. This method of tying on can be every bit as efficient as an eyed hook in everyday use. A lot of fishermen think that the iron lies out from the nylon far better with this kind of hook. Lastly, the hook that comes already whipped to nylon by a multitude of tackle manufacturers. The ladies that perform the function of tying are far more adept at doing so than the average angler, especially when we consider difficulties involved in tying sizes below 20!

Many anglers think of patterns of hook in relation to the fish that they expect to catch. This is wrong, for the hook to use is one that is perfect for the bait to be offered in terms of size, thickness of the wire and kind of bend and shank. In simple terms, a hook should penetrate the bait, such as maggot or caster, but not split it. Size bears a relationship to the amount of bait being offered. A single maggot needs only an 18 or smaller. Double-maggot hookbaits might go better on a 16 or one could fish a bunch of grubs to a 12. A lob-worm needs a hook of at least size 14 to enable it to take hold properly. Anything smaller would tear out from even a small worm on the cast. Bread baits, like flake or crust, really demand a minimum size of 14 to give an effective hookhold on soft baits.

Bait presentation, hook penetration and a good hold; all three hook types should meet these requirements.

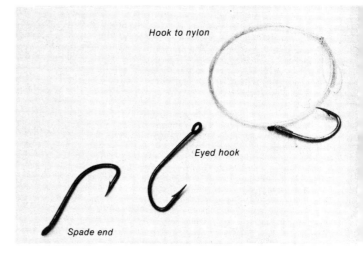

Hook shapes

The shape of the hook is important also. Worms fit best onto hooks with slightly longer shanks, enabling part of the hook to be passed through the body of the worm where it gives extra holding power effective during a punched cast. Maggots, on the other hand, are best put onto a short-shank hook. A longer shank suits the particle baits that are becoming very popular. A thread of sweetcorn fits admirably on a long-shank, whereas one would have to increase the size of hook used if a short-shank pattern was chosen.

Hook faults

Take a look at the barb before buying hooks. Sometimes the barb is too deeply sliced, causing a definite weakness. There are some on which the barb is too far way from the hook point. Both faults would need excessive force to ensure perfect penetration. A lightly sliced barb, not too long and really close to the point, will give the best striking efficiency.

Artificial lures, spinners, plugs and suchlike are all fitted with treble hooks when bought. Without questioning the wisdom of the choice of a treble, it should be pointed out that all the problems associated with single-shank hooks are also found among trebles. All too often they are too thick in the wire with suspect points and barbs. Make a similar check on the furnished hooks when treating yourself to new spinning baits. Pike, particularly, have very bony jaws that repel all but the best hooks unless excessive force, involving over-strength tackle, is used when fishing for them.

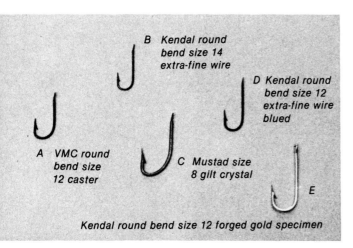

B Kendal round bend size 14 extra-fine wire

D Kendal round bend size 12 extra-fine wire blued

A VMC round bend size 12 caster

C Mustad size 8 gilt crystal

E

Kendal round bend size 12 forged gold specimen

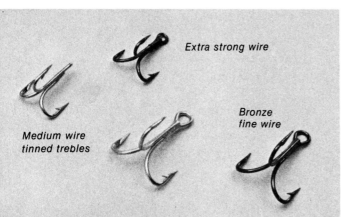

Extra strong wire

Medium wire tinned trebles

Bronze fine wire

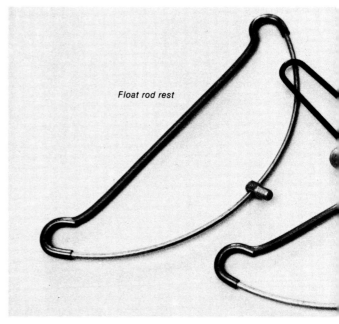

Float rod rest

Rod rests support the rod without damage or line snag.

Swimfeeders

This groundbaiting accessory is utilised normally by attaching it as a leger weight. It consists of a nylon or plastic perforated container, into which the angler places the groundbait, normally in the form of maggots or cereal particles. The maggots gradually work through the holes in the small tube container, and are drawn down through the swim by the current. This has much the same effect as loose feeding on the surface and upper layers of the water, only it offers the angler who wants to fish a bottom bait, the chance to draw fish to his hook bait.

The method is mainly used for streams, but can also be effective on stillwaters, where the maggots crawl out of the container to be picked up by grazing species, hopefully locating the angler's bait in the process.

Rod rests

These do not, as might be implied, save the lazy angler from holding his fishing outfit, although it no doubt happens. Rests assist the angler in several ways!

To position the rod so that the tip is adjacent to the water surface, and angled so bite indication, when legering, is simplified even if windy.

To adjust the height of the rod parallel to the bank and water surface, irrespective of the topography of the bank. As a support as an alternative to the underarm position or laying the rod on the bank, where the ingress of sand or dirt might impair the working of the reel: useful during rebaiting, or changing the terminal rig.

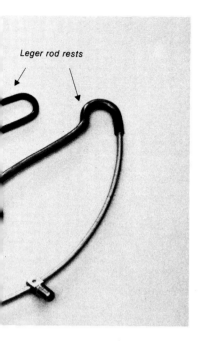

Leger rod rests

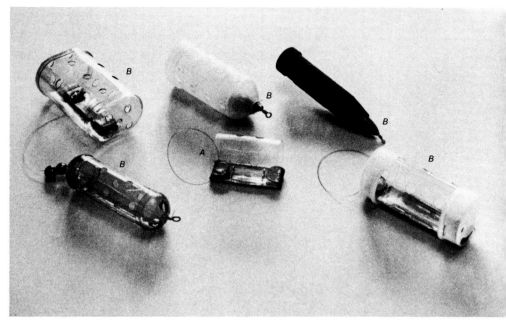

Swimfeeders come in all shapes and sizes open-ended (A) and block ends (B).

Depending on the circumstances, the angler will use either one or two rests per rod. When specimen hunting, this also allows the angler, where permissible, to use more than one rod. Coupled with an electronic bite indicator, this application is most used by carp anglers fishing at night on stillwater situations. Most rod rests are made of light tube or rolled metal, with a spiked end for an easy fix into the banking. Do not necessarily go for lightness, as some of the cheaper rests on the market can fail under pressure caused by an over-energetic angler trying to push the rod into banking which is too stony. Rubber tubing is generally used at the business end to protect the rod. For boat use, or where the banking is unsuitable for the spiked variety, rod rests are available with clamps, for fixing to the gunwhale of the boat, or to the angler's box.

Landing nets

The criteria for any landing net are that it should be of sufficient size for the fish which you hope to catch, with a handle long enough to suit your location and situation relative to the water being fished. Thus, in a boat, the angler will not require as long a handle as the fisherman who is located on a steep bank well over his fish. The length of rod being fished also has a bearing on net handle length. It is easier with a long rod to draw a fish over a long-handled net, than a correspondingly short one, and most anglers, especially match anglers, prefer a long handle, even if this means some underarm tactics and laying the rod down to draw a larger fish back in to the bank once in the net.

The diameter of the net should be large enough to accommodate most fish expected. A screw-in type of net of 18 in to 2 ft diameter will meet most requirements

and this can be matched with a variety of handles. Telescopic handles are also available, and the angler has a choice of both metal and fibreglass. A specimen-sized net is invaluable for both carp and pike fishing, and many anglers prefer a triangular shaped net to a circular one. This allows the net to be placed into the water, even if weedy, and the bigger fish can be drawn or slipped over the net. A circular net in a similar situation stands the chance of becoming entangled in reeds and weed growth, with the possible disastrous consequences of a lost specimen.

Draw the fish over the waiting net — never scoop!

Keepnets should keep fish healthy — a hundred pounds of roach from Denmark's Ansager require two large nets.

In landing fish too big to be swung out to the angler's hand, for preference always draw the fish over the net, rather than slide the net under the fish. This means positioning the net first, and using the rod to slide the fish over the waiting net. Any movement of the net is likely to excite the fish still further and lead to a possible breakage of line and a lost fish. Watch the relationship of line length to rod length, as there is a tendency to retrieve too much line, resulting in the angler being unable to draw the fish close enough to net, without overreaching. Mesh size should relate again to the fishing carried out, but in general terms, the newer knotless nylon meshes in smaller sizes are less likely to cause scale damage, and also prevent escapees. With the finer minnow meshes, there is some additional danger of the hook being caught in the mesh, and if this occurs near the rim, and a big fish twists, the danger exists of again saying cheerio to a specimen!

Keepnets

Keepnets should always be large enough for the catch, and the species you fish for. There is no use compromising on price, if it is likely to lead to big fish, such as bream, being damaged in a net only suitable for smaller species like roach. With an exceptional catch, the angler may very well require more than one net for his fish. Mesh quality has improved tremendously in recent years, and most commercially produced nets do an excellent job. Metal hoops have also been replaced by plastic-coated frames.

After fish are returned to the water, keepnets should be laid out on the bank and allowed to dry. This can be facilitated by fixing one end, or asking a neighbouring angler to hold the base while you spin or flap the other end in a circular motion, to shake off excess water and speed up the drying process.

Tackle boxes

Boxes come in all shapes and sizes, and in a variety of materials. Some double as angling seats, although these have the disadvantage that the angler has to get up if he needs a particular piece of tackle which hasn't already been set out. This can be critical during a match, and can cost time and fish to the competitor.

A tidy angler is generally a successful one, although for some inexplicable reason (is it bad luck?) the opposite can be the case. A good tackle box will have compartments for keeping everything neatly in its place, and most work on the 'tool box' principle of a series of fold-out layers, each with a series of boxed or elongated compartments, with or without lids. Tackle boxes, which have lids on some of the sections, can

A disgorger ensures small fish are returned unharmed.

prove their worth, especially on a difficult, steep bank, where there is always the danger of an overturned box. It can be infuriating if things like hooks, small floats, and weights become dislodged, and mixed up.

The balance of the box, for this same reason, should be good in the open and closed position. It is surprising how many boxes become unstable when left open. A good box will utilise the top as a double base when open, so that the rows of trays are supported firmly with little chance of the whole thing tipping over, even in a wind. The most successful boxes are either made of fibreglass or wood, in the case of box seats, or reinforced plastic. Any metal, such as hinges or supports should be wiped clean, and kept lightly oiled to prevent rusting. A good broad base, with either tapered sides to a smaller opening top or parallel sides, is to be preferred to the less stable boxes which are tapered from top to narrower bottom.

The clothing for the job

Nothing can be worse than having to fish in the wrong gear be it in warm, dry weather, or on a cold, wet, blustery day. Knowing the uncertainty of the European weather pattern, it often pays during the summer, even during a heat wave, to carry sufficient waterproof clothing, especially for that surprise thunderstorm. The weather on the other hand can and does frequently change for the better, and if you go out dressed for the cold, without packing or wearing something lighter underneath, it can be an equally uncomfortable experience.

Over garments should be light enough to prevent excessive condensation, and allow the angler to move.

Loose feed can be catapulted when fish are at distance.

Float fishing on rivers ar

Late afternoon on a breezy River Shannon at Lanesborough.

streams

Float fishing in running water can be separated into two basic forms of technique: fishing a moving bait or holding the bait in a particular place. If we accept that a float will give an indication of a bite while presenting the bait at the correct depth and giving greater control over the way in which the bait fishes, we then set out to arrive at a method which will cope with the type of water and the species that are inhabiting the water.

Trotting the river

Most river fish lie in wait for food that is brought downstream to their territory. Within limits, usually dictated by the underwater topography, presence of predators and suitability for supporting life, our river fish will not venture far. Trotting a bait down a river is a prime method for catching fish without disturbing the territorial behaviour of the shoal by a bankside presence. The object is to fish from at least 10 yd, or so, above the place in which you think fish will congregate. Recognition of a fish-holding swim is the most important decision to be made before trotting.

The ideal swim would give a trot of 30 yd, either clear of or between weedbeds. The bait is presented by shotting a running water float in such a way as to get the bait down quickly through the water. The float, which could be an 'Avon' for rough water, or a stick when fishing less turbulent conditions, is set to trip the bait along just above the bed of the stream. Fairly large floats can be of assistance in that the shot carried helps to take the bait down quickly as well as allowing perfect sight of the float tip at distance. It is a mistake to think that a correctly shotted but light float is more sensitive than a larger, more heavily shotted one. The added bulk, of a large 'Avon' will give a much smoother ride through rough water, without reacting to every wave and sudden surge that water can show.

Cast out the terminal tackle with an underarm swing, let the float settle and begin to trot downstream. Apply a little resistance to the float's passage. This can be done by light finger pressure on a centrepin or a similar action as the line dribbles over the rim of a fixed-spool. Doing this will ensure that the bait travels slightly ahead of the float. Holding back the float oc-

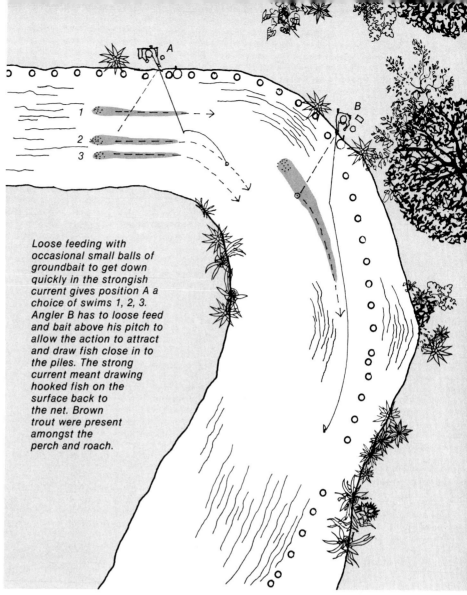

Loose feeding with occasional small balls of groundbait to get down quickly in the strongish current gives position A a choice of swims 1, 2, 3. Angler B has to loose feed and bait above his pitch to allow the action to attract and draw fish close in to the piles. The strong current meant drawing hooked fish on the surface back to the net. Brown trout were present amongst the perch and roach.

casionally will keep the bait fishing correctly and cause it to swing up momentarily from the river bed. This slight lift, to the hookbait, is very attractive to waiting fish. It helps them see the bait before it trips past them at the speed of the current. Remember that river-dwelling species expect to see food and other items coming toward them at a set speed. Anything that varies from the normal will be suspected. Only the small members of the shoal will rush in to grab at an unattractive offering . . . juvenile exuberance! The larger fish are also wiser and demand a more expert presentation if they are to be fooled into taking an angler's hookbait.

Plumbing for accurate depth is rarely possible when trotting a river. The bottom isn't always regular and there will be downstream obstructions, like patches of weed. So, arriving at the correct depth setting for the float is a trial and error situation. A couple of swims down will soon establish the average depth of water. The perfect trot would have the bait tripping along just clear of the riverbed, but fish will be aware of the hookbait if it travels slightly higher in the stream because trotting is always accompanied by a planned

practice of loose feeding. This involves throwing a few examples of the hookbait that will trundle downstream alongside the bait. In addition, an amount of ground-bait can be fed into the head of the swim to cloud the water with particles that can be seen and smelled. Fish lying further downstream than the float is being trotted will travel for a short distance to investigate the source of the food stream, although the urge to proceed out of their known territory may be halted by fish feeding further up the river. There is a pecking order among fish which can be clearly seen on game rivers where bigger trout and salmon lying in the best lies will at times defend the perimeter of the pool against

Angler A Above: has an even flow across the river and can swim the stream close in, middle or far bank, or trot down to next swim. Angler B has a stronger current into the bank, and long trots close to the piles.

Top left: This swift-flowing Danish stream has undercut the near bank, and the piling offers cover and feeding for the perch and roach, and sport long trotting.

the arrival of a newcomer. Whether the incumbent feels that the new arrival threatens the food availability in the case of trout or seeks to steal the best lie is difficult to say but the defender always seems to gain strength from possession. Chub are a coarse species that can be observed chasing smaller fish out of a favoured lying place.

Long-trotting calls for power in the tackle. After all, there may well be 30 yd of line off the reel when the bait is taken by a good fish. That means a hefty strike to pick up the floating line and set the hook! A 12-13 ft through-action rod is admirable for most species to be caught using this fishing style. Ideally, one would use a centrepin reel, but the fixed-spool reel has become the angler's standard equipment over the years. Use a line of 3-5 lb on the reel for trotting. The hook length can be lightened to about 2 lb, but there will be few situations where that breaking strain would give a better strike rate. Trotting gives fish little time to inspect line diameter; they are too busy watching for food!

With stick or 'Avon' floats the reel line is fished along the line of the float by fixing it with two rubbers. Alternatively, use a single rubber with the line passed through a ring whipped to the base of the float. The line needs to float on the surface, reducing the amount of drag imparted at the moment of strike. There will be times when the stick or 'Avon' float will not travel downstream at the required speed or with the control expected. In conditions of turbulent water and anything but the fiercest downstream winds, the balsa gives that shot carrying capacity to beat the water and wind. It will ride down steadier than either the stick or 'Avon', while coping with the heaviest shot load needed to get the bait down before the float is swept off. Size of float does not affect sensitivity providing the shot pattern is correct for the strength of flow.

Swimming the stream

There are occasions when long-trotting is out of the question for a variety of reasons. The river may be too twisting or prior knowledge may have established that fish are in isolated pockets that have to be fished from a particular position. Then we swim the stream. This means that the floatfished bait is cast to a point slightly upstream of the angler's position. It is then allowed to travel downstream, past the angler, to swing round in an arc at the end of what is thought to be the tail of the swim. Obviously, as the fishing takes place immediately in front of the pitch, some attention must be made to keeping a low profile. Fishing ought to be from a seated position, as unobtrusive as possible.

Most lengths and types of float rod can be used with a fixed-spool reel as first choice. The rod is held

Top: An akward situation; lively roach, a strong current and difficult reach with the net over timber piles. Swift-flowing, medium depth swims can mean that the angler has to slide his catch back to the net. Above: Casters beneath a balsa float produced these superb Trent roach.

64

The rudd of Lanesborough

The rudd is one of our most attractive species in the British Isles, its large scales coloured golden, through bronze to pale brass depending on habitat. The fins are a bright vermilion, and the eye is a brilliant red . . . lending the rudd the nickname of 'Red Eye'. Unlike the roach, the rudd has an underslung jaw which gives the mouth a distinctive turned-up appearance. Distribution is throughout England, Wales, the south of Scotland and Ireland. Most of the rudd population in Scottish waters is of fairly recent origin, with several fisheries developed in the last decade, especially in the Solway area. The dorsal fin foredge lies behind a line from the pelvic fins, whereas on the roach, the dorsal leading edge is ahead of the pelvic fins. In Ireland, the two species are further confused by the incorrect use of 'roach' when referring to rudd.

In Ireland, the rudd is prolific, and unlike England and Wales where distribution is far more sporadic, catches are frequently taken not only on the lakes, but also from the slower moving rivers such as the Shannon at Lanesborough, and the canals only a short drive from Dublin. In early spring, rudd, along with bream, and even tench, congregate in the warm water outfall to the power station at Lanesborough. The bream are there right up in the fast water, cleaning themselves after spawning. The rudd can be in a feeding mood, too, and large nets of plump, well-conditioned fish are not uncommon. The warm water outfall at Lanesborough is a fairly deep channel, parallel to the main river, and a long cast to the other side. The rudd lie at distance, tending to feed to the far side of the channel into the reeds. As with the lake situation, they have to be drawn from their cover by groundbaiting. This requires a good throw, using balls of compacted groundbait, with chopped up worm and maggot hook bait included. As the groundbait drops through the water, particles of the hook bait break off. By loose feeding with maggots using a catapult, the rudd can be gradually drawn away from the far side, within easier casting range of the angler.

The Shannon at this section is very exposed and often blustery, windy conditions make for difficult casting, and even more awkward bite identification. While legering is successful for the bream further up towards the warm water outfall, float fishing produces a better response from the rudd.

This is how match angler Ken Giles approached the problem during his fishing session: Choice of float is a waggler, attached bottom ring only, so that the line sinks below the surface and will not catch the wind. As the fish grow confident and start to feed more vigorously, hook size is increased, and loose feeding with catapulted maggots keeps a concentration of the hookbait at casting distance away from the reeds to draw the rudd, even with the windy conditions.

throughout the swim-down, keeping the line clear of the water to avoid a belly forming that would cause the float to veer across the water. The method is suitable for slow-flowing water where delicacy of presentation is important. Direct contact with the float is vital, so a tight line must always be sought. If the rod tip is raised as the float comes through from its cast-to position and then lowered again as the float travels downstream, this can be achieved.

Casting must be done with minimal disturbance for the fish could very well be under the rod tip! Some of their fears can be allayed by constantly loose feeding to a point upstream of the angler's pitch. Then the feed will have time to hit the bottom before it arrives in front of the pitch. It is a good idea, after hooking a fish, to lift it fairly quickly away from the rest of the shoal so that it can be played out in clear water, and not disturb other fish. Try not to let any hooked fish tear through the swim scattering the other occupants. Once scared, it will take time before the fish come back on to the feed. Regularly loose feeding half a dozen maggots before each cast will keep the swim worked up and the fish intent on feeding.

In an upstream wind and medium flow conditions, the balsa-cane stick float will be a perfect choice giving the ideal balance between buoyancy and bite detection qualities. Shot should be applied as a string of 'shirt buttons', evenly spaced between float and hook. Graduate the shot, with the heaviest pinched on just under the float rubber. Most floats sold today indicate their shot loading with a transfer along the body of the float. Sometimes this loading is accurate but not always. Better to arrive at a loading yourself, at home, without the pressures of fishing. Say the load capacity works out at 3 BB, you have then to split this into a manageable pattern of smaller shot that make up a 3 BB loading. The split shot chart (see tackle) will explain how split shot is sub-divided by size and weight.

There will be times when the flow is slow but the wind is directly downstream, then the bodied waggler becomes the correct float choice. It has the further advantage that it can be used at slightly greater distances than would be suitable for the stick float. The shot pattern differs markedly in having the bulk shot, those which stabilise the float, pinched on either side of the float ring, for the float is attached bottom ring only. Below halfway to the hook pinch on further bulk shot to take the bait down in the current. A telltale shot, No. 6 or 8, fixed at about 6 in from the hook completes the rig. Cast the float out, onto the line of the trot, with an overhead action. Properly shotted, the rig will not tangle as it flies through the air. The float will settle upright but high in the water. After a few seconds, the mid-cast bulk shot will take effect causing the float to settle where the cane insert joins to the sacandas body. Finally, the telltale shot will take the float down to leave just the insert showing. This is an extremely sensitive rig, for bites *on the drop* will be shown by the float not settling to its correct depth. Lift bites will also be clearly indicated as the fish takes the weight of the telltale. The body of the float emerges as the buoyancy of the float body takes over.

Laying on

There are fishing situations on any river that call for a static bait, but the angler does not want to turn to legering styles. Laying on is a method of float fishing, using a float for bite indication and control of where the bait fishes but keeping the bait absolutely static. This is achieved by choosing a float that will ride the current happily even though there may be a fastish flow. A stick or small balsa will cope with all but the heaviest water. Set the float at least half again overdepth. Shot down the line to about 12 in from the hook. Both shot and bait will lie on the bottom. The float is held on a tight line so that it rides, head up, showing an inch or so for bite detection. It is a good idea to cast and let the float swing round, in the current, to adopt its best lie against the flow. Then tighten a few turns on the reel, to establish perfect

A steady hand and careful pressure on the rod to play a specimen roach back to the bank. It is early in the season, but already summer riverbank growth is lush and green.

Left: The results of the afternoon's sport, a net of healthy roach all topping the pound mark, and well recovered from the recent spawning activity in the gravelly shallows.

Right: Concentration, as this holiday angler enjoys both sun and sport. The very shallow swim, and clarity of water dictate a low profile and pole tactics.

contact. Bites are shown by a vigorous plunging of the float, when a fish turns downstream with the bait, or a noticeable lift almost shooting out of the water should the fish rise with the bait in its mouth. Often the float will lie flat on the water's surface. This happens when the bait is taken up, removing just a small amount of the tension placed on the shot and bait by the current at the riverbed. Laying on can be a successful method when fishing a stream in which there are long trailing beds of streamer weeds or underwater obstructions to the free passage of a trotted bait.

Stret-pegging

This is really a method of laying on where the bait is moved downstream in stages. The system and tackle are the same using a buoyant float, but one that is not too bulky, to support itself against the flow. After casting and establishing a line for the float to follow, the bait is allowed to fish for a few minutes. Then, by raising the tip of the rod and letting a yard of line off the reel, the bait is fished statically slightly further downstream. This technique will let you fish a river progressively, like trotting, yet give shy fish a real chance to see the bait.

Holding back

In this method we use a trotting style, holding back the passage of the float momentarily to encourage fish to move up to a bait that flutters, enticingly, above their heads. After trotting through in the normal fashion where you may have experienced bites that were missed, holding back can be the answer to more positive bite creation. An increase in the length of trail, between hook and telltale shot, will ensure that the bait is swimming within reach of bottom-grazing species.

Float paternostering

Here we have a style for fishing a static bait, within a current flow, that is clear of the bottom. Perch and chub are species that will attack a bait that is just clear

of their heads. Sight of the offering is all important. The method comes into its own on the small stream, where there may be holes into which fish are attracted or undercut banks that prevent trotting or swimming a bait round with any degree of accuracy. The rod can be poked through reeds or between bushes to drop the bait, quietly, through the water. Use an 'Avon' float that will not pull under in the current when tethered. An 'Arlesey' bomb big enough to hold the ground, against the current, keeps the bait in position and allows enough weight to cast, underhand, to those difficult lies. The hook dropper can be formed by tying in a blood loop, although a tied-in swivel (or three-way swivel) to which a hook length is attached is probably safer when using fine nylon. Do not go down too light with either the reel line or the hook length as small streams do occasionally have a lot of branches and sunken obstructions in the water. A good fish on a small stream has to be held; any slack line and it will dive into the safety of snags it knows the position of . . . you don't know where they are, so a strong, effective tackle make-up will remove the possibility of a lost specimen and the resultant bad humour!

When holes are really deep, such as one might find below a weirpool, the float paternoster technique can still be applied by altering the rig slightly. A sliding float, of the same buoyancy, is employed to give a direct contact through to the hook. There are two occasions when the paternostering method cannot be readily applied: when the stream has a very fast flow close in to the bank or when the distance to be cast is greater than a couple of rod lengths. Both conditions will cause the line to belly round, pulling the float under. Fishing in easy water, close in or at distance, is readily accomplished by keeping the rod tip fairly high so that the minimum of line touches the water surface.

In all float fishing styles the important thing to remember is to use the correct float, properly shotted and set to the right depth. A bait must go to where the fish are . . . they can be fed toward the angler's pitch but this both takes time and removes the fish from its home territory, which makes it less inclined to feed in a positive fashion.

A magnificent catch of chub taken from the River Trent at Muskham; a strong terminal tackle make-up is needed for such specimens.

The angler has chosen a waggler in the windy conditions, holding back on the trot to induce bites from the shy roach. The roach is drawn gently over the rim of the waiting net.

Perch — the striped ghost that haunts the dark shadows

Perch are the craftiest of fish and Nature has complemented their predatory instincts with body colouring that gives them perfect camouflage. They can lie up alongside a reedbed, from where they strike in ambush. They are difficult for both prey and other predators to see, with the bronze-green bars on their flanks matching perfectly the underwater stalks of their favourite lies.

Perch are not only good sport and powerful fighters, but are relatively easy to catch when shoaling, so obliging in fact as to be the ideal beginner's fish. How many youngsters had a perch to thank for their first catch. Perch are also very catholic in their choice of baits and the angler's methods are equally varied. They can be lured on small blade spinners, wet flies and nymphs, artificial reservoir lures, minnows, worm, maggot or grubs.

While shoaling, perch tend to mix of a size, and once located can offer hectic sport, providing the shoal isn't disturbed or doesn't move on. Big perch however . . . really big perch, upwards of 2 lb have to be searched for! They don't readily show themselves, and are either loners or move in small packs. Infuriatingly, they always seem to haunt the most inaccessible places as far as the angler is concerned . . . holes and gaps in the reeds where it's difficult to cast an artificial lure to or drop a minnow or worm over the fish without too much disturbance. One successful method involves creeping along the river or lake banksides, dropping a paternoster baited with worm into each likely hole.

A fairly long rod is required. A 12-ft coarse fishing float rod with fixed spool reel, loaded with 4 lb b.s. nylon is ideal. The terminal rig, shown here, is perfect for the job. Attach the baited hook length about mid-way between the lead and the float. This is because invariably, perch swim in mid-water and the worm has to be clearly seen by the fish that you are stalking. The float should not be too heavy; perch, although eager feeders, can be put off by the wrong gear, and that means anything which causes unnatural resistance when the fish takes the bait.

The lead, lying on the bottom, will keep your tackle in the chosen swim position. Adjust the float to give a tip showing about an inch or so. With the rod tip poking out through the reeds, it is possible to impart life to the bait, by lifting the rig occasionally, then letting it settle for a minute. If fishing a river, this will place the bait a few feet downstream, and using this technique, the whole of a long stretch of riverbank can be effectively searched with the minimum of moves by the angler. Where the flow is slight or on a stillwater, when there is little wind to move the bait, the lead can be kept to a minimum, sufficient to hold the worm in the desired vicinity of the perch's territory. Perch can at times be easily frightened. This is often the case when a shoal of fish is travelling or feeding near to the surface. The unsuspecting angler can approach without realising the location of the shoal, and the first thing which indicates their presence is when they 'sound' or dive away from the intruder, causing, as they go, an effect on the surface of the water similar to somebody throwing in a handful of stones. When perch are moving close to the surface in this manner, careful observation will often give the angler a chance of spotting the fish, before the perch see the angler. Polarising lenses ▶

Left: The paternoster rig suits minnow as well.

can also help spot the perch just below the surface, or in calm conditions the fish leave a wake caused by their dorsal fins. What the angler has to do in such circumstances is to intercept the shoal. If he is on the bank of a river or lake, it may mean moving quickly up the bank ahead of the shoal and anticipate where and when they are going to arrive, ensuring that his bait is already in position before the arrival of the fish. Perch can cover a lot of ground, and even a clumsily-cast bait over the top of the shoal will scatter them in all directions. By pre-baiting a swim ahead of the fish, however, the lucky angler should be able to hold the fish for some time, with the chance of taking a good net full of perch.

One of the most effective methods for catching really big perch is using freshly-killed minnows. Live minnow is used extensively on major waters, and is particularly effective on the deeper lakes such as Windermere. Rather than using livebait — the ethics of which are not discussed here — a deadbait fished sink and draw can be even more effective. The angler has more control over the fish, and can place the bait exactly at the depth and position he wants. Since a bait simulating an injured or sick fish is much more likely to draw a response from a predator, the sink and draw method of working a deadbait is just as effective if not more so than a livebait, without creating the possibilities of criticism by anyone.

River Tweed below Norham Bridge

Dace of the North

The most northerly distribution of the dace in Scottish waters is restricted to the lower Tweed and its tributaries. The streams in the Coldstream area up to Norham Bridge, and the Leet Water are relatively unfished by experienced coarse anglers, and it is only in the last ten years or so that there has been much activity. Float fishing with maggot or casters is the most widely-practised method here, although the dace will also take small-hackled flies readily during mild conditions.

These slim, silvery fish require light tackle tactics and take a bait with lightning speed. The average on a good dace water might go 6-8 oz, with a pound fish very good indeed. A 1½-2 lb hook length and matching reel line is not too heavy considering the speed of the take and fast water which the dace is fond of. Any lighter and the angler risks a breakage against the current and speed of the dace. When feeding well, dace will virtually hook themselves, and all that is required is a quick but smooth raising of the rod against the pressure of the fish to secure the hook.

A fish for all seasons

There are a surprising number of venues and locations where big roach remain relatively easy to catch, fisheries with no great pressure from intensive angling. The River Erne and the Cork Blackwater are two Irish examples, and lower Tweed and Tay in Scotland both offer coarse anglers a good chance of 2-lb plus specimens.

In the heavily-fished match waters and club fisheries of the Midlands, the roach, even small fish, become very hook and tackle shy; skill is necessary to locate and hold the fish. The roach, as well as giving the angler good summertime sport, is a true winter fish, continuing feeding right through the coldest months, even when there is ice forming on the water. Not only is the angler fortunate in having roach which are widely distributed, but he has a fish for all seasons!

In late April and May, roach begin to congregate in the shallows in readiness for spawning. They develop breeding tubercles similar in appearance to those on the bream. In the rivers, roach move up into the very shallow streams to deposit and fertilise their ova. The eggs are laid in gravelly redds, buried from predators and the sun, until the eyed ova hatch into fry. In a mixed fishery, the roach spawn will suffer from a variety of fish, notably eels, perch and trout.

Above: Delicate bait presentation trotted down the far bank will be effective here.

Above: A superb perch, with an equally colourful array of floats, designed to catch the angler's attention rather than the fish.

Left: Float fishing for roach and perch on the River Endrick.

Legering in running wa

Winter spate conditions mean coloured water and a stron,
static bait presented where the fish can see it is the ke

er

rent. A
success.

Legering is an allround fishing style that can be adapted to suit most rivers and streams. The idea is that a lead weight gives sufficient holding effect to fish a bait right on the bottom. Whether the bait is intended to roll across the riverbed or hold a static position, the sinker chosen must never be too heavy or be fixed in a way that would transfer its weight to a taking fish. The most simple type of leger rig is one where the leger weight slides freely on the reel line. It is prevented from running down to the baited hook by a split shot or small swivel, pinched onto the line. The distance between sinker and hook depends upon the type of water fished. In a strong current the bait will wash around downstream extended from the tethering leger weight, which can be attractive to fish seeing the hookbait waving in the flow. In a slow-moving river a smaller trail is advisable as there may not be enough current, at the bottom of the stream, to get the bait extended. If the line between rod and bait isn't tight the fish will have the possibility of removing the hookbait without its movements showing to the angler.

The rolling leger

This is a technique for covering the whole of the riverbed, finding the position of fish across its width. The leger weight, a drilled bullet, is fished with the reel line running through the lead. Stop the bullet lead with a small split shot or by tying the smallest of barrel swivels into the rig between sinker and hook. The latter method is probably better because it is less likely to jam. The baited rig is cast across the river. After settling on the bottom, the current begins to have an effect against both leger weight and line. The rig trundles across the stream, its movement indicated by subtle motions of the rod tip or bite indicator. Deciding when a vibration is caused by a fish grabbing the bait, rather than the leger jumping over the bottom, is a matter of experience. If the leger stops in its travel across the river, it could be hung up or there may be a fish that has taken the bait, thus halting the weight's arc of movement.

One of the best bite detection methods is the *touch leger*. This means that the angler holds the line as it leaves the reel, between thumb and forefinger. Bites and rolling movements are easier to define by feel than by sight. After a cast has been fished round, the next cast should be a yard or so further down the river. Each further cast ensures that the riverbed is searched progressively.

Applying a rolling leger system to fishing a small stream has another value: it does not frighten fish in shallow water when they are feeding in the middle of the stream or in toward the angler's bank. A lead cast directly to the fish would splash through the surface, above their heads, creating both an audible and visual

Top: No wonder chub have healthy appetites! With a mouth that size, they make quick work of most hook baits.

Above: The River Avon at Stratford where the predominant species is chub. They respond to a legered bait as well as trotting.

Left: A barbel from the River Severn at Arley noted for specimen fish of a number of species. Dace splash in the shallows but it is in the deep water at mid-stream, that the barbel lurk among the weeds.

75

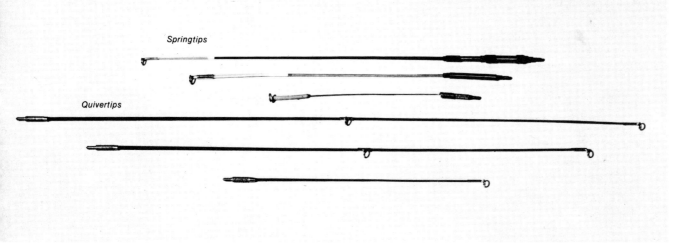

Springtips

Quivertips

Quivertips — a sensitive leger bite indicator for most situations.

Legering below a weir on the River Dove, Walton's favourite river.

disturbance that could cause chub and roach to scatter downstream. The rolling leger is cast away from the holding ground, it then rolls around silently bringing the hookbait in a natural swimming fashion.

The leger weight can be fixed in a number of other ways. If the stream bed is known to have a number of obstructions, a link leger will help in releasing a rig that catches up. It is very easy to form the link. A small piece of nylon is folded over the reel line, then the number of swan shot necessary to give casting weight and bottom-holding power are pinched onto the nylon link. The link is prevented from slipping to the hook by a small split shot. If the leger catches in an obstruction it can be released by a steady pull on the reel line. The swan shot will pull off the link, releasing the hook

link . . . which could have a good fish attached!

Legering a static bait

Most legering is done with a bait that is intended to hold in a definite position down on the riverbed. Similar leger weights can be used, although fish have all the time in the world to inspect and take the bait, so the rig should be as sensitive as you can make it. That means the sinker must not be felt by a fish. Having the leger weight on a separate length of line is one way to minimise the possibility. A small three-way swivel, used as a junction between hook link and sinker link, will complete the rig in a way that ensures the bait contact is direct to the rod tip without passing

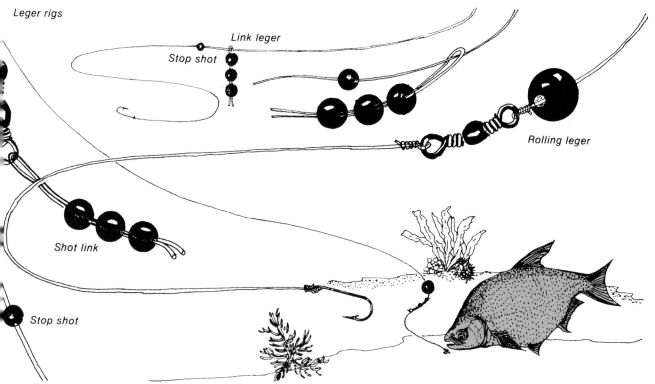

Leger rigs

Link leger

Stop shot

Rolling leger

Shot link

Stop shot

Link leger for a static bait; the rolling leger needs even current and a clean bottom.

The correct attachment of the swimfeeder to prevent tangling the rig.

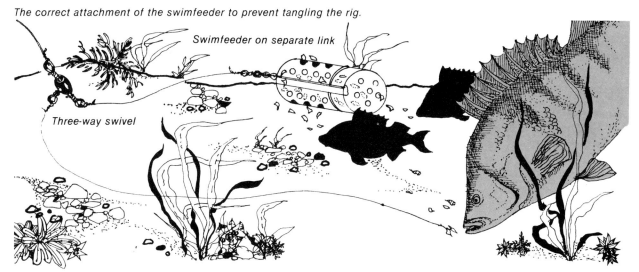

Swimfeeder on separate link

Three-way swivel

through a lead weight. Another rig system is for the sinker to be attached to a short length of nylon, say about 12 in, which is then tied to a small barrel swivel. The swivel runs on the reel line, stopped by a split shot or another swivel. This rig would be equally useful as a rolling or static leger.

Groundbaiting is an integral part of legering. Ideally, we need the feed to be slightly upstream of our hookbait. One cannot throw out groundbait with that degree of accuracy so the answer is to use a swimfeeder forming a part of the terminal rig. There are a variety of swimfeeder types. Some are known as *open-end* feeders. They are used to deposit groundbait particles as the current washes the feed out from the celluloid tube. Sufficient weight, to hold bottom, is built into

the swimfeeder as a strip of lead attached to the side. Casting groundbait with a feeder ensures that the attractor feed is lying exactly where the angler wants it to be. If there is a drawback to the use of feeders, it is that they form an obstruction to the current, setting up a strain to the line and rod. Line strength must be raised to accommodate the swimfeeder while a suitable rod should be used. Some of the resistance to current flow can be overcome by using streamlined *block-end* swimfeeders. These are designed to feed maggots in a stream down to the hookbait. The small holes, punched out of the feeder body, allow the maggots to wriggle through a few at a time. Manufacturers are constantly producing new shapes to improve the efficiency of their feeders with a view to cutting down resistance to current flow.

Groundbaiting with a swimfeeder is the best way to bring fish onto the feed and keep the feed in a defined area. Little but often is the golden rule of groundbaiting . . . so, to position it close to the hookbait must make sense. It isn't always necessary to match hookbaits to groundbait. One can feed cereals while using a worm on the hook or use breadflake in conjunction with breadcrumb feed.

Detecting bites

Fishing a river or stream assumes that there will be a current of sorts. On a slow-flowing stream, the swingtip can be used because the current flow can be counteracted by the chosen weight of indicator. Trouble comes when the current speeds or is irregular, for that will make the tip move accordingly. The angler has to sort out what is a bite and what movement is caused by the flow. If you then add a breeze of wind, the swingtip dances unmanageably. These conditions call for a springtip or quivertip and either of these bite indicators can be matched to the prevailing conditions by choosing one with the correct tension characteristics. Both are screwed into the tip ring to provide a more flexible rod tip extension. Length and diameter of material settle the uses of quivertips whereas the length and number of coils to the spring, determine how a springtip will react to the pull of a biting fish.

Obviously, either of these rod tip indicators will react to current flow but experience will tell how much of the adopted bend is current and how bites differ from the normal indicator attitude. What must be done is to make certain of the actual fishing position, in relation to the rod. Fishing ought to be at right angles to the direction of the reel line as it cuts through the surface of the water. It is no use pointing the rod toward the bait. That stance will be suitable for a swingtip but show little movement using a quivertip, that can be reacted to.

For those occasions when big fish are expected in a strong flow, one might think of using the rod tip as the only form of bite indication. Most modern rods have very sensitive, slender tip sections that give a perfect indication. This style, perhaps coupled with the reel line held, as a touch-legering addition, can be as sure a method of successful bite detection as any other!

Striking the fish

As legering is normally conducted at greater distances than floatfishing techniques, it follows that there will be more line out with all the stretch that that infers. Striking effectively means that we have to overcome the natural elasticity of nylon, shift the leger weight

Top right: The best swim in the pool. Unlike the anglers fishing the far side, the angler's choice of swim on the near bank allows him to leger on the edge of the stream, the backwater caused by the tree producing a fish-holding eddy.

Below: This lively chub was hooked on a rolling leger and sweetcorn bait fished under an overhanging tree, shading a deep gravelly swim scoured out by the current.

and set the hook into the fish. A short, sharp strike will not prove effective. A long, swept back strike is vital. The rod back *and* high position must be held to first feel the fish and then a few turns of the rod handle need to be made to take up the length of line gained by the strike. Then the rod can be brought round and toward the fish while the line is continuously recovered onto the reel. Perfect contact is all important as this is the time when a great number of fish are lost. A few moments of slack line after the initial strike motion is made, enables the fish to *bounce* off the hook. Whether legering or floatfishing, the quarry must always be fighting against the pressure of the rod arc.

Many authorities advise the angler to set his slipping drag adjustment to match the power of a big fish that may be too much for the fisherman to handle during the early stages of the fight. On the face of it, good advice. But, it is infinitely preferable to make your fish fight the rod, not the mechanics of a slipping clutch! Certainly, make the drag setting a sensible match to the breaking strain of the line but keep the attitude of the rod correctly . . . held high, so that the fish lunges against the sweetness of the rod's action . . . never with the rod tip pointed toward the hooked specimen. Our sporting pleasure is in using the vibrations' pull of a hard-fighting fish, to test skill and tackle make-up, not in hearing the burr of slipping drag washers!

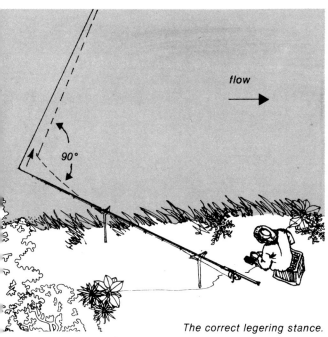

The correct legering stance.

Free-lining on small streams

In a small stream where there is little current flow, the splash of a leger weight, however small, will send a vibration running through the pool. Casting a small piece of breadflake, using an underarm swing, will make less noise and yet have enough weight to hold bottom. The method has the advantage that by raising the rod tip the bait can be dropped downstream as a few yards of line are run from the reel. Waiting fish may see the bait as an arrival of food in a perfectly natural fashion. Maggot baits have little weight for casting or holding position in a gentle flow so the addition of one BB shot, at about 24 in from the hook, will be necessary to fish effectively. Bites are detected by watching the bow formed in the line. The angler should respond to any straightening movement by an immediate strike. When fishing directly downstream the touch legering style can be equally effective.

Spinning on rivers

Early morning and the frosty mist lingers in the stillness of the valley.
Pike lie in wait.

The art of spinning for coarse fish encompasses a variety of techniques, using an equally diverse collection of spoons, plugs, lures and natural fish baits . . . all of which don't necessarily *spin* in the water. The technique and ultimate goal will be, however, to lure the fish into believing that it is taking a sick or injured fish. Whether the bait is one of the hundreds of artificials available on the market, or a natural dead bait, it will be mounted so that the lure works in a life-like if erratic manner.

Most coarse species at some time or another will take an artificial bait, fished on a spinning rod and reel to imitate a small sick or injured fish. Few anglers, however, deliberately fish for carp, bream, roach and rudd with spinning tackle, and rightly so. When such species decide to take a spinning bait . . . as they often do, then the fun is in the surprise element rather than the capture or fight. Those species which interest us most include the grayling, chub, zander and those two formidable predators, the perch and pike.

Sink and draw

Eels live sedentary lives on the bottom, and will seldom move any great distance to take a bait. Eels will occasionally take a small dead bait, on a spinning mount. A legered dead bait is a far more common method though, but especially when there is little response to this technique, spinning can be an effective alternative. A small minnow or dace can be mounted either on a spinning flight or wobble tackle, and is then fished slowly, sink and draw along the main lies. Underwater snags can prove a problem in both instances due to the slowness of retrieve. The method has the advantage over legering, that far larger areas of water can be covered by the angler, with an increased chance of finding a willing fish.

Sink and draw is not really a method of spinning, but is an excellent method of working a natural bait on spinning rod and reel, especially useful covering lies close in to the bank. While effective for eels the method is used far more when after chub and perch, and is discussed fully under these species.

Choice of rod and reel

Few anglers nowadays fish with a centrepin or the traditional side-casting reels developed by Alvey of Australia, where the spool is turned through ninety degrees for the cast, and then returned to the normal centrepin position for the retrieve. This type of reel has the disadvantage of kinking the nylon, unless the angler reels in left and right handed on consecutive casts. Even then, the reel line does take unnecessary twist, which inevitably weakens the nylon. The most

popular spinning reels undoubtedly are those of the fixed-spool variety. There are numerous good reels on the market, and the choice is normally a personal one. However, the size of reel should match the rod chosen, and also the breaking strain of line to be fished. It is no use fishing four pounds nylon for spinning for say perch, and load a spinning reel, more suited for pike fishing, which won't have a sensitive enough slipping clutch to allow a fish to take line without causing a breakage. The closed faced fixed-spool reel is favoured by some anglers, especially for light threadline work, and is generally used on top of a short cranked-handled bait casting rod. More popular, especially for

Thumb pressure on the multiplier ensures a smooth delivery when long casting, and prevents over-run.

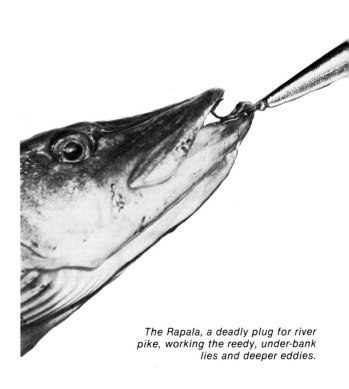

The Rapala, a deadly plug for river pike, working the reedy, under-bank lies and deeper eddies.

heavier work, is the multiplying reel, simply called a multiplier. The multiplier demands rather more concentration from the angler if casts are to be made efficiently. Even with modern braking systems, it is still all too easy for a careless angler to produce a disastrous overrun, caused by the spool accelerating faster than the line is travelling out with the bait. The tension on the multiplier has to be adjusted to suit the weight of the lure or bait. The small, compact lightweight multipliers fished with 8-10 lb line or sometimes less, will handle small spoons and plugs weighing ⅜ oz or so, but for normal multiplier use, baits of between ⅝ and 1½ oz are more normal, and help balance the mechanics of the cast.

Rods vary from short 5-ft baitcasters with cranked handles, to about 10-11 ft for pike spinning or capable of casting a fairly hefty dead bait 30 or 40 yd. Techniques and choice of tackle and lures to suit are dealt with by species, allowing for a natural overlap, where the angler would expect to catch perhaps more than one type of fish at a particular venue.

Dace — playmates of the salmon

On this particular occasion I wasn't out for coarse fish, but was on the lower Tweed below Norham Bridge. Tidal influence is still noticeable this far upstream, and with a low river, I was hoping that one or two salmon were holding in these lower pools, waiting for rain before venturing farther upriver to spawn. There were a few fish lying below the bridge, but they proved uncatchable, occasionally walloping the surface in a display of boredom. Several were very red and had obviously been in the pool for some time.

Below the bridge, the river takes a broad glide down through some fairly shallow, weedy streams; beautiful dace and roach water this, but today, of no interest when after salmon. At the tail of the broad shallow flat, the river gathers again at the head of an island, and it is here that the first real chance of a salmon happens for the flyfisher. The fast stream from there down to the tail of the island is again full of dace, but a little too fast for the roach. Towards the tail of the stream on the right bank — English side — is an enticing eddy.

The swirl of the water on the edge of this cauldron means it is virtually impossible for the angler to distinguish whether the salmon will be lying facing upstream or at times downstream depending on the lie of the current; the backwater was also full of dace, and by the evidence of the regular splashing of big fish, there was no shortage of salmon either. Then something extraordinary happened. The salmon stopped jumping, and after several minutes of quiet, the whole eddy burst into spray as dace *en masse* erupted out of the water and scattered in all directions . . . perhaps fifty or more. My first reaction was that there was a wily pike in the swim. Although seldom taken on rod and line, pike are to be found on lower Tweed. This wasn't a pike at all, but the salmon . . . not just one fish, but several.

I retraced my steps back upstream and crossed over to the far bank, and sat quietly watching. Sure enough, the same exercise was repeated, the pattern unmistakably caused by four or five salmon having a bonanza, chasing these dace for their lives. Since salmon don't feed in freshwater, there was no doubt in my mind that this was just a form of play or amusement for the salmon, although I doubt if the dace were of the same opinion.

I had beforehand tried unsuccessfully to interest the salmon in a variety of baits and flies . . . the traditional Tweed patterns such as Yellow Dog, black and yellow bucktail, and black and orange. I had cast a small copper spoon across and a Zebra black and gold Toby, to no avail. This was early September, so spinning was still allowed for the salmon. I crossed back over, but this time tied on a Silver Wilkinson, hoping that the flash of silver would remind the salmon of their 'friends', the dace. I waited until the action returned. Immediately after the rumpus had died down, I cast my cheeky 'dace' into the edge of the eddy, and drew it in short jerks across and onto the edge of the stream; wallop! The line drew, and I tightened into a lively fourteen pounder, which was duly landed. Whether the fish had taken the fly as an impudent dace I don't know, but perhaps it had been the dace which were disturbing the salmon and not the other way round.

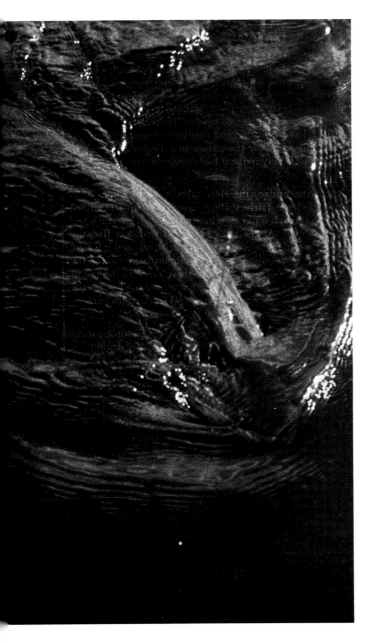

Plug fishing for pike

Plugs in their smaller sizes can be effective for chub and perch, but generally, most plug fishing is associated with pike. Plugs can be floaters, sinkers, jointed or of single piece construction. The bigger the plug, the more hooks it is likely to have. The more battle-scarred the plug is, the more the fish seem to love it. The freshly-painted specimens from the tackle shop undoubtedly catch more anglers than fish, but the real signs of a successful lure are the teeth marks in the wood or plastic. Most plugs are of the floating variety, and the depth at which they swim is governed by the diving vane at the front of the lure. Some of these baits have adjustable vanes, so that the angler can choose the depth at which he is fishing. If pike are not taking at one depth, the angler can alter the depth and speed of retrieve of the plug by adjusting the vane without changing the lure.

Unlike spoons, which flutter, dive and dart, the plug has a more readily defined action, often a side to side wobble, which, like the blade spinner, sets up vibrations in the water simulating an injured or sick fish. Since the directional movement of the plug is more stable, strikes tend to be equally positive, and pike are more likely to take hold on the first hit. Plugs also tend to be slightly larger, slower moving baits, and are also easier for the pike to hit.

One of the difficulties related to plugs, especially those with more than one treble hook atached, is the unhooking of the pike. Big fish should be handled with care, and a gag used carefully, to ensure that the mouth remains open while the hook removal operation takes place. A pair of forceps can help the operation, or one of the proprietary mechanical disgorgers. The angler has to take care that during the removal operation, the pike remains still. A slip can cause one of the free hooks to become lodged either in the angler or elsewhere on the fish. For this reason, multi-hooked plugs should be avoided, and two larger trebles at the most, rather than three smaller ones, used on the bigger plugs.

Jointed plugs have the added attraction of weaving and swimming in a snake-like fashion through the water. Unlike a longer, single piece plug in larger sizes, it cannot be used by the fish as a lever. A 4-5 in plug, made in one single piece of wood or plastic with rear treble attached, can act against the angler on a hooked fish, which can sometimes work the bait free of its hold.

Where to fish

The pike angler quickly identifies those areas where he is most likely to find his fish. On the river, this can be near any underwater obstructions such as old jetties, dead trees or reed beds, or along the edges of banks, where the water drops off from shallows into deeper water. Here, the fish can lurk in the shadows, over a weedy bottom.

Perch

Perch are avid takers of spinning lures, at times following a bait in shoals. Often, the largest fish are leading the pack in V-formation, and on the retrieve in clear water, it can be exciting observing first one then another perch take a quick snatch at the lure. In such circumstances, it needs only one fish with the courage to make a grab, and then one of the other fish will dart up in a burst of acceleration and take the lure firmly. Often the shoal disperses as the hooked fish starts to fight, but once the unlucky fish is netted, and the angler casts again over the same area, the fish will have frequently reformed the shoal, and the exercise can be repeated several times, before the perch retire cautiously, and the angler has to look for a fresh shoal to which to turn his attention. Bigger perch do tend to be loners, and are far less likely to be fooled by an artificial. Here, the natural minnow will again score over spoons or small plugs, although in the right circumstances a jigged bait will still prove effective.

Drop minnow

Where the angler can actually fish from such structures, a drop minnow can be even more effective than an artificial. The bait is threaded onto the cast, using a needle where the eye has been cut, so that it can be nicked onto a nylon loop or small swivel, which then passes through the bait fish, by the head, and either out from the vent or near the tail. Even a small swivel will tear the flesh and skin at the tail of a small bait, and this method should only be used with a swivel if the fish is large enough. Where the bait is threaded on, with the line back out through the vent, the tail portion can be secured with a little elastic thread, red or black for minnows or small perch, and white for dace or small roach. The terminal hook can be either a small treble, single or double, again depending on the size of the bait used, and the mount can incorporate a small barrel lead threaded onto the line immediately above the hook. The angler can improve on this tackle, by using a spade end, long-shanked hook

which will allow the lead to slip over the end of the hook, and improve continuity. Where the lead remains separate from the hook, a soft bait can soon break up with the action between weight and hook at the eye of the hook which acts as a fulcrum. Without the weight, a bait can tend to fish too high in the water, and even with a lead further up the line, will tend to float rather than work in a lifelike manner, below the surface.

Since this method of fishing is generally done with a short line, and the angler is fishing with the line at a fairly steep angle between bait and rod top, the weight inside the bait aids the action, rather than in a spinning technique where it would tend to dull and impair the movement of the lure. This can be clearly seen in the action imparted to a sink and draw bait as it is worked back along the bottom, towards the angler. The area of water immediately in front of the fisherman should be covered first of all; and then gradually, working in an arc, lengthening the line, all available spots can be covered from the one position, without unnecessarily disturbing the water or the fish.

Left: Beware of the pike which appears to be played out; they can make a sudden lunge and snap the line.

Below: This youngster's casting technique is wrong. The rod should be held at the point of balance which, in this case, is at the reel seat giving directional accuracy and control.

Plugs that dive, plugs that float, wobble and flutter — even a jointed plug that wiggles!

The bait is allowed to settle on the bottom; and then by means of a lift on the rod tip, and retrieve, the bait which is head first, tail up off the bottom, backs off this 'feeding position' and then as the rod tip is dropped *swims* back down to the bottom. This method gives the bait the appearance of a feeding fish rather than an injured one, the series of bobbing movements, always with the head down, giving the impression of a small fish grubbing for food on the bottom, and then backing off. It is often 'on the drop' that the chub or perch strikes, that is, while the angler's rod is in the drop position, and the line slack. The angler either feels the fish on the end of the line, as he starts his next lift, or sometimes the line visibly moves off. Either way, the strike should be delayed slightly in order to let the fish mouth the bait properly. If the line draws on the drop, then the fish has probably taken the bait well down in any case, and a firm strike by lifting the rod should set the hook. Further delay can cause a deep hook hold which may prove difficult to get out without damage to the fish.

The nearest thing to the natural action of the diving minnow is the American jigbait. This normally consists of a single, long-shank hook with a lead ball head which can be painted white, red or yellow with contrasting eyes. The hook is dressed with dyed bucktail. Again, the most popular colours are yellow, white and red. Fished on spinning tackle, the jigbait can be cast from the river bank or side of the lake and worked back sink and draw, similar to the diving minnow. From a boat, the lure can be dropped to the bottom, and worked with the rod top, in a jerky, erratic fashion. This method is similar to pirking for saltwater fish, and is effective for perch in deep water. Small pike will also have a go, so heavier nylon on the trace will help prevent breakages.

Jigging

Spinning the natural minnow is also an attractive method for taking chub. In the river situation, accurate casting is necessary, as many of the best chub lies will be under tree lined banks, in the undercuts

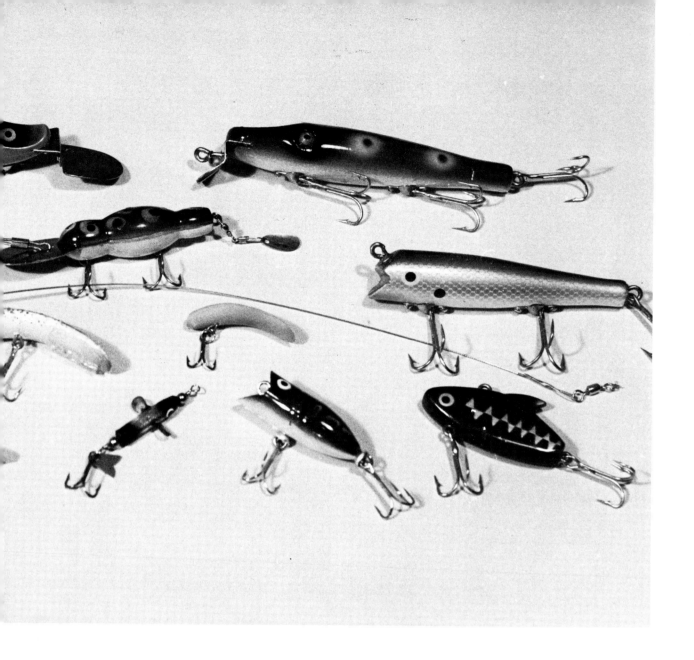

formed by the erosion of the river, and lying under overhanging trees. Where there are a lot of trees and shrubs, under which the angler hopes to place a bait, it is important to use a sidecast, to keep the trajectory of the bait as low as possible. This in terms of distance and direction is a more difficult cast to achieve correctly compared to the overhead cast, where the rod can be virtually pointed at the target. With a light outfit it is possible to use the thumb on top of the rod, stopping the backcast at the 12 o'clock position similar to that used in fly fishing. The rod tip progressively coils the spring; the angler then follows through with the forward cast in the same line as the rod originally pointed. The spring of the rod releases the bait and the target is accurately hit. This method can be adopted with either a short drop from the rod tip or a longer 'pendulum' drop for slightly heavier baits. Either way, the bait will follow through smoothly, providing the angler keeps his elbow in during the cast and the rod in the vertical plane, once the direction or trajectory is chosen.

Landing fish

All smaller species, with the exception of eels, should be netted if possible. Even with specimen pike these days, fewer anglers are using a gaff in preference to a 'specimen-sized' landing net. If the angler uses a gaff, then it should be used properly, so that no damage occurs to the fish. Whereas in salmon and sea angling a fish is normally gaffed cleanly across the back, a short distance behind the head, a pike should be thoroughly played out and brought quietly in towards the bank or boat. There the fisherman can slide the fish on the surface towards the waiting gaff by drawing it in with an arm movement and the power of the rod. As the fish is moved towards the angler, the gaff is inserted cleanly under the chin, with the fish drawn smoothly into the boat or onto the bank. Then, before the fish has time to kick, risking the gaff twisting into the flesh, the instrument is quickly withdrawn. This method works best when bank fishing, and the pike can be either beached or drawn onto the bank. For boat fishing, it is

far better to use a net. For the wandering angler, fishing the river bank or a lake, a collapsible gaff or wading gaff possibly offers him more convenience than a net, although there are now adequate folding nets which will accommodate most pike up to and including twenty pounders.

Grayling

The grayling is most frequently taken either on the fly or by trotting a worm or maggot bait on float tackle or free-lining. They will, however, frequently take a small spoon or lure. Light tackle is required, and the bait has to be small as grayling have very small mouths.

The rod and reel ideally will be capable of fishing light baits, and should be used with lines of 3-6 lb breaking strain, depending on the size of river and strength of current. Grayling tend to lie in quite fast water, or on the edge of streams.

Directional casting

The angler has the choice of either fishing across and down the current, allowing the strength of the stream to bring the lure across the fish in a lifelike manner, or casting across and upriver. Fishing upstream, the angler has to allow the bait to sink for a second or two before beginning the retrieve, which has to be faster than the current, in order that the bait works properly. A small, bladed spinner is most effective for this work, as the blade will operate with the minimum of friction, even when the retrieve is only marginally faster than the current. For upstream fishing the slower, more evenly paced stretches will prove easier; although the experienced angler will find great satisfaction in working a lure back downstream at a fast rate, *feeling* for the eddies and current as he works his bait back down over the tumbling whirlpools created by underwater boulders and weedbeds.

The quarry will often lie either behind or immediately in front of larger boulders, holding station in the

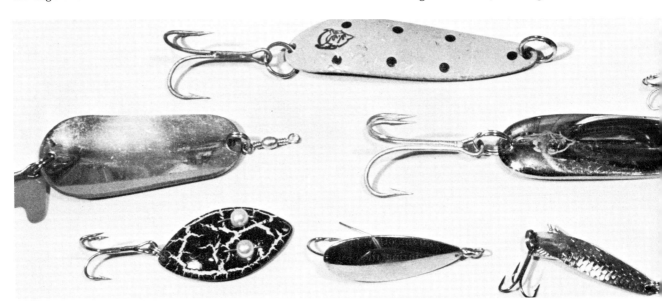

neutral pockets of relatively calm water, caused by the pressure waves around the obstacle. Grayling are reasonably fast moving fish, but won't travel any great distance to take a lure, and so the more accurate and deliberate the angler's technique the better. Chub are similarly inclined.

Fishing the stream

Let us take as an example a fairly wide stream with a good current and clean, gravelly bottom, broken here and there by weed beds and boulder-strewn lies. If the angler spends a little time observing the area, he should be able to spot where the fish are lying. They may be surface feeding on flies, or they may be observed holding on the edge of the current — a shoal of grey ghosts. If the angler adopts the method of downstream spinning, allowing his bait to move across and down the lies, he may spot fish moving to the bait, without actually taking the lure. He may also experience small plucks. Unlike pike spinning, where a faster retrieve normally induces a firmer response, a

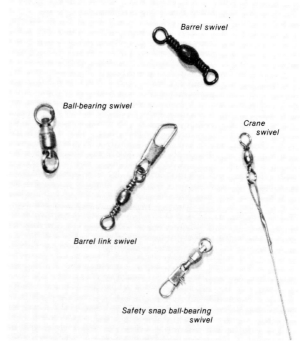

Barrel swivel

Ball-bearing swivel

Crane swivel

Barrel link swivel

Safety snap ball-bearing swivel

A big enough choice of spoons for even the most fastidious pike.

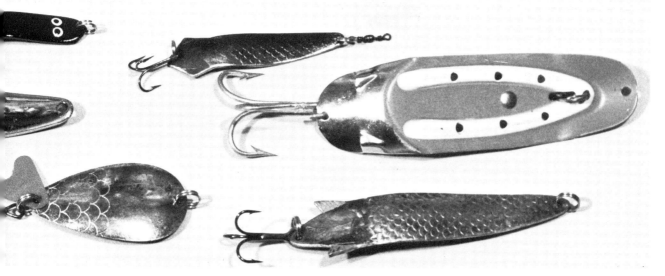

89

temporary delay in retrieve, lowering the rod top and stopping reeling for a second or two, often allows stream located species to move round and take a firmer hold.

Dorsal power

On hooking a grayling from the upstream position, the fish will almost without fail back off downstream, using its magnificent dorsal as a sail against the current. Rather than attempt to hold this first run, the angler should allow the grayling to move off down current. With the fish away from the rest of the shoal the angler, if wading, should come out of the water to follow the fish down the bank. If moving position would also disturb the grayling left in the shoal, allow the fish to work on a long line and then, as it tires, lead it into the bank below the rod position. Then retrieve line until the fish comes within reach of the net.

The angler who chooses to fish upstream, will find his technique less likely to disturb the main shoal of fish. As the spoon or lure flutters over the grayling, one or perhaps more interested fish will break away from the shoal, and turn onto the bait. If a grayling is hooked, its instinctive reaction to back off down current will naturally and without effort lead it away from the shoal and back towards the angler. Keeping a tight line on the fish, to ensure that the grayling doesn't get slack and therefore risk losing the hook hold, the fisherman can then virtually lead the grayling back towards him, and finish playing it firmly on a short line. It is then a simple matter to lead the fish into the net, and safely onto the bank.

As previously stated, grayling have small mouths, which are also very soft, and the angler has to appreciate the power and weight of a big grayling in the current, and the fight shouldn't be rushed by over-eagerness to get the specimen into the net.

A Toby spoon is quite a big bait, but this nice perch was intent upon swallowing it!

Top right and centre: If it moves, wobbles or lurches, pike will have a go. The pike above right, has taken a rubber and metal wobbler. Bigger and slower pike will prefer the sink and draw action of a deadbait; the one illustrated here is a smelt, fished with single treble hook.

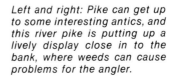

Left and right: Pike can get up to some interesting antics, and this river pike is putting up a lively display close in to the bank, where weeds can cause problems for the angler.

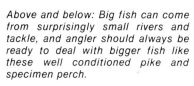

Above and below: Big fish can come from surprisingly small rivers and tackle, and angler should always be ready to deal with bigger fish like these well conditioned pike and specimen perch.

91

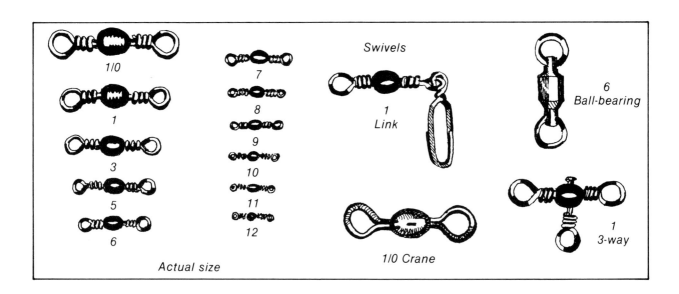

Swivels

1/0

1

3

5

6

7

8

9

10

11

12

Actual size

1 Link

1/0 Crane

6 Ball-bearing

1 3-way

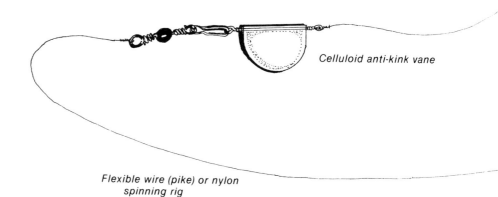

Celluloid anti-kink vane

Flexible wire (pike) or nylon
spinning rig

Chub

If the grayling has a small, soft mouth, then the chub has to be the complete opposite with its blunt head, big, tough, rubbery lips and cavernous mouth. It can be an exciting experience, fishing a small surface lure over a lie, and to see a fat lazy chub rise from the depths in an almost leisurely fashion to grab the bait. You can often spot the opened mouth before you actually see the fish! The temptation then is to strike too soon, and the fisherman should always delay the strike until the chub turns back and completes the 'rise'.

Chub, because of their shape, bulk and general feeding characteristics, are far more lethargic than other predators such as the pike and perch. They will

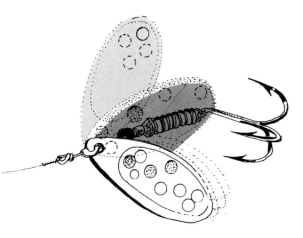

take a spinning bait readily, but won't go to any great lengths to chase a lure, if it isn't close enough, or moving too fast. The chub, too, will take up station in the swim, in quieter water than the grayling. It will be lying further down the pool, on the edge of the deeps, or under the bank, in the shade of the trees which give him much of his food. Chub will also lie at the tail of weed beds, moving out into the main current to intercept food, and raid the occasional shoal of minnow, and small fry if they get too close for their own good.

Smaller chub, those up to 2 lb or so, are far more ready to take a fast moving lure than the bigger fish, so if the angler has his sights on a specimen, his bait and pace of retrieve should be adjusted accordingly. Big chub are not so easily fooled either, and a natural minnow, bleak or small dace will prove far more effective on a wobble tackle or spinning flight than a spoon or plug. A slightly longer rod can be used for chub, with lines up to 6-8 lb breaking strain. Bladed spinners which work well even in a modest current, are better hookers than the bar spoons. They do tend to kink the nylon line though, and ball-bearing swivels, with an anti-kink vane, are much more effective than ordinary swivels. They prevent both frayed line and tempers.

For the deeper lies, it may be necessary to use either a bigger or heavier lure, or add weight to the line. The advantage of adding a weight to the line is that the angler can continue to fish a light lure, without impairing the action in the water. A heavier lure, or one where weight is added close to the bait, results in a relatively dead movement through the lies. A weight ahead of the lure by some 1½-2½ ft will allow the bait to impart a lifelike action, responsive to the topography of river bed and the variations in the current, important if the bigger chub are to be fooled by the fisherman.

A big chub when hooked will frequently come across stream towards the angler, and the fisherman must be prepared for this move, ensuring that the rod tip is kept up, and the line tight all the time. This may require some fast reeling on the retrieve, but beware of the sudden lunge back away from the angler, or a change in direction which can snap the line, if the slipping clutch isn't adjusted properly on the reel.

Chub are generally found in rivers, but there are a number of stillwater locations where chub can be found, and here they will often take an artificial lure even better than in the river situation. Again their preference is for some shade, in or near reed beds, underwater obstructions where they can shelter, such as fallen trees, or along the drop off between shallows and deeper water. If there are any timber piles or jetties, then chub, along with perch, will be found nearby.

The ubiquitous maggot: where would we be without it?

Fish will eat practically anything that lives in or falls onto the surface of our rivers and lakes. Both, animal and plantlife are acceptable as food. Some species prefer a totally live diet in the form of plankton creatures. After growing a little, they develop a taste for daphnia, which is a larger water flea that clouds the water in profusion at a time that coincides with the juvenile fish needing maximum food availability.

The young fry of mixed species then separate. Some fish will continue to find larger food animals in the upper layers of water while others sink down to begin a life of searching amongst the mud and silt for wormlike animals. The young of the pike and zander will now start to predate upon the fry of shoal species like the roach and bream. Of the millions of eggs that hatch, very few immature fish will survive the juvenile stage of their lives. The wily and the strong grow fast to become the angler's quarry of tomorrow.

Into this eco-system, the angler introduces a variety of hookbaits. Some are immediately accepted by the fish as food that they recognise; worms, that are always being washed into any watercourse, as well as maggots that the fish accept as grubs of the many flying insects that frequent the waterside. Bread, however, has a more difficult place to explain in a fish's diet. No way can it be said that fish expect to find bread *naturally*. Probably the attraction is first that it can be easily seen, and secondly, tiny portions of the hookbait tend to break off as the bait falls through the water, introducing a mini-groundbaiting effect. Fish undoubtedly have a learning capacity, so bread baits become acceptable.

The ubiquitous maggot

Most anglers use maggot baits today. Whether they are more successful than other forms of livebait is debatable. Their popularity comes from the ease with which they can be obtained. The maggot is bred on a bait farm where millions of flies are contained in sheds, feeding and laying eggs on meat and fish offal. The flies 'blow', that is lay their eggs on the meat which is then taken to feeding sheds. The eggs hatch into larvae which immediately begin to feed on the meat or fish. They grow fast and at a defined stage in growth drop off the carcases to be gathered in trays. The maggots are cleaned, by letting them wriggle through trays filled with sawdust.

Several different kinds of maggot are produced for the angler. The bluebottle, that buzzes around the house in summer, gives us the most common hookbait. Greenbottles provide the *pinkie,* so called because of the faint rose hue that colours the body of this small grub. Pinkies are used as feeder maggots, thrown into the swim to attract the attention and hold feeding fish. Canal fishers, who may be forced to adopt ultrafine fishing techniques, use pinkies as a hookbait fished on fine wire hooks of size 20-24.

The common housefly is pressed into angling service, giving us a tiny maggot called the squat. These are also used as feeders, when the angler is fishing a larger commercial maggot on the hook.

There is considerable attraction in coloured maggots. Both anglers and the maggot producers will dye the grubs in a range of colours. Red, yellow and bronze are the standard hues which may be more easily seen, by feeding fish, in coloured water. The dye is introduced to the feed on which the maggots are growing or as a powder added to a batch of maggots that have newly been taken off the feed.

The next stage in the life of a maggot is for it to turn into a chrysalis (or 'caster'); the time taken depending on age of the grub and the temperature at which the grub is being stored. Unless stored in clean sawdust or bran at low temperature, the caster stage will soon appear. Casters are a good hookbait on a lot of waters. Roach, bream and other shoal species take them well. Fishing with caster demands immediate reaction to bites because the take is incredibly fast and casters tear off the hook all too easily. It is a sound idea to combine a caster with a maggot, as a cocktail hookbait . . . bites are slower as the maggot cannot be torn off the hook quite as easily, so we get a better chance to meet the bite.

Bread

A loaf of bread will produce at least four forms of fishbait. The outer, crisp casing can be used as pieces of crust. The soft, inner textured bulk of the loaf is pinched onto the hook as flake. It fluffs up when in the water, breaking into tiny particles that spread across the bottom. The same inside part of a loaf can be soaked and kneaded to make a stiffish paste. This was a common hookbait in the past but seems to have lost favour with many anglers. When the loaf becomes stale we can dry it thoroughly in the oven. Crushed and ground to fine crumbs, the stale bread makes a good groundbait. So, nothing need be wasted.

Seeds

Most seeds will attract fish. Grains of wheat, hemp, sweetcorn and tares all take their toll of fish and it is not difficult to see why. Surrounding almost every fishery we find vegetation. Fish become conditioned, at various times of the growing season, to seeing seeds fall on the water.

Likewise, all manner of animal life lose their seasonal foothold. Some fish, chub are an example, deliberately lie under over-hanging trees to collect the natural food that presents itself. If we add the creatures that crawl among the damp bankside plants, quite a list emerges. Slugs, snails and caterpillars are baits that can be gathered and used, the only problem is that the method of presenting them to the fish must match the way in which the fish expects to see them arrive. A degree of natural presentation is vital.

At some time or other most freshwater fish pass through a predatory phase in their lives. To use fish fry as a hookbait is both difficult and slightly unethical to coarse fishermen. We expect to go for pike with a fishbait, but few anglers would set out to net minute fish to use on their terminal rigs. If there are exceptions, it will be the use of a minnow to attract large perch and trout.

Three-in-one: flake, crust and paste

Bait additives

Additives are becoming popular to the modern angler. Mixed with groundbait or the prepared hookbaits of specimen hunters, they take the form of high protein materials that give taste and smell to the standard cereal mix which forms the bulk of the feed. Tinned catfood, ground hemp, soya flour and meat meal all find their way into the water. Experience has shown that additive feeds produce that extra attraction on hard-fished waters or where fish, such as carp, have to be turned away from the natural food that a fertile carp water grows in profusion. Luncheon meat, cheese and sweetcorn are used with similar effect on a number of rivers. Species sought are barbel and chub.

Clockwise top left: hemp, sweetcorn, tares, wheat

The purpose in developing these hookbaits is to establish selectiveness in fishing. Baiting by size and type gives the angler the opportunity to fish for specific species. Conventional baits, maggots, bread and seeds, are taken by most fish so the specimen hunters are continually seeking hook offerings that will guarantee particular species interest. If the price of maggots continues rising, coupled with the difficulties that bait farms have in running what is a smelly business that is constantly frowned upon by local residents, we might well find more efforts from bait suppliers to provide man-made hookbaits. These could be cereal based with the essences of natural creatures, such as maggots, used to bind the materials together.

Worms

The lobworm or garden worm is a large mouthful for large fish. The really big, black-headed variety will take barbel, chub, specimen perch, zander, tench, bream and eels. If you are lucky enough to fish rivers containing large barbel, a lobworm can be an effective lure. Carp, if not over-fished, will also take a good-sized worm bait, legered on or just off the bottom. In coloured water, such as during a spate, the lobworm can be supplemented with a couple or more maggots, making the bait more visible to the fish.

Garden worms vary in size, and it is useful for the angler to grade those that he digs or catches, into moss-filled boxes, so that he can select his bait of the day, depending on which species he is going after.

While digging will generally produce an ample supply, an easier and more interesting method is to go out on a damp night. All you need is a torch, a receptacle for the worms, and a quick but patient arm. Moving slowly and steadily, work over a suitable lawn. The amount of success, seen within minutes, will depend on the warmth of the night and the dampness of the grass. There are signs beforehand, of course, such as those well kept lawns which show up clearly the worm casts . . . the little mounds of soil extruded from the burying worms. The more casts, the more worms.

For the uninitiated, worm catching, while not an art, can be great fun, and almost as much a sport as fishing itself. Once you spot a worm on the grass . . . beware; it's not just a simple case of lifting it up and popping it into the jar. Nine times out of ten, it will still have its tail firmly in the ground. The method is to hold the lamp steady while crouching quietly and slowly towards the worm, until within arm's length. Then, with a quick and accurate movement, snatch the worm firmly about its middle, but don't jerk . . . or you'll end up with half a worm or nothing at all. The worm's initial reaction is to make its escape back down the hole, but by steady pressure, it eventually gives up,

and can then be drawn back out of the hole and popped into the bait box. Worms also mate on warm, wet nights, and while not wanting to spoil anybody's fun, this coupling offers a double chance. One or other, or even both worms are likely to have their tails still in the ground, and therefore the snatch has to be central, and then hold on as the tug of war commences. If all this sounds rather involved for what should be a relatively simple method of obtaining bait, by all means buy them from your local dealer; it will, however, be much more expensive, and not nearly so much fun.

If your bait catching exercise doesn't run to nocturnal activity, then a wet sack, thoroughly soaked once in position over some suitable grass, and left overnight,

With so much vegetation, insects, grubs and worms will find their w

Perch, roach, flounders and sea-trout kelt, all taken on legered worm from the tidal River Tay at Perth.

can be lifted after a day or so. In the scramble that follows, you should be able to gather enough worms for your needs. An extra pair of hands will help ensure that few of the worms will escape, although they are less likely to be lying with their tails in the ground.

Small, red worms and brandlings are also easily gathered. They are found in compost heaps and in the farmyard midden. The brandling is a small reddish-brown worm with yellow stripes. It gives off a foul, yellowish substance when handled, which leaves a nasty smell on the hands. Whether this also puts the fish off is unlikely, as they are an excellent bait for grayling, perch, roach and rudd, and seem to do just as well as red worms, and even better in coloured water. Both the red worm and brandling like the

warm, damp environment which results from matter decomposing and generating surprisingly high temperatures in manure tips. Even in the cold, frosty winter, break the initial hard crust and turn over the layers with a garden fork; the vegetation and straw is warm to the touch, and the worms won't be too far below the surface.

Compost heaps and manure produce far more brandlings than the ordinary red worms or 'reds', but grass cuttings or rotten wood left lying in a grassy or soiled area will produce good quantities of the reds. While a sandy soil adjacent to the river or pond seldom offers good sized lobs, the soil around grassy roots will often produce enough reds for some sport. If you have access to a hen-run, look no further. Redworms love chicken runs, and appear to thrive on the droppings. Rake the soft areas in the run, and check any loose objects such as bits of wood or bigger stones, and there should be ample supplies of worms under them.

If you want to collect and breed your own worms, without having the space for a compost heap, you can utilise a couple of large polythene fertiliser sacks filled with manure or damp peat, mixed with animal feed or cereal roughage such as oatmeal. Of the two, red-worms are the better leger bait while brandlings produce rather well when trotted as a moving bait.

Wasp grubs

These delicate and lively offerings would be more popular if readily and easily available. Alas, wasp nets are neither prolific nor safe.

July and August are the best months to look for nests; one clue to their whereabouts is spotting wasps flying in a straight line, as they will normally be heading back to the nest. A chemical preparation for destroying nests is available from any chemist, but beware of any wasps in the near vicinity, or during treatment; they are very dangerous.

Wasp grubs are a deadly bait for chub, with the bigger queen grubs the best of the lot. Either fished singly, or for bigger fish as a bunch on a No 10 or 12 hook, wasp grubs are generally fished float style, while the 'cake' is used as a leger bait, due to its buoyancy. Wasp cake can also be deep frozen and used successfully during the winter, fished on the bottom to No 4 or 6 hook.

Docken grubs

Found usually in the roots of large docken plants, this grub can also be dug up in surrounding soil. It is a very soft bait, which will only keep alive for short periods. Keep dockens in sphagnum moss, and fish on single

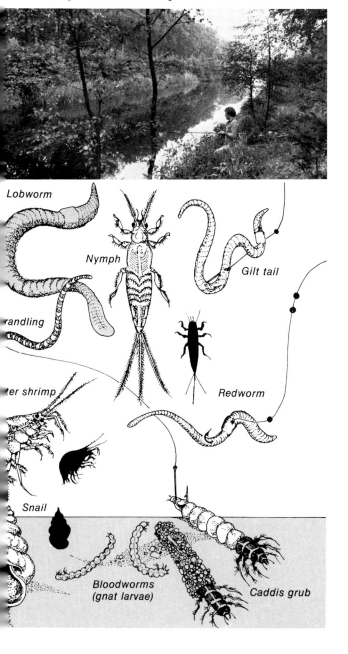

he water and give excellent feeding for the fish in this Dutch canal.

Lobworm

Nymph

Gilt tail

randling

ter shrimp

Redworm

Snail

Bloodworms
(gnat larvae)

Caddis grub

hook ranging from size 14-16 for smallest grubs up to size 6-8 for a really big mouthful. The bigger grubs have a distinctive orange-red head tipped dark brown or black, and a fat, juicy, segmented body. Docken grubs require careful hooking either lightly through the skin behind the head, or threaded onto the hook, if distance casting is at all involved. The bait does not cast well, however, and threading a docken grub onto the hook is both messy, and seldom presents such an attractive bait. Docken grub is an excellent choice for river fishing, and will take chub, perch, big roach and grayling. The best method is either freelining on a short line in streamier water, or on float tackle trotted down the edge of the current.

Crayfish

This is another excellent bait for chub. They can be gathered under the banks and along rocky ledges and crevices. Small crayfish tails will also at times take grayling in water where the two are found together such as Yorkshire's River Wharfe.

Freshwater mussel

These can be gathered in fast flowing streams and in certain ponds, and make excellent large baits particularly attractive to tench. Freshwater mussels are gathered as far north as the River Tay and tributaries in Perthshire. The roach and perch of the lower reaches are seldom fished with this bait, which tends to be found further upstream in the middle reaches of the river.

Freshwater shrimp

Together with the small saltwater brown variety, this can be an excellent bait for big fish, especially chub and river perch. The larger saltwater shrimp is also a popular bait with salmon and sea trout anglers, so coarse fishermen should use this method with discretion on mixed coarse and game fisheries.

Snails

Many rivers and lakes produce large quantities of snails which are swallowed whole by a variety of fish including grayling, chub and roach. This results in bottom feeding, and to catch them, the angler has to either trot the swim or leger. The difficulty of imitating or presenting a freshwater snail is a major problem, however. Some success has been achieved with an artificial, tied fly-style and fished on a sinking line and fly rod, otherwise the angler has to find enough snails big enough to shell and present on a hook. Since most of these snails are tiny, small hooks, size 18-22, should be utilised, depending on the size of bait presented.

Berries

A variety of berries will take coarse fish, notably chub which love to lie under over-hanging bushes; during windy weather the shrubs and trees shed their fruit onto the water, where chub either take them on the surface or as they sink downstream. Freelining such a bait can be an exciting experience, as the chub's rubbery lips break the surface in a spectacular, slow-motion rise to your bait. You have to delay the strike, and allow the unsuspecting chub to drop back into his lie before tightening the line and setting the hook, which should be done by a firm but controlled lifting of the rod.

Grasshopper and daddy-long-legs

Both baits can be deadly, but require the flyfisher technique of dapping for most success. A longish 13-14-ft float rod can be utilised, especially on an overgrown bank, by dancing the bait on the surface of the water. Special hooks can be obtained for fishing the grasshopper or 'daddy' live — a deadly method for grayling and chub.

Caddis grub

The larvae are found under the stones in streams, where they make their homes by cementing together tiny pebbles and sand into a protective tube. In Scotland, the caddis is known as the 'gadger', and is a favourite bait for grayling and trout on the River Clyde. Here, the bait is fished normally on a fly rod, with 8-9 ft leader of 2-3 lb nylon, using a roll cast across and upstream, allowing the bait to trundle naturally over the gravel on the current. As a grayling takes, this is registered by the fly line stopping or moving across the stream, and the angler strikes. The coarse fisherman can also fish the caddis with a 12-ft float rod, 2-3-lb reel line, and size 12-16 hook depending on the size of the bait. As well as grayling, the caddis grub will also take roach, perch and chub.

Groundbaiting

When groundbaiting, it is always advantageous to include in the mix some of the hookbait. In the case of worms, these should be chopped up and used sparingly, otherwise the fish might become over-fed and refuse the hookbait. Moderation in feed should ensure the fish become interested, but not satiated. A little and often is a good guide, and where maggot is the hookbait, an occasional handful, loose feeding to supplement the balls of groundbait, will keep the fish on the feed. By alternating with balls of groundbait and loose feed, the angler can draw fish at any depth and keep them interested. Flatten the groundbait into a pancake or pendulum shape and this will swing through the water, breaking off small pieces of bait at all levels of the swim.

Right: The freshwater mussel, found in rivers and stillwaters; excellent for tench.

Below: While some food comes from the river itself, such as aquatic insects, surface flies and small bait fish, the river bank holds its own larder.

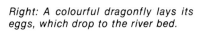

Right: A colourful dragonfly lays its eggs, which drop to the river bed.

Below: The freshwater crayfish is an excellent bait for chub.

101

Action all the way to the net on the North Muskham Fishery, Nottinghamshire. The angler was fishing at distance with straight antenna and single maggot bait.

Floatfishing on lakes and ponds

Within the governing factors of depth and distance, floatfishing is a delightful technique for stillwater fishing. The approach should be one of delicacy allied to a choice of method that will cope with the swim and its occupants.

Fishing the lift float

Summer time conjures up visions of early morning mists drifting lazily across a limpid pool. In the quiet water, near to dense weedbeds, the tip of a peacock quill shows above the surface. Every coarse fisherman's idea of opening day you might say? In these conditions tench and bream might well be the fish sought. The closed season induces a period of trust of the angler's bait by both species. We can make use of one of coarse fishing's pleasures . . . the lift float.

1 in float tip shows

Fishing the lift float

Lift

AAA split shot

6 in

The insert waggler

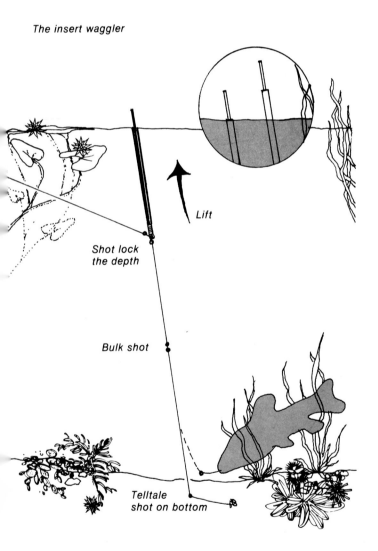

Lift

Shot lock the depth

Bulk shot

Telltale shot on bottom

The tackle make-up is one of the simplest. A single swan or AAA split shot is pinched onto the reel line within 6 in of the hook. The depth is plumbed for absolute accuracy to set the float showing only an inch of tip. When a fish arrives, the float will probably dance

a little. This happens because the fish's body or fins touch the line. A feeding fish will take the bait into its mouth which, when we consider the body shape of either tench or bream, means that they have to approach the bait nosedown. In mouthing the bait the fish lifts the weight of the single shot taking its cocking value away from the float. The angler will see the float rise up in the water, then fall over to lie flat on the surface. The strike should be made as the float begins to fall which indicates that the taking fish still has the bait in its mouth. Delaying the strike, until the float is horizontal, gives the fish time to spit the bait out.

Inevitably, fish become aware of the baits offered and the noise or vibration above their heads caused by anglers moving. Within a short time the fish change their biting behaviour. They take time to inspect offered food, whether it is loose fed or on a hook! The manner of presenting baits has to be more subtle. We don't have to leave the lift float method completely, just improve the sensitivity of the rig while reducing the amount of weight that a feeding fish might feel.

An insert waggler is pressed into use. Shotted down by locking the depth, with a shot either side of the float, the bulk shot are attached at mid-water. One other shot is pinched on to rest on the bottom. The shotting has to be accurate, so that lifting the telltale shot will raise the waggler considerably. The best way to arrive at correct shotting is to practise the art at home, using a rain barrel or deep vessel, to enable you to know exactly the amount of weight the float will take.

A variety of wagglers ought to be carried in the float box so that the water and weather conditions can be matched with the lightest float possible. In a breeze the float may well need changing to a stillwater antenna. Fished bottom end only, the diminished buoyancy of a fin-stemmed antenna will require a lot less shot to enable the angler to fish the lift float style. A No 6 telltale shot produces an appreciable lift that can be seen at reasonable distance.

The lift float style is by no means confined to fishing for tench and bream alone. Carp will give a fair lift to any float, especially when the fish has any size to it. At distance the style has to be altered yet again. A float is chosen that carries at least two SSG shot without cocking. The lengthy cast is made after roughly judging the depth. Let the bait sink on the bottom and the float lie flat. The rod is laid in its rests and the reel wound in slowly until the line tightens down to the shots, cocking the float to sink it down till only a fraction of tip shows. Put one of the shot at 6 in from the hook and the other at about 24 in above it. In extremely deep water the float can be fished as a slider, because the depth at which the float is stopped, by its knot, doesn't matter providing that setting is a couple of feet over the depth of the lake which allows the reel line to be drawn back at an angle to cock the float.

The over-shotted float style

Shy biting fish will often pull at a suspended bait, feel the buoyancy of the float, then drop the bait. The over-shotted method helps to mask the inherent buoyancy of the float while preserving a delicacy in the rig. Used when fishing up to two rod lengths out, the basic requirement is a light float that will carry about four No 1 shot to cock it correctly. The depth is plumbed to allow a fifth shot to rest on the lake-bed. A trail of about 6 in of nylon leads to the hook. The telltale shot lying on the bottom does not contribute any weight to the float until a fish takes the bait into its mouth. Doing so, it lifts the small shot which adds its weight to those that already cock the float . . . and so the float sinks away. It is very doubtful whether a fish feels the weight of just the one No 1 shot although the float will react to the extra weight immediately.

Slow-sinking baits

Not all coarse fish feed on the bottom throughout the season. There are times when rudd, roach and skimmer bream will rise to feed on small plankton creatures in mid-water. Loose feeding will bring the fish closer to the surface and get them excited. A maggot, fished on a standard bottom rig, will take the

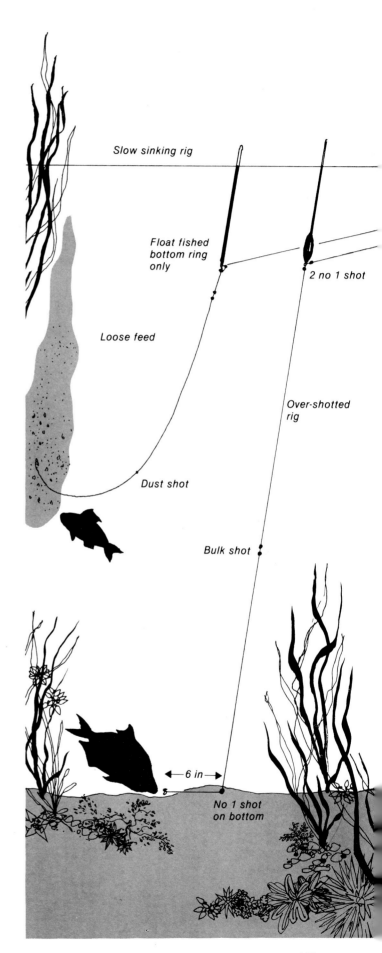

Slow sinking rig

Float fished bottom ring only

2 no 1 shot

Loose feed

Over-shotted rig

Dust shot

Bulk shot

6 in

No 1 shot on bottom

minimum of time to get down to the bottom. Mid-water fish detect that there is something unusual about the way in which the grub falls. Possibly, it lacks the energetic wriggling of the loose fed creature. We can simulate the free falling attitude of the bait by forming a rig that has all the shot necessary to cast and cock the float attached just below the float. Alternatively, a self-cocking float can be used with a dust shot to take the bait slowly down.

Unimpeded by split shot the bait's movements will prove most attractive to fish that are brought to an awareness of feed by the throwing in of a few maggots. Shot the float down, whichever one is chosen, to show a minute tip section. The dust shot will add enough weight to sink it so that it dimples the surface. When that happens, the bait has reached the depth setting. Retrieve the bait and cast again, but inspect the maggot before doing so. You may find it sucked flat, with all the body juices removed by a fish. Some 'On the drop' bites will always go undetected!

Wind action

Fishing in stillwater has one main nuisance . . . wind, that blows the float across the surface or places a curve in the line causing a lack of direct contact with the float. All but the strongest breezes can be overcome by sinking the line between rod tip and float. Always attach a stillwater float bottom end only unless you are fishing almost under the rod tip. The sunk line is achieved by first overcasting the spot that you want to fish. Let the float settle for a moment then plunge the rod tip beneath the water. Make a few winds of the reel to draw back line. You will see the nylon cutting through the surface tension. Set up the rod rests so that the rod tip is in touch with the water. Wind cannot have any effect on a line that is completely below the water. If the float continues to move across the water you will have to change fishing style to one that anchors the bait to the lake bed.

Laying on

There is little difference between laying on in stillwaters or in rivers of slow to medium flow. A stick float is fixed onto the line using the float ring and a rubber at the top of the float. The depth is plumbed and the float set to be about 2 ft over-depth. Shot is attached so that the bulk will lie clear of the lake bed with two smaller shot resting on the bottom. Leave a foot of trail between these shot and the hookbait.

Cast beyond the area in which your feed is lying. Place the rod onto its rests and carefully wind in. The float will travel flat across the surface until cocking with a slanted attitude. The trail will let fish mouth the bait with confidence, letting them move off without feeling any weight or resistance. Positive bites are registered

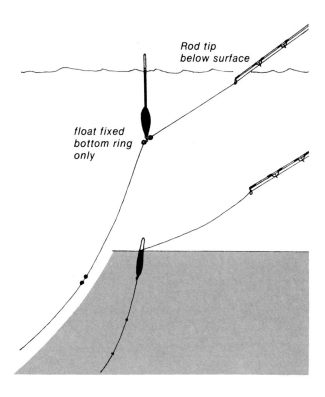

Wind effect

Rod tip
below surface

float fixed
bottom ring
only

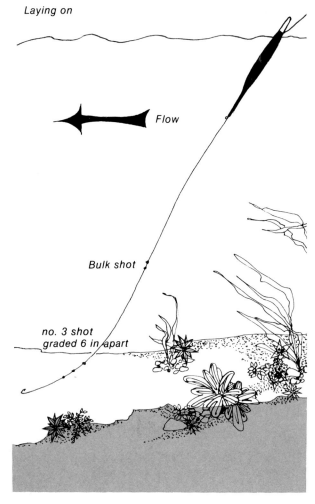

Laying on

Flow

Bulk shot

no. 3 shot
graded 6 in apart

The canal fishery

Canals were the product of the Industrial Revolution, used to transport raw materials and manufactured items between industrial towns. However, the Grand Canal, County Kildare, was dug for a military purpose for transporting British troops from the Eastern seaboard of the Republic of Ireland across to the Shannon in Napoleonic times. Because of the lack of barge traffic, the canal has tended to silt up, and has become naturalised. There is little, if any, water flow other than that required to maintain water levels and avoid the hazards of flooding. The Grand Canal between Sallins and Edenderry has established itself as a first class fishery, and in the area of the small village of Prosperous we find some of the best rudd fishing. As well as the shoals of specimen rudd, the canal contains some splendid rudd-bream hybrids, bream, perch, tench, pike and occasional roach which probably entered the canal system via the Shannon Harbour, migrating down from the Erne catchment.

Because of the popularity of the Grand Canal at Prosperous as a match fishing water, floatfishing techniques have become the dominant style. Canals throughout Ireland are of even depth, 4-5 ft being the norm, and there is little growing weed on the bottom, since the controlling local authorities pursue a policy of annual chemical control. On the major systems, there are innumerable cut-off sections where weed growth has taken hold, providing a perfect habitat for the fish species to reproduce.

The canal in the area under discussion is between 30 and 40 ft wide, with a depth which varies only slightly from 4 to 5 ft. The canal runs across the Midland Plain to the west of Dublin, is fairly straight, and lacks any real cover to prevent winter weather having a cooling effect on the water. For this reason, the canal's environment does not begin to fish before about late April or early May.

Fishing canals effectively is a delicate operation. Float fishing is always the style, with very light tackle methods the order of the day. There is very little current on the Grand Canal as the boat traffic is light, but in order to establish the water levels, the lock-keepers periodically drain water along the canal length. This, unfortunately, has the effect of moving ultra-light tackle with the water flow, but the run off is rarely of more than a few minutes' duration.

The canal rig uses a light quill float equipped with a bottom end ring, which is stopped by the use of two No 6 shot; at a point just above mid-cast, a further two No 3 shot give casting weight and stability to the rig. A No 6 anchor shot, giving at least 6 in trail to the hook, is used to present a slow sinking style, and give enough weight to the cast. The float can be locked to its depth with a single rubber, but this can give a lot of disturbance on the strike, as the float hurriedly turns over to change direction. The slightest wind, particularly from left or right of the angler, will have an effect on the behaviour of the float, and for this reason, the rod tip should be sunk with the reel line below the surface of the water.

Light rigs using quill floats are only really of use when one is fishing from one to one and a half rod lengths out from the bank. Should the approach method be concerned with fishing the far bank, the quill float should be changed in preference for a dart float which has a partial loading and better casting characteristics. However, the light shotting arrangement would not alter.

'A lost lough'?

I suppose that every coarse fisherman's dream is to find a stretch of water that nobody has ever fished before. Apart from the wilderness areas of the world, that vision is never likely to be fulfilled. But, on rare occasions one does find something that is virgin water. More often than not, finding such a fishing location is pure accident . . . although I recently happened on such a place by a combination of good luck and research.

Hearing that the Irish Coarse Fishing Championship was to be fished on Lough Garradice, I headed up into the lakeland of Cavan to take a look at what was an unknown quantity to me. A few words, with locals in the tiny bars of Ballyconnel, established that Garradice had huge pike together with a sprinkling of bream and rudd . . . a fair mixture in Ireland, where there has always been a perfect balance between predator and prey.

My first sight of the lough indicated that finding fish wouldn't be easy because of the sheer size of the water. A quick circuit, using a boat and echo sounder, showed that the lough has relatively shallow margins dropping off sharply into deep water. So, armed with that information I elected to fish in two ways: for roach and rudd from the bank and an evening session using the boat to troll a big, copper and red spoon for pike.

Garradice proved to have average fishing only. The rudd, roach and bream would not move onto the shallow marginal shelf. Firing out feed, liberally laced with pinkies, produced about 20 lb but nothing startling. So, I loaded the boat with all my gear to fish the river that flows into Garradice from the north. In motoring under the road bridge that separates the lough from a much smaller, reeded lake, the idea came to me that here was a river that I didn't know much about. It winds through meadows, far from the roads, joining a necklace of small lakes.

It happens to me often . . . once I start chuntering along with the outboard humming merrily, I tend to go further than I plan. Well, I'm glad that I did. For within a couple of miles the river broadened into a shallow lough, fringed with dense beds of reedmace. I couldn't see the road, and I imagine that infers that the lake is totally hidden from the searching eyes of anglers as they pass by to the popular Cavan waters.

An inspection seemed to be in order. So, I made a quiet circuit, with the sounder ticking away, to get an idea where fish might be. At first there was no depth at all. Three feet seemed to be the maximum. Then, having completed a circle, the flashing neon began to move around the dial to show slightly deeper water where the river flows out on its journey to the lower lakes. About 6 ft was indicated, which seemed the spot to let the anchor go. My float rod was already made up with an insert waggler, shotted to drop a single maggot slowly through the depth. First cast and I was into a fish. Nothing large . . . a hybrid of about 1 lb took the bait and tore off toward the reeds.

I must, at this stage, admit that I wasn't alone. A pal, Trevor King, had patiently allowed me to indulge myself in the business of acting as his waterborne tourist host! I think that he was on the point of giving up the idea of ever settling to fish . . . as ruined castles were passed and

▶

Float fishing at distance requires concentration and a pronounced

...ake.

rapids were negotiated. The hooking of my first fish broke his grim expression into a broadening grin as he got to the task of getting depth and baiting up. By now I had another fish into the net and was stuck into something a good deal heavier. A muttered 'Magic' and 'Fantastic' drifted back to me as Trevor realised that we were, at last, catching.

I won't say that our catch was the best that Ireland has ever given to us, but what we achieved that day will be imprinted on the cerebral diary as a bonus experience . . . one that had a pioneering flavour because *nobody had been there before . . . ?*

Burbot . . . the freshwater cod

This rare fish, with two dorsal fins and a barbel below its chin denoting membership of the cod family, was once fairly common throughout the Fenland drains and stillwaters of East Anglia and counties farther up the East Coast of Britain. Said to be a delicious eating fish (Houghton: *British Freshwater Fishes*, 1879) it may have suffered severe predation by country-dwelling folk. The species is still quite common on the Continent and parts of Canada.

Why it disappeared from our waters nobody really knows but one reason could be that since the time of Houghton's writings the Fens have been methodically drained. There is little entry for saltwater, apart from the seaward ends of the Norfolk Broads. Whether the burbot was entirely a freshwater fish has not been recorded, so the fish remains a mystery!

[signature]

by the float sliding away below the surface. If a fish picks up the bait and continues to move in toward the angler, the float will rise and fall flat as the cocking effect of the shot is removed.

Laying on is a method to use when fishing a bait just touching the bottom or lying with a short trail when all else has failed. Sometimes the fish detect the weight of shot or they touch the perpendicular line, which tells them that something is wrong. The bait laid-on has to be taken before the fish feels any part of the angler's tackle make-up!

Weed problems

There will be times when a lake to be fished for the first time is found to be full of weed. The blanket variety that covers the bottom to a depth of several feet will give the biggest problem to the angler. There are two ways in which the lake can be fished: to suspend a bait above the weed, taking a chance on whether the winds will blow the float about, or to tether the bait through the weed.

Float paternostering over weed

The depth of weed has to be assessed. Then a hook dropper has to be tied into the reel line below a float capable of cocking with one SSG shot. The shot is pinched on to the end of the reel line. It is intended to settle through the weed, onto the lakebed. The hook link lies on the surface of the weed or can be tied in to fish so that the bait hangs just above the plant growth. Fish taking the paternostered bait will rarely cause the float to dip below the surface. Usually, it bobs and moves away to the side as the fish wanders off above the weed. A shot that goes foul in the bottom can be released by a steady pull on the line, always providing that the shot hasn't been squeezed on too harshly. The method is attractive when fishing a worm or live minnow to perch or a piece of flake to patrolling carp.

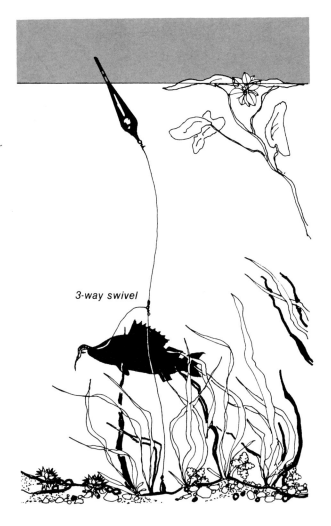

3-way swivel

Floating baits

Carp and weeds seem to go together. There isn't really a need to incorporate a float within the carp rig. It can be a simple matter of tying on a hook direct to the reel line. A crust is then pulled onto the hook and the rig cast out to float above the weedbeds. Carp will rise in the water to suck it down, failing to spot the nylon line, sitting in the surface film.

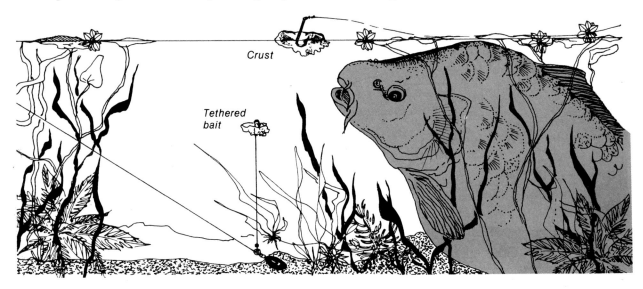

Crust

Tethered bait

A mixed net of tench, roach, stillwater chub and dace from a Severn Valley fishery.

Spawning fish and angling ethics

In Ireland, where the rudd is widely distributed, the angler has no closed season for coarse fish, and opinion differs as to the moral issues of fishing for species during and immediately after spawning activity.

It is debatable whether one should be prevented from fishing for these species in an area which doesn't have a closed season on the basis that it is unlikely that the fish will be harmed in any way, when handled properly. If a gravid fish does exude eggs or milt during handling, these would normally drop into the water anyway, and since rudd are haphazard spawners it is unlikely that any harm is done at all.

If fishing during this time, always ensure that you have a suitably large landing net, so that any specimen sized fish can be netted with the minimum of fuss or damage.

Heavily gravid fish will not take an angler's bait in any case, as they are far too pre-occupied with the rigours of spawning. They do not elect to feed at this time, and it is only the fish which are coming up to spawning or are cleaning themselves after spawning which will grab a bait keenly.

In the rudd, spawning is indicated obviously by body shape, but also by the possession of tubercles on the head and gill cases of the fish; these are present as tiny black dots. Fish in general, but the rudd in particular, take part in a noisy spawning ritual. Spawning activity is seen as a group of fish in a highly agitated fashion, rising and splashing on the surface, generally in the shallows and reedy margins, often well inside the reeds. Rudd break surface, slapping their tails, doing little jumps and turning over in the water. It seems there are two reasons for this. The ecologist would suggest that this behavioural pattern is necessary to let the fish know as a shoal that spawning is about to take place or *needs* to take place. It stimulates the activities of the heavy spawners, those not quite ready for spawning and lets the immature fish know that this activity is necessary and that in the future they would be part of it. More important to survival though, this activity is an essential part of the egg fertilisation process. Spawning is on an indiscriminate basis, with males and females coming together in groups without particular mates, often with one fairly large female being attended by a number of smaller males in a frenzied orgy of egg dispersion and fertilisation.

It is fascinating to watch a situation where, within a few yards of a spawning group of rudd, another shoal parades in only a few inches of water, in a clear area surrounded by reeds and rock, and is prepared to take a hookbait readily in only a foot or so of water.

The sliding float in use

The deep swim that vastly outspans the length of the angler's rod is the situation that causes most trouble for the average fisherman. In these circumstances, he might well turn to legering. It is worth considering the use of a sliding float to overcome the depth problem. Some sliders are fitted with two small rings, one at the side of the float body and another at the base. There is a good case for using a float, of the bodied waggler variety, with only a small bottom ring. Then the line can be sunk to beat wind as well as depth!

Begin to make-up the rig by running the float onto the reel line. Then tie a hook directly to the line. Take a guess at the depth and tie into the main line a stop knot. Attach your plummet and cast out to get the depth. When it has been gauged accurately, shot the line with the bulk at about 3 ft up from the bottom. A telltale shot will hold the bait tight on the bottom if pinched on at 6 in from the hook. Add a further small shot 2 ft above the bulk weights to stop the float touching them where there is a possibility of the hook trail coming back to wrap around the float on the cast.

Cast out with an overhead punch. Let the float and terminal rig settle before closing the bail arm. At first the float will lie flat on the water while the line continues to slide down through the float ring before stopping at the knot. Keep the rod tip sunk below the water while this is going on so that the line remains buried after the float cocks. Reaction to a bite must follow a definite pattern. The rod *must* be swept right back over the shoulder in what may seem to be an exaggerated strike. The vigour is necessary to impart a strike through the right angle of line to float and down to hook. Take the rod back and keep it there while reeling line in to establish contact with the fish. Depths over 10 ft or long-distance fishing means a lot of line stretch has to be taken up before a hook can be set.

The same sliding float technique can be used to fish very deep, slow-moving waters. A float with large shot-carrying capacity is vital as the heavy shots will get the bait down fast before the float trots out of sight!

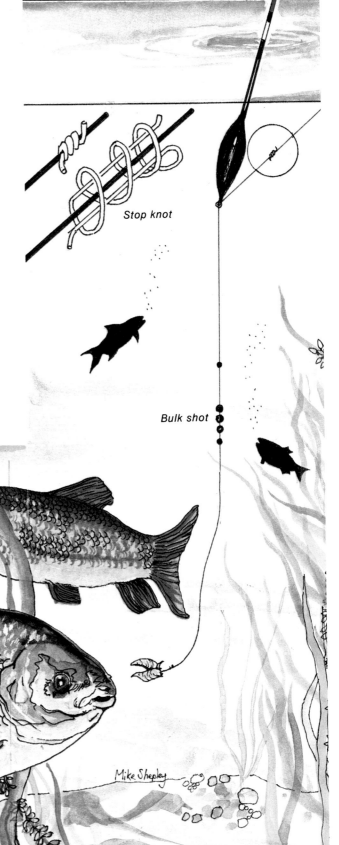

Stop knot

Bulk shot

Mike Shepley

Water lilies, bankside reeds and underwater weed growth make for a fertile Fenland fishery.

A Fenland Lake in East Anglia

In Britain, during the 17th and 18th centuries, peat workings were established in East Anglia, which have resulted in the Norfolk Broads and a number of other Fenland Lakes. The area also has innumerable gravel workings and marl pits which have now flooded and have become a naturalised addition to the lowland landscape.

Lincolnshire has a number of waters containing huge shoals of rudd, common bream and a sprinkling of that near-related species, the silver bream. As well as these rudd and bream, there are roach and hybrids between these three species, along with tench, carp and three predators . . . the pike, perch and zander, the latter a relatively recent introduction from Central Europe. Float and leger techniques are used to fish for these species in the extensive Fenland waters. This is a description of an actual rudd fishery in Lincolnshire which has become naturalised from this combination of early peat and gravel workings. The depth of the water close in to the margins is about 4 ft, dropping out from the banks gradually into 8 or 10 ft of water, with isolated holes up to 30 ft deep.

The lake, surprisingly, only produces quality fish, including bream, roach, carp, tench, pike and rudd. There are shoals of fry and first-year immatures of all species; then there seems to be a gap between them and rudd of 1½ lb - 2 lb class. The roach run to much the same size, again with a gap between the small fish and the specimens. Tench of 6 lb and pike up to 30 lb make this an exceptional fishery for specimen-sized prizes.

This Lincolnshire water is typical of the Fenland situation. As with a lot of stillwater fisheries, particularly those in the east of the British Isles, the lake is rapidly and radically affected by temperature change. Due to the exceptional clarity, fish can also spot anglers more easily than they themselves can be seen by the fishermen. Fishing has to be done therefore at long range.

In a situation like this, one cannot draw the fish, even with groundbaiting, closer than 30 ft. What the angler has to try and do is to lay a carpet of groundbait on the top of the soft blanket weed from about twenty to thirty yards out. The distance is based on the optimum length for good casting with a degree of accuracy. Then, the style is to fish with a float presenting either bread or worm baits to lie on top of the carpet weed. Anything heavier, or any attempts at using a legering technique, won't work, because the bait and lead sink into the weed, and the rudd are unable to find the bait. As well as the tail of a lob or bread flake, bunched maggots can also be successful for rudd, with the groundbait supplemented by loose feeding with maggots. To get the distance, a catapult will be necessary for loose feeding over the main part of the swim.

Rudd are not too difficult to get into feeding mood, especially in the autumn when we generally fish this water, but they can be disturbed by over-zealous anglers, who don't approach their sport with an element of care. In the diagram, you will notice that fishing is done at a range of around twenty-five yards. That, however, doesn't mean casting to that distance. Rudd are scary, and it's necessary to overcast . . . say thirty-five yards, and draw back so that your bait is positioned amongst the fish, without disturbing them.

On the correct tackle, rudd give a good account of themselves, are quite powerful, but don't bore. They come to the surface fairly easily, and seldom get their heads down and stay near the bottom. The rudd is a much slower fish than the roach, and this can perhaps be explained by its heavier build, more solid, but without the sustained fight that a roach or hybrid between the two is capable of giving.

Stillwater chub from a Nottinghamshire lake.

Above: If the fish don't want to feed, there is no reason why everyone has to starve; steak with wine at lake temperature to celebrate 16 June.

Left: Sheffield angling writer Bill Bartles admires his first chub of the day taken at distance when adjacent swims failed to catch. Concentrated heavy groundbaiting attracted, then held, the shoal and Bill took fish steadily all day.

*: Five beautifully conditioned stillwater chub from Walter Bower's fishery at North Muskham.

Left: The chub were introduced gradually into the fishery from natural stock caught in the River Trent. The huge resident population of sticklebacks in the lake quickly disappeared and the chub grew fit and fat.

Below: The swims on this particular part of the fishery are cut through fairly wide banks of reeds, with 6-8 ft of water immediately off the reedbed. Several times, the lively chub made powerful runs into the snaggy shelf as they came towards the angler resulting in lost fish. Firm pressure and delicate reel control are master of the situation.

Legering on stillwaters

A warm summer's day and bream bubbles are rising.

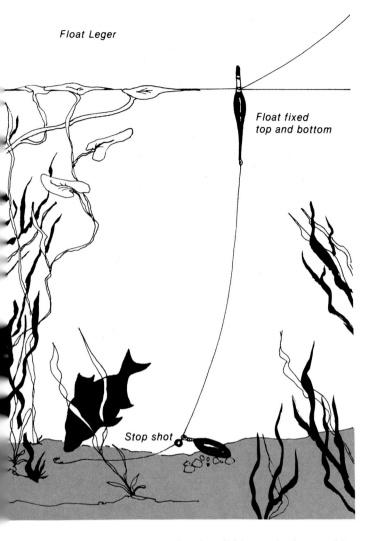

Float Leger

Float fixed
top and bottom

Stop shot

It has developed as a 'Big Fish' method of angling and experience has shown that there is good reason to believe the style to be better suited than a float fishing method. The hookbait certainly gets to where the larger fish are *and* stays there! Over recent times the rods, used for the style, have changed. Where once a 10-ft rod was in everyday use we now find that swingtipping and quivertipping have brought about the introduction of much shorter rods. It can be argued that an 8 or 9-ft rod will give a speedier transfer of anglers' reactions to the rod and down to the bait, but there can be a price to pay in that the shorter rod will not hit fish at long distance, setting the hook perfectly, nor is the control over a hooked fish quite so easy. Aesthetically, a longer rod can also give more pleasure in playing fish to the net.

Rod action

Two distinct types of rod action are found in the rods used for legering on stillwaters: a fast-tapered blank for the long distance casting and hooking, fairly thin in the wall, that gives both punch to launch a bait and the power to set the hook positively into what can be a bony jaw. The shorter rods, used with finer lines for the smaller species and for casting short distances, tend to be thicker walled and slower tapered. Most modern rods are accurately described with a test curve that lets us balance the rod to the most useful line breaking strain. Balance between rod and line is vital on all leger rods but particularly so when a shorter rod is being used. A useful starting point is to multiply the test curve by five. So, a rod having a test curve of 1 lb balances to a reel line of 5 lb. It is common practice for anglers to lower the breaking strain of the length of nylon between the hook and a swivel incorporated within the leger rig. This must be remembered when leaning into a good fish. A far better system is to tie the hook directly to the reel line with no lessening in breaking strain other than that imposed by the one knot necessary.

At its simplest, legering is a fishing style that enables us to present a bait, hard on the lakebed, at greater distances than would be possible using a float. It also beats the problem of wind as 100% of the reel line can be buried beneath the surface of the water. A legered bait, used in conjunction with a swimfeeder, puts both bait and groundbait or samples of hookbait where the angler needs them to be.

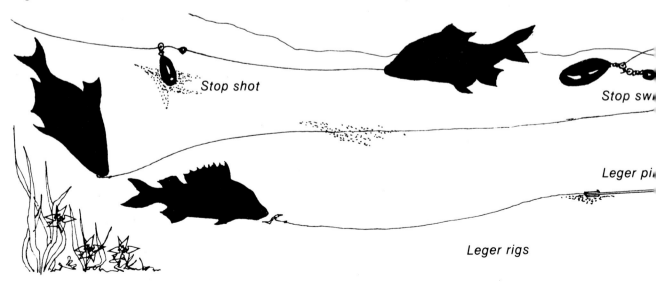

Stop shot

Stop sw

Leger pi

Leger rigs

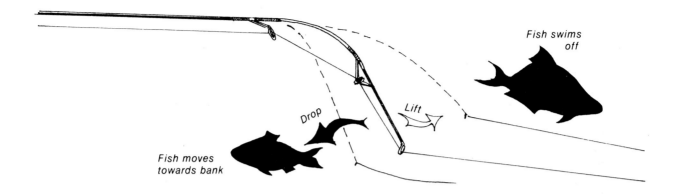

Fish swims off

Drop

Lift

Fish moves towards bank

Reel choice

The fixed-spool reel reigns supreme among legermen. It is versatile, casts well with heavy or light baits and offers a reel line quick change facility using interchangeable spools that is invaluable when fish are shy to bite. Several spools, carrying different line strengths, can be at hand to cope with the vagaries of the fish while still preserving the line strength through to the hook. There is another important aid built into the fixed spool, that is the bale arm. It can be left open so that line will peel off the drum unhindered. Fish, like the carp, are generally given time for the bite to develop into a run before any attempt at striking is made. Then, when a positive move off is seen, the bale arm is closed and the fish struck as the line tightens. The only friction likely to be felt by the moving fish, is the line running through the rod rings. There is little that can be done about that. Nylon is partially self-lubricating and, of course, a wet line will be eased through the rings quite smoothly. Rings, on the leger rod, need to be strong. Generally there are less of them than we would find on a float rod of comparable length. This is because the leger weight pulls the line off the reel and through the rings more easily as there is always a reasonably-sized weight used.

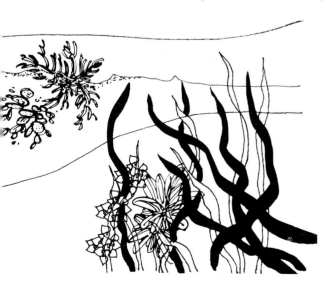

A fight worth remembering . . .

The eel is not always a welcome visitor as far as the coarse angler is concerned, but it nevertheless does attract that fanaticism associated with the specimen hunter. The mysterious excitement of fishing for big eels at night can give the successful angler great satisfaction. Eeels are powerful fighters and have equally powerful jaws. They seldom prove shy feeders once in the mood, and once an eel bite is identified, the angler who waits too long before striking will find himself with a lot of slimy trouble, and an inevitably lost hook, gorged right down by the eel.

The common eel (*Anguilla anguilla*) lives in freshwater and migrates to saltwater to spawn. In the sea, they take on a silvery appearance and are called silver eels; they are caught by shore anglers fishing in estuaries for codling and flatfish. The eel frequents lakes, rivers and ponds; in running water, it prefers the slower, quieter stretches, living amongst the weed beds, and on the silty bottom, preferring sand and muddier stretches to clean gravel. Commercial eel traps have been supplemented by fishermen 'dibbling' for eels, using a pole-like rod, and fixed line, with a bunch of worms teased with wool, dropped into likely eel holes. The eels are then lifted out, sometimes two and three at a time, knocked off into a barrel or other useful receptacle and transported alive to the market. For the angler, the method is not dissimilar. Once an eel hole has been located, legering with a lob-worm bait, often consisting of more than one worm, on a running trace, or using a small deadbait such as minnow, immature dace or bleak will attract the bigger eels. Where the eels are plentiful, it can sometimes be necessary to catch some of the smaller fish before finding the specimens. The alternative is to use a bait which is going to prove too big a mouthful for the smaller eels. Night time, or early morning and dusk are by far the best times to look for specimen eels. Unless the angler is particularly fond of eels for the table, or has a market for them, he will seldom be interested in the messy 'sport' of catching bootlace eels, which are not only virtually impossible to handle, but will cover everything and anything in a nasty smelling slime. The bigger specimens over 4 lb, however, can give the eel-enthusiast a fight worth remembering.

A bream hotspot at Silvergrove near Ennis in Western Ireland. Because of the shallow margins, anglers fish at long range on the leger.

Tackle make up

The stillwater leger rig can be a simple affair, made up in much the same way as one for fishing a river. But, there is a good case for incorporating subtlety. Unlike the running water situation, where the hook length is stretched out by the current flow, a stillwater rig needs to be pulled out to establish direct contact between angler and hookbait. It is preferable to avoid running the sinker on the reel line for two reasons.

1. The lakebed may have a layer of soft mud or silt into which the weight can sink, drawing the line down with it, where the bite is masked by the soft mud.

2. Stillwater fish have all the time available to inspect and mouth a bait. The slight friction caused, as line is drawn through the lead, could be detected resulting in the fish rejecting your offering! The leger rig can be made up in two ways to avoid introducing unnecessary friction on the lakebed. Either one can terminate the rig in a three-way swivel, so that hook link and sinker link can be tied to separate eyes, or a swivel and long length of nylon to the sinker can be run freely on the main line. Both systems give a fish freedom to take the bait and move off a small distance without feeling any resistance to their feeding.

Many anglers use far too heavy a lead. The ideal is one that will carry the bait out to where it is needed, tethering it against any slight underwater currents that the lake could have. Legering is not a 'Chuck it and chance it' operation but a delicate technique that ought to match the float fisher's styles.

Hook penetration is vital when fishing at distance. The hook ought to be strong yet fine in the wire, with a short, sharp point and a low-cut barb. Rank hooks that have high, thick barbs will bounce out of fish. You strike with them, feel the fish momentarily and then it has gone. Do not rely on the manufacturer, take a hard look at the hook, testing its strength and sharpness before tying it on to the rig.

Right: A rudd-bream hybrid from an Irish water. It has the scaling and body shape of the bream; fins give a clue to its partial rudd parentage.

Left: Swingtipping for bream at Bridget Lake, Co. Clare.

The dough bobbin

The simplest method of detecting bites when legering is to attach a clearly visible object to the line. Most anglers choose to pull down a loop of line, between the butt and first intermediate rings on which is hung a coloured object of light weight. Previously, a traditional method was to pinch a bread paste on at the same position.

When a fish takes a bait into its mouth, a slight pull on the line will cause the bobbin to rise. It is a reasonably efficient system when large fish are about; but with smaller species, the friction caused, as the line is pulled through almost all of the rings, may be felt by the fish.

I much prefer to have an indicator, whether attached to the rod or fixed to the line, at the rod tip. There is, for me, a hypnotic effect when using a butt indicator. Far better to see the tip bite indicator against the backdrop of the lake or river where there is always a lot to see that may well contribute to the fishing.

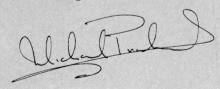

Above: A fine tench, neatly lip-hooked on running leger rig. Tench have to be handled with care to ensure the protective coating of slime isn't disturbed.

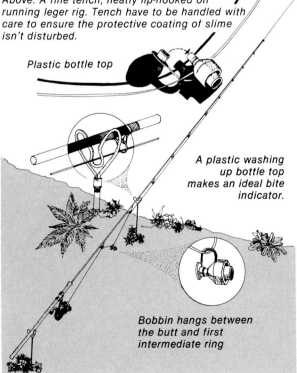

Plastic bottle top

A plastic washing up bottle top makes an ideal bite indicator.

Bobbin hangs between the butt and first intermediate ring

Another customer which requires a lot of room in the keepnet, an 18 in diameter net will provide the space and protection.

Bite indicators

Now that we have a made-up rod plan, the question of the right bite detector to use is important. Most people look for a device at the tip of the rod, and a good idea that may be. The swingtip will give perfect bite detection in two ways: the move off bite and the drop back bite. It also allows a bite a slight chance to develop as the swinging arm will move with little resistance to the taking fish. The swingtip's only shortcoming is when the wind is blowing, then the tip has either to be sheltered from the breeze or loaded with weight to overcome the movement caused. Either way the tip will not perform at its best.

A fairly long, pliable quivertip could be the answer. It is unaffected by a breeze and provided it is not too stiff, will give perfect bite indication. The quiver is also easier to cast with at any time. They are made in a variety of diameters and materials that can be chosen to match the prevailing conditions. One can always fall back on the butt indicator. This can be a sophisticated affair, like the Amron Indicator that functions perfectly in any gale of wind, or as simple as

An ideal bite indicator, above, for legering in stillwaters.

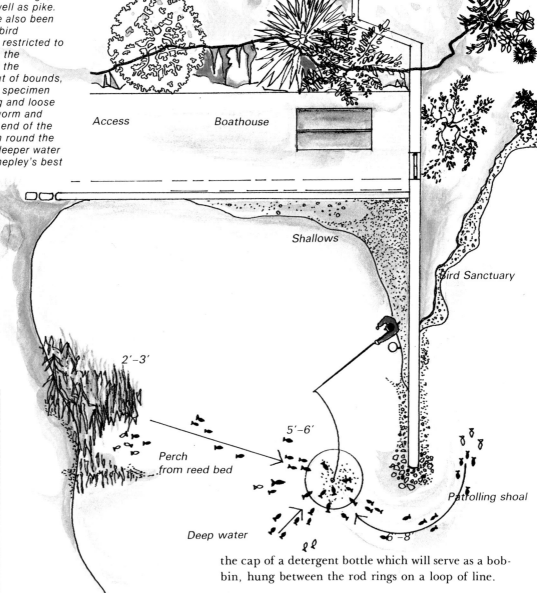

Duddingston Loch, Edinburgh, holds big perch as well as pike. Roach and carp have also been introduced. Being a bird sanctuary, fishing is restricted to the bank adjacent to the roadway. The wall at the boathouse is now out of bounds, but used to produce specimen perch. Groundbaiting and loose feed with chopped worm and maggot close to the end of the wall drew perch from round the wall, and also from deeper water and nearby reeds. Shepley's best perch from the loch went over two pounds. Efforts have been made by the authors to re-open the area at the boathouse for fishing, as it provides ideal access for children and disabled anglers.

Access

Boathouse

Shallows

Bird Sanctuary

2'-3'

5'-6'

Perch from reed bed

Patrolling shoal

Deep water

6'-8'

Left: Duddingston Loch, Edinburgh, viewed from Arthur's Seat in the Queen's Park.

Below: A very young Shepley with a 2 lb perch from Duddingston Loch.

the cap of a detergent bottle which will serve as a bobbin, hung between the rod rings on a loop of line.

The length of trail or hook link is always a bone of contention among legermen. Whether there is a material advantage in having a short or long hook link rather depends on the species present in the lake and their varying feeding habits. The quick biters, roach, small bream and rudd, are best given a shortish hook link so that their bites are easily detected on a tight line to the hook. Tench, big bream, carp and larger specimens of the former group are slower to take a bait which is a good reason for using the longer hook trail that will encourage them to take in their own time. They are also less likely to spot or feel the leger weight. Body shape with some species determines how they feed. The portly bream almost stands on its head to grub a bait off the bottom. If, in doing so, it feels a tension on the line the bream will drop the bait. Going tail up then returning to the horizontal must cause the fish to move the bait and pull the line a small amount, so the longish un-tensioned trail will help overcome the fish's suspicions.

125

Big fish . . .

Heading for trouble; this angler has hooked into a heavy bream, and there are snaggy old tree roots close by and a narrow channel of clear water back to the net.

Stillwaters will always produce the largest fish for coarse anglers. The lakes, particularly those in lowland, fertile areas, have the food producing potential capable of supporting the enormous shoals and appetites of specimen fish. To grow large fish there have to be perfect conditions in any water. Lakes and ponds must be constant in depth, without any pollution which would prevent the growth of weeds and the accompanying food animals. The water needs to have both area and depth to allow sufficient space for fish to establish territory and avoid winter kill.

Large freshwater fish have a unique angling following. Specimen hunters, as the fellows that pursue the larger fish are called, have taken fishing into a new area of thinking. They have developed the tackle bait systems and planned attack to finely honed techniques that have resulted in greatly raising the number of specimens landed, each year. This type of fishing really started with the exploits of Richard Walker, in his efforts to land big carp in the early 50s. Along with his specimen hunting companions, Walker found and exploited the potential of Redmire, a Herefordshire lake, that had everything just right for growing large carp. Richard Walker, because of his fishing activities and ability as a writer, became a leader of opinion and technique. Even now other specimen hunters continue to use his methods in the many waters that have been discovered. For, without doubt, the big fish waters do still exist. Increased fishing, over the last few years, has brought many new fisheries to light, a lot of them in places where big fish were not known to be! One of the things brought about by the specimen hunter has been the opening up of new waters. For they, along with match anglers, serve to introduce tackle systems and angling methods that are then adopted by the pleasure and club angler.

Specimen hunting does not always mean that carp or pike are the quarry. Specimens are any large fish of any species . . . so a roach of over 2 lb becomes as important as a carp of 40 lb. What matters is that the wily fish (and surely one of any species that attains better than average weight for its kind must have learned something) can be caught by the angler that observes,

closely, all that happens during the course of his days spent at the waterside.

Carp must be our most exciting stillwater specimen. No other fish has the same sustained fight or requires the degree of angling application. The tench, pound for pound, is a worthy adversary with a fight near approaching that of the carp when fished for with tackle that matches the fish's ability to test tackle and angler. The common bream, often regarded as a sluggish, stolid fighter, can be equally difficult to cope with. What matters, with all of these species, is that the run-up to the angling . . . finding the fish, baiting the swim and actual tackle presentation, is as important as hooking and playing a large specimen.

Fishing for carp

Carp, like any other freshwater fish, come in a range of sizes. The tackle, rod, reel and terminal rig, must be balanced to whatever is contained in the water. Obviously, prior knowledge of any water is useful in gauging how to approach the fishing, but that information isn't always available. It is best for the intending carp man to carry two sets of gear. A rod of 10-11 ft, with a test curve of 1½-2 lb, will cope with all but the monster fish. Lines of 8-10 lb on a fixed-spool reel balance perfectly. Attention must be made to the hook, it probably is the most important part of the tackle make-up when carp fishing. Sharpness of the point to take up a good hold is vital, but the point must not be too fine in the wire, otherwise the metal may well turn in a gristly jaw. Seek hooks that have small, low-cut barbs. Too rank a barb will prevent the hook drawing into the rubbery lips of this species. A medium shank combined with strength and a neat eye complete the hook requirement.

The tackle can be presented floating, suspended on a float or as a legered arrangement. The floating crust technique calls for nothing more than a bait on the hook, which is tied direct to the reel line. As carp are suspicious of nylon, particularly when it lies under the water's surface, it is a good idea to grease the line to make it float. This prevents approaching carp from

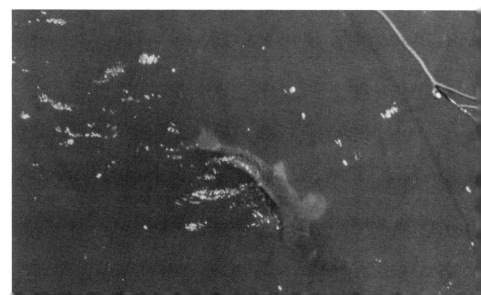

Left: No disputing the skill of this fisherman; the beautiful kingfisher . . . a lightning streak of blue and orange.

Right: An 8 lb carp on a 4 lb nylon with snags, means delicate control on the other end of the rod.

brushing against the line as they inspect a floating crust. Insert the hook so that the eye and knot emerge from the hard side of the crust. The softer, flaky texture of the bread will be attractive to a fish seeing it from depth and, of course, the flake will break off gradually as a rain of inviting particles that also act as an attractor. The floating crust should be fished at the edges of floating weedbeds, lily pads or at the margins of reeds. Carp inspect these areas continuously for food where their arrival is seen as a broad wake, pushed ahead by the bulk of the fish's body or as a dark shape rising like a submarine from below the weeds.

Carp suck in the bait at distance. Sometimes the fish will nose up to the bait, clearly suspecting its presence. This especially happens when the bait is offered out in open water. The classic take is when the fish sucks the crust down from below, displaying a whirling vortex on the water's surface. It is at this moment when carp detect the presence of the hook. Often the bait will be ejected at great speed. Some of the fish's natural suspicions can be allayed by throwing a few small crusts out onto the water to act as a ground-baiting attraction and to give the fish something to inspect!

Not everyone realises that most carp are hooked on floatfished baits. Small fish, and that means the majority of carp taken by pleasure fishermen, are caught on baits intended for other fish. It is very difficult to provide a selective bait for carp when there are other species in the lake. Big carp are an entirely different proposition because bait size provides the selectivity required.

Floatfishing for this fish only differs in that the line strength must be capable of holding the carp. Lift-float or laid-on techniques will take the fish where they are known to be searching the lakebed. Carp in mid-water can be attracted by a float suspended bait or a bait with buoyancy can be legered, which has the effect of tethering the crust in a mid-water situation that is suited to fishing over bottom-growing weeds or a thick layer of silt, into which a conventional legered bait would disappear. In all these systems one thing must be done. The hook should be tied direct to the reel line giving only one knot in the entire tackle. Carp of any size test the tackle, so the minimum of knots will preserve line strength. To go up in line breaking strain will more often cut down the takes from feeding carp . . . they soon learn about lines!

Most serious fishing for large fish is done by legering methods. Again, the breaking strain is kept by having only the knot at the hook. Leger weights should be used in a way that gives the weight to cast and hold it on the lakebed but not in such a way as to create friction that the fish will feel if it takes the bait and moves off. Avoid running a leger bomb on the reel line, far better to have it suspended on a separate nylon link.

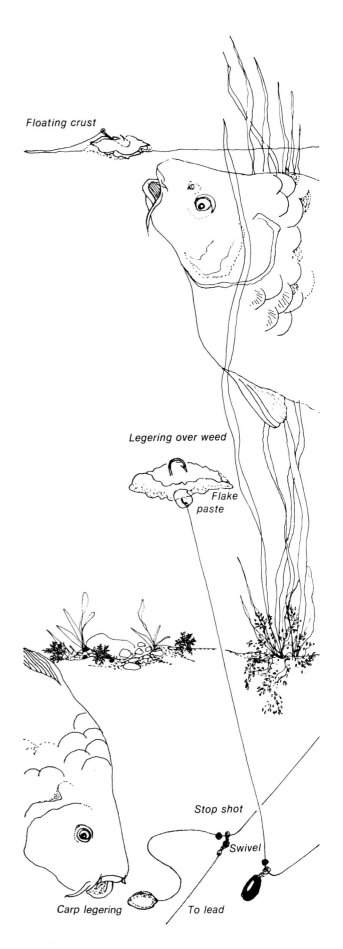

Floating crust

Legering over weed

Flake paste

Stop shot

Swivel

Carp legering

To lead

With a number of baits, potatoes, paste and the high protein hook offerings, no sinker may be needed to cast. Providing that the distance to be cast isn't too great this style of bait presentation ensures that a feeding fish will feel no resistance to the take at all. Back at the rod end of the tackle, the same care needs to be taken to ensure a freely-running line off the reel. Careful positioning of the two rod rests, using heads that have a deep V cut that lets the line run through, is a must. It is best to position the rests in such a way as to point the rod along the direction of the line as it enters the water.

The bale arm is left open with either a piece of paper lying across a drawn-down loop to act as an indicator or passage of the line can be watched by the angler. Neither system is perfect as the concentration needed throughout a fishing day is too much for the average angler. Most specimen hunters use a bite detector on the leading rod rest for their carp fishing that gives a light and a sound signal to indicate that line is running off the reel. Certainly, night fishing cannot be a realistic idea without the help of one or another of the electronic aids. The 'Buzzer' has one drawback in that if two rods are being used, there have to be different sounds for each rod indicator.

Hooking and playing carp

The carp is a fish that bites in so many widely differing ways: the crashing run, where the fish picks up a legered bait and immediately begins a long run. The soft, mouthing take has the indicator rising and falling for several seconds before the positive bite develops. Twitching bites can keep an angler in a state of frustrated animation for minutes; although many of

Three splendid carp on opening day 1981 from the Trent at Newark.

these twitch bites are, in fact, imparted movements to the line where the fish are probably nosing the bait around on the lakebed. Whatever the bite, the hardest decision to make must be when to hit it! Apart from ensuring that the fish does have the bait within its mouth, there is the added problem of striking with sufficient force to set the hook at what can be a considerable distance.

Experience of detecting and successfully hitting a few bites will indicate the right moment to strike, but one piece of advice would be to hit anything that is continuously moving. If the indicator jumps, followed by line moving off the spool an immediate strike will meet the fish's movement through the water. The twitch bite is hardest to meet with a positive strike as these

bites vary, fish to fish and water to water! Strike with a powerful motion that sweeps the rod back over the shoulder. Keep the rod held high while getting a few winds on the handle to take up any slack between the fish and the rod tip. Keep the rod held high against a fish that is static or running. Sudden movements, from any large fish, can only be effectively met by the cushioning of the rod arc. It is doubtful whether presetting the clutch to a playing drag can really cope with the tremendous changes in direction, power and sudden rushes of a carp. The best system is to keep the anti-reverse off and play the fish *on the handle*! Backwinding and using the power of the rod blank is a positively measured way in which to control the fight. Drag setting varies, particularly when line diameter, on the spool, runs down during a fight where a lot of line is taken off by the fish.

The direction that a fish moves to dictates the playing position of the rod. Held high or used to place side strain, the rod must always exert the maximum pressure on the fish. Never allow a slack line or give a heavy specimen a rest. The object must be to keep the fish moving, for while it moves against the rod it must be tiring. Pressure applied against a static fish tires the angler, however!

Netting a carp efficiently is a two-man operation. The net should be large and well sunk. Get the net into the water long before the fish shows within a few feet of the pitch. Then raise the rod to steadily draw the carp over the rim of the net. Raise the net *only* to effectively trap the fish within the funnel of meshes. Then it is time to lay the rod down to lift the net onto dry land.

The hook should be removed with the fish lying in the net. If it has to be lifted, give support to the belly of the carp. One hand grasping the underjaw, with the other arm and hand across the fish's back, give added security to lifting it. Artery forceps are the only real means of removing a hook without stress or damage to the fish. If the hook is deeply embedded, grasp the hook shank with the forceps, apply a little twist and steady turning pressure to remove it.

Everybody wants to photograph a good fish. To do this the carp are often kept within a keepnet. This is not the best treatment for a large fish as they could be stressed, so make certain that the net is large enough and never put more than one carp in any net. Better to get the pictures taken quickly and make an immediate return to the water for the fish.

Left: A lively double-figure mirror carp, from a farm pond, which fought well.

Above: Into a carp in snagging conditions. Steady side pressure is required.

Scottish carp

Scotland has few carp, and most lochs and ponds where they can be found have either been stocked by the monks many years ago, or have been relatively recent introductions by English anglers, in some cases fishermen who have moved to Scotland and developed their own fisheries such as the one near Lochmaben at Hightaemill Loch.

One of the few accessible waters on the East Coast is Danskin, near Gifford in the Lothians, little more than half an hour's drive from Edinburgh. The loch contains a small head of good tench (another rare Scottish coarse fish), and large numbers of wild carp. These fish have been caught between 9 or 10 lb in weight, but are known to grow larger in the water. The average is around 3-4 lb.

The best method is to leger a natural bait, such as a lobworm. The fish are not hook shy, but swims are rarely baited, and therefore the fish are not really accustomed to the variety of angler's high protein, bread, par-boiled potatoes and other delicacies offered by carp specialists in England. The wild carp of Danskin are much less sophisticated than carp of established fisheries in England, and once on the feed, can produce memorable sport throughout the day. Early morning and dusk, however, are still key feeding periods when sport can be spectacular. With relatively cooler temperatures, Scottish carp fishing has a shorter season, and is best generally through the warmest summer months from late June to the end of August.

Mirrors, commons and leather carp have been introduced in a few small waters in Dumfriesshire and the surrounding countryside along the Solway. They don't grow large, however.

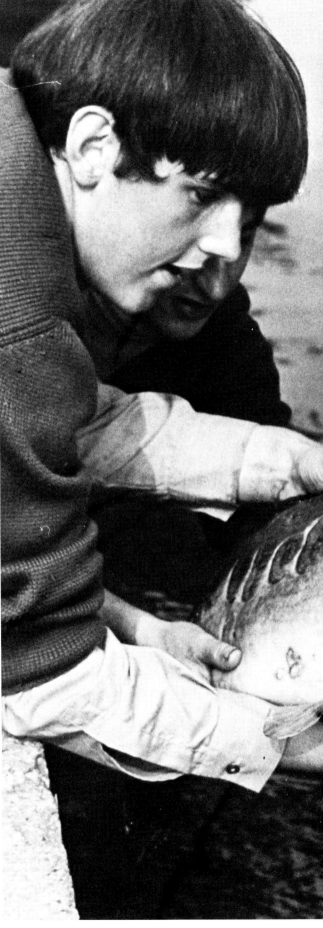

A young angler returns his mirror

er. The 24 lb specimen was caught from the Thames at Staines!

Clerical carp!

The carp *Cyprinus carpio* is found in many freshwater habitats throughout the British Isles. Although absent from much of Scotland, the species has been introduced into a number of lowland waters.

Recently, the Inland Fisheries Trust have made efforts to produce carp for lakes in Ireland. Introducing the carp to new environments is part of a continuing saga of seeding freshwater environments. It began in the Middle Ages, when the fish was brought to Europe by the clerics of that time; placed into stews, on a fish-farming basis, the fish was used to augment the diet of the monks.

Because of the popularity of the carp as a food, many countries in middle Europe experimented with the production of fast-growing varieties that could be brought to marketable size more quickly than the common variety. Anglers have benefited from this animal technology in that it has produced leather and mirror carps of tremendous depth and girth, fish that annually give us the huge specimens that make headlines in the angling press.

So we now find that there are four distinct varieties of *Cyprinus*: the fully scaled, deep-bodied lake fish; a slimmer version that inhabits slow-flowing rivers, called 'river carp' or 'Wildies'; a partially scaled fish, with a number of enlarged scales, normally along the lateral line, named 'mirror carp', and a fish devoid of scaling carrying the title 'leather carp'. All of them originate from the Asian stock that came to us many centuries ago.

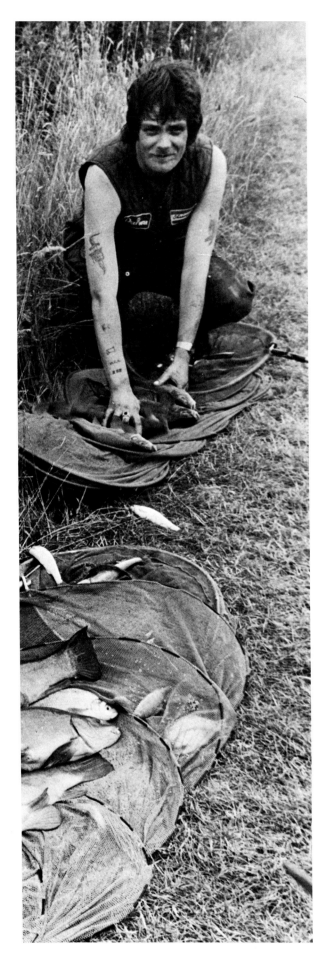

Fishing for tench

One can floatfish or leger for this fish of the summer, but a bait presented using a float gives a satisfaction that legering could never compare with. Tench are a species that feed in a way suited to float fishing technique and a visual reaction on the part of the angler. They grub around on the lakebed, sending up clouds of minute bubbles to mark their feeding area. The fish can be encouraged to feed by careful groundbaiting of the chosen swim, coupled with some judicious raking of the bottom.

Both the lift-float and laying-on styles are suitable for bait presentation. For the bigger fish one needs to use a straight-through line breaking strain; the hook tied on to the reel line. Only enough shot to cock the float and give the weight to cast need be attached. In swims without serious underwater snags, 4 lb line would handle all but the largest tench. Where a swim is thought to hold very large fish or the lakebed is snaggy, a 6 lb reel line would give that extra strength to enable the full power of the rod to be used. Tench are strong fish that fight right into the net, so a rod of at least 1 lb test curve is a must. A rod of 11 ft will give the control necessary to handle a tench close-in to the bank.

The hook size rather depends upon the bait chosen to offer to the fish. Worm must rank as a premier bait but the tench will take flake and maggot baits. A size 8 hook is about right for the average lobworm with a 12 for a bunch of maggots. Hide the hook within a bread bait as tench are fond of mouthing before swallowing a bait. The species reacts to a well fed swim, but the feed should be slowed down as soon as a fish is hooked. Add enough, in small balls, to hold the fish within the baited area. Keep surface disturbance down to a minimum by feeding fairly loose groundbait. It is also a good technique to overcast the swim by a few yards, drawing the float back to cock it while not scaring fish that are moving in the swim. Once you get the fish feeding *with their heads down*, little will scare them.

Handle the captured tench with care. It is a slimy fish that can be a little difficult to handle, said by oldtime writers to possess medicinal properties when the slime is rubbed onto a wound. If possible, the fish should be held in a damp cloth to prevent removing the slime which protects the tench against the entrance, into its body, of water diseases. The bream is a similar fish, slimy but slightly harder scaled.

Tench can be fished for with the leger. Certainly, long range fishing would demand that approach if the tench could not be fed in toward the angler's pitch. Accurate groundbaiting can be achieved by casting out using an open-ended swimfeeder, repeatedly drop-

Ballycullinane, Co Clare

This lough is a centuries old peat working with an average depth of 12-14 ft. The lough is totally naturalised, and fringed with dense reedmace and stunted vegetation. There are acres of long-established water lilies, and the whole of the lakebed is covered with a variety of bottom-growing water weeds. If anything, the lake tends to be acidic, and for this reason, pike, rudd, perch and a small population of brown trout are indigenous.

The Irish Inland Fisheries Trust confirm that in the late sixties/early seventies, the lake was stocked with common bream, and this fish, together with the rudd, supports a high population of predators. The weed growth and its type gives maximum cover for the rudd, which ensures the survival of large specimen fish. As well as affording the rudd protection from the marauding pike, their fringe environment does not conflict with the common bream population, which tends to be concentrated over the deeper, mud-bottomed regions in the main part of the lake.

While bream have often been sighted on this lake during various visits, they have proved difficult to take on the rod, possibly due to the proximity of my angling activity to their spawning activity. One bream weighing in excess of 9 lb, however, took a Little 'S' plug bait being trolled for pike at 6 am on a warm, calm day in early summer.

Since the rudd tend to be in the shallower margins, well into the cover of the reed beds, it is necessary to draw them out into the open, where they can be caught on the relatively light tackle needed to fish for them. The most successful method adopted at Ballycullinane is to draw the rudd from their hiding with the use of cloud groundbait. This colours the water, and attracts the fish, which can then be held by loose feeding maggots or chopped worms into the cloud, depending on the choice of hook bait.

This groundbaiting method has the effect of not only attracting the fish by sight, but it produces a suspended smell in the area of the hook bait. The rudd can be gradually worked upwards towards the surface. After a good feeding pattern is established, the angler can change from 1½-lb reel line direct to a No 20 to 2½-lb line, and a bigger hook. A No 16 with bunched maggots or bread drawn close to the surface will take some of the bigger specimens.

Because of the weed growth, both surface and demersal, float fishing is the only effective way to produce rudd of any quality and quantity. Legering is unsuitable due to the excessive vegetation normally associated with the rudd's environment. One of the most difficult aspects of rudd fishing is in fact the location of the shoals, and then drawing them from cover and into a feeding pattern.

Left: The float slips away and Mike Shepley hooks his first tench of the season.

Right: The male tench has rounder, fuller fins than the female.

The neater fins of the female tench.

Bottom right: A superb tench, the perfect picture for opening day.

Below: Nearly in the net, bringing half the bottom weed with it.

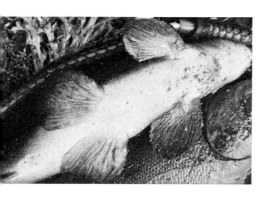

Above right: Gently does it; the coating of slime which protects the tench can be easily disturbed.

A critical moment. Landing big bream, even in snag-free water, requires skill and care. Draw the bream over the waiting net; never scoop at the fish.

Right: a good net of fish, including some well-conditioned bream, from a canal in the Midlands of Ireland.

ping a cereal onto the chosen area. A sharp striking action will clear the feed from the feeder. The hookbait could then be a similar based material, either flake or a malleable bread paste. If maggots are chosen for the hook, a block-end feeder would ensure that maggots are fed within close range of the hookbait. Alternatively, the loosefeed can be fired out, using a catapult.

Big bream on stillwaters

If there is one major difficulty in catching big fish from any water . . . it is in finding them in the first place. The common bream is more of a shoal fish than the former species. They tend to shoal up according to

Landing nets

The standard coarse fishing net, where the mesh is gathered at the bottom and fixed with a hoop or clasp, should be regularly checked. I once lost a specimen bream pushing double figures due to the cord holding the bottom of the net together working loose and spilling the fish through the loop. Before I could put the fish back through the damaged mesh, the line broke on the rim of the net. I had not checked the net beforehand as it was completely new and presumably had been checked and passed by the manufacturer.

the size of the individual specimens. The shoals are constantly on the move, investigating every part of a lake, searching for enough food to satisfy their needs. Bream are said to graze a lakebed like a flock of sheep. Massive amounts of groundbait are necessary in order that the fish find it and that it holds their attention long enough for the angler to get the big fellows.

Like the tench, this fish advertises its arrival into a baited area by emitting clouds of bubbles as it feeds. Whether the bubbles actually come from the bream or are as a result of its sifting the mud for food, cannot be definitely stated; but we can often see clouds of muddy, suspended matter after bream have commenced their banquet! They feed rather like the tench, standing on their heads to nose down among the littered bottom. So, the lift-float is a perfect fishing style for bite indication. Inevitably, there will be a succession of tiny lifts and dips on the float as the line is struck by the various fins and bodies that make up the shoal. 'Line bites', as they are called, can be frustrating but are a penalty to pay for the floatfisher.

Above: The results of patience; this bream went better than 5lb.

Left: Waiting for the telltale movement on the swingtip. The tip will drop if the bream picks up the bait and moves towards the bank, or lift if the fish swims off to deeper water.

143

Right and far right: Legering in a Danish lake near Skive, Mike Prichard draws a good mixed bag of bream and roach.

Below: A good sized bream to test your tackle. Their reputation as poor fighters doesn't always hold with Irish specimens.

Greater fishing distances can be coped with on the float by laying on. Depth of water will determine whether the float is fixed or fished as a slider. Either way, bites will most often be seen as a slight rise as the fish lifts the bait, followed by a purposeful sliding away as the fish moves off. In any shoal there must be terrific competition for the available morsels lying on the bottom. Such competition will induce fish to grab the bait, but this is more likely among the skimmers and smallish members of a big shoal. The older, bigger fish have become crafty in their feeding. Often the quiet bites, that hardly move the float, are the only indication of the arrival of a monster.

Bream cannot be said to match the fight of either the carp or tench. If they have a claim to fame it is in the dour, stubborn drawn out battle as they use their flattened body across the water. Although this species grows to heavier weights than most tench caught to date, the tackle strength need not be much altered. A standard float rod, coupled to 4 lb line, will handle all but the largest fish or the difficult swims. As much of the bream's natural food is made up of tiny organisms, water larvae and vegetable matter, small baits will be taken by any size of fish. This feeding behaviour forces us to respond with the choice of rod; one that has the steel to set a hook positively, yet not so stiff as to break out of a big fish, is required.

Legering presents the same problem that the hook has to be set in a thick, rubbery jaw. The rod must be capable of absorbing the shock load as the strike meets with a bream's ponderous weight. An all-through action will match the fine line and smallish hook.

Bottom right: Six well-fed specimens from Silvergrove, Co Clare; four of them are bream. Johnny Woods and tackle dealer Trevor King make up the sextet.

144

145

Trotting the River Dove

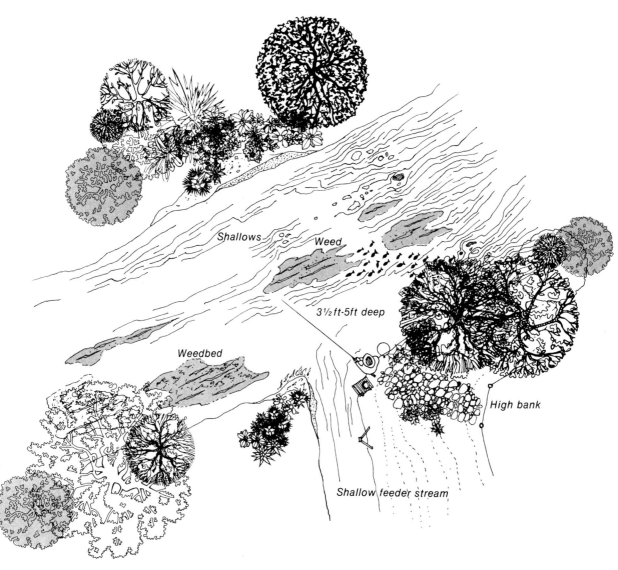

Shallows

Weed

3½ft-5ft deep

Weedbed

High bank

Shallow feeder stream

Right: A net of well conditioned chub. A streamy swim on the Dove is just as likely to produce grayling amongst the blunt-headed chub.

Left: By holding back the float the angler can make the single hook maggot bait lift enticingly off the bottom, working down the swim adjacent to the weeds which harbour the chub.

Below: The River Dove here flows swift and shallow through lush banks of submerged weed. The small feeder coming in on the right bank creates a deeper glide where the angler has attracted chub by loose feeding along the edge of the weed.

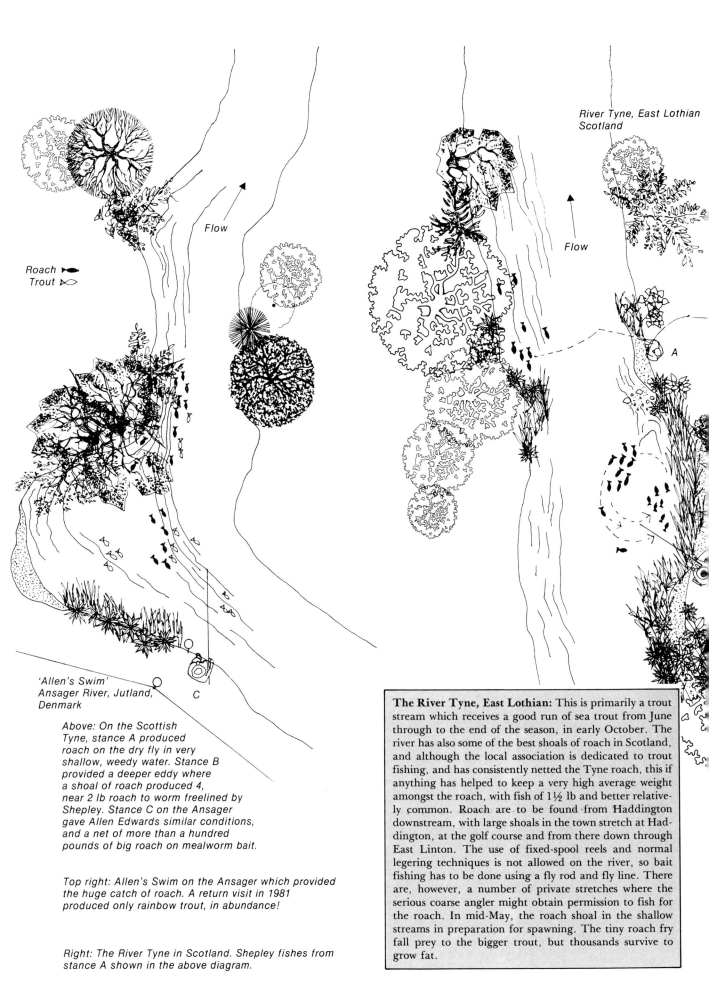

Flow

Roach ▶━
Trout ▷━

River Tyne, East Lothian
Scotland

Flow

A

'Allen's Swim'
Ansager River, Jutland,
Denmark

C

Above: On the Scottish
Tyne, stance A produced
roach on the dry fly in very
shallow, weedy water. Stance B
provided a deeper eddy where
a shoal of roach produced 4,
near 2 lb roach to worm freelined by
Shepley. Stance C on the Ansager
gave Allen Edwards similar conditions,
and a net of more than a hundred
pounds of big roach on mealworm bait.

Top right: Allen's Swim on the Ansager which provided
the huge catch of roach. A return visit in 1981
produced only rainbow trout, in abundance!

Right: The River Tyne in Scotland. Shepley fishes from
stance A shown in the above diagram.

The River Tyne, East Lothian: This is primarily a trout
stream which receives a good run of sea trout from June
through to the end of the season, in early October. The
river has also some of the best shoals of roach in Scotland,
and although the local association is dedicated to trout
fishing, and has consistently netted the Tyne roach, this if
anything has helped to keep a very high average weight
amongst the roach, with fish of 1½ lb and better relatively common. Roach are to be found from Haddington
downstream, with large shoals in the town stretch at Haddington, at the golf course and from there down through
East Linton. The use of fixed-spool reels and normal
legering techniques is not allowed on the river, so bait
fishing has to be done using a fly rod and fly line. There
are, however, a number of private stretches where the
serious coarse angler might obtain permission to fish for
the roach. In mid-May, the roach shoal in the shallow
streams in preparation for spawning. The tiny roach fry
fall prey to the bigger trout, but thousands survive to
grow fat.

Man has seldom, if ever, improved on Nature, and the systematic culling and human predation on pike in particular has done little to help those waters where it has been attempted. Even on trout fisheries, the presence of pike is generally a natural controlling influence. While likely to predate to some extent on the trout stocks, pike will also effectively reduce the numbers of other coarse fish, which compete directly with the trout for available food, particularly roach, rudd and perch, and help maintain an acceptable balance of species at a realistic level. On a mixed fishery, the pike will feed much more readily on the slower-moving coarse species, rather than chase the faster and more solitary trout. Where these shoal fish congregate, the pike fisherman is most likely to meet with success. When spinning from the bank, the angler is unlikely to find many vast depths inshore although rocky headlands can produce this sort of water. These deeper areas, however, are often reached more readily by the boat angler. Most of the shoreline activity will be concentrated in the shallower areas of the lake where the shoaling species congregate.

Streams and rivers running into or out of a stillwater always attract the predators, and offer an excellent chance for the angler to contact a good fish. Any reeds and visible weed banks will harbour pike and perch, although at times, the reeds will frustrate the angler's approach to the better fish. Where a likely looking stretch of reeds cannot be fished from the bank, the angler has to revert to boat tactics. One trick which can be used is to chase the fish out of the reed bed by bombardment with earth clods or stones. This not only pushes the pike and perch out into the open water, but tends to irritate the fish into snapping at the first available object, which hopefully is your lure.

Predators in stillwaters

Have you ever watched a pike feeding? This particular incident occurred on the River Teith in Stirlingshire, a major tributary of the River Forth. As the Teith is primarily a salmon and trout water, no Sunday angling is allowed. What does the angler do on such occasions? Being on holiday, I went for a walk upstream. With plenty of nearby pike lochs, and the slow nature of the river, it came as no surprise to discover that the Teith also holds pike.

I came across a small backwater, little more than an eddy of stillish water close under the bank, protected from the strong sunshine by an overhanging bush. In the shadows I spotted what at first sight looked like a sunken tree branch; but this was a pike . . . not big, but a fair size for a river pike, and quite capable of making a dent in the local fish population.

I had brought with me an old wine bottle, and some bread, with the intention of catching some minnows for the following week's game fishing. Needless to say, there were few minnows swimming near the pike. Moving a few yards upstream, it didn't take long to find a likely spot, with plenty of fat minnows moving in the shallows. The bottle quickly sunk to the river bed with its feast of breadcrumbs, and one or two bits of bread scattered around the trap soon had the minnows feeding and nosing into the inverted entrance to the bottle. In no time at all, I had about twenty or so plump minnows.

Back to the overhanging shrub, and sure enough the pike was still holding station, motionless. I emptied my catch, and quickly tapped each minnow smartly on the head as a *coup de grâce*.

There was little current, and the first aim about 2 ft from the pike, caused no reaction as the little minnow fluttered down through the clear depths, and settled onto the sandy bottom in about 3 ft of water.

The second minnow, however, produced an immediate response. As it hit water, I could see the dorsal and tail fin of the pike take on an urgency, as if the fish was poised to strike; it moved almost imperceptibly, but still didn't attack. The minnow was no more than 6 in from the bottom when the pike, in one movement, dived and charged forwards, striking the minnow sideways to engulf it, ignoring the first minnow still on the bottom. The third and fourth minnow barely hit the water before they, too, were attacked and devoured. Eventually, like all good gourmets, the pike found and *tidied* up the first minnow.

I kept the rest of the minnows, for the next day's trouting, vowing that I would return and take this unwanted *Esox* out of the river; but of course pike have an uncanny knack of melting in with the shadows. Not only is their camouflage complete, they can also do an excellent disappearing act. If anything, I was pleased when I returned to the spot and found the pike had gone . . . a satisfied customer. I never did like killing pike.

Undercut banking is less likely as a feature on the stillwater than on the river, where the current scours out the bank, forming excellent lies. However, due to wave action and bankside trees and shrubs also encroaching over, and at times, into the water, adequate cover and shaded haunts are produced which suit the predator. By identifying these ambush points, the angler will quickly get to know the most likely taking spots on any fishery.

Bays, rather than headlands, are the shallow areas where pike and perch shoals will congregate. Piers and jetties also give cover and shade so liked by big perch. It is there, too, that the minnows and smaller fry feed. Surprisingly big pike will often foray close inshore, lying motionless under cover of jetties or moored boats, waiting silently 'on the fin' for food fish to move close enough for a strike.

In such shallow, weedy situations, the angler's choice of lure is very important, if he is not to lose an excessive amount of tackle. Weedless spoons, where the hooks are guarded by wire springs which fold if a fish strikes, but are strong enough to bounce the bait over any weed or reed obstacle, will ensure a snag free retrieve in difficult spots. The floating plug will also allow the angler to work the pockets of clear, snag free water among the reed beds, although the subsequent extraction of a good pike can prove difficult.

The angler who goes spinning on a lake or reservoir rather than a river immediately has a major problem of locating his fish. Reading a stillwater, and identifying where the fish will be, poses rather more difficulties than on the stream and larger river, where current and above-water features help in establishing the position of better lies.

No matter how good or well stocked a stillwater may be, not every square yard will hold fish of quality. The two major species of interest to the spin fisher will be pike and perch. As major predators of smaller fish, they are most likely to be interested in the angler's spoons and plugs. Since big pike also predate on small jack and perch of any size, the two fish are inseparable and can turn up together at any time. This poses little trouble when a perch takes your lure intended for a pike, but the converse situation can be extremely frustrating when a spun lure, intended for perch, is grabbed by a good pike, often resulting in a breakage.

While many features which will attract and hold perch and pike are not visible to the angler above the surface of the water, there are plenty of indicators along the shoreline which guide the thoughtful fisherman to the most likely places. The major guiding factors inevitably relate to the availability of small shoal fish as

A pike grabs the sink and draw deadbait right at the bank.

An ox-bow lake in Perthshire

A series of lakes lies just south of the city of Perth, and only about 3 miles from Bridge of Earn on the Tay's lowest tributary, the River Earn. The main lake, known locally as the Deadwaters, lies on agricultural land. Permission to fish is required from the local farmer, and as always when in the countryside, the courtesy of being given permission should be matched by care with all gates into and out of the farm land. Attention must be given to crops and livestock, the banks of the fishery and above all in ensuring that all bottles and other rubbish are taken away with you. In the past, a few thoughtless individuals have, as with many other accessible fisheries, caused permission to be withdrawn by the riparian owner. If you had livestock and valuable crops at stake, wouldn't you do the same?

The Deadwaters are typical of the ox-bow lake; shallow, weedy and overgrown, with reed beds forming smaller pools and holes where pike can lurk waiting for the shoals of perch. Locals will tell you there are tench in these pools, although I've never seen them myself. There again, I was also told there was one big old pike, so ancient and large that he had moss growing on his head. What the

chap had probably seen was indeed a big pike, and the moss no doubt was a touch of fungus caused by an infection! The place itself almost invites such stories, though. Dark, mysterious, as its name suggests, some of the trees have died and fallen into the water creating underwater labyrinths which scream 'PIKE' to the angler.

As you work your lure or bait along the margins or adjacent to the sunken trees, you can almost sense the stirring of the pike, the eyes that are following the progress of your bait along through the clear depths. And then that excitement which always comes as a heart-stopping surprise no matter how much it is expected, as the mottled green freshwater shark hurls itself without warning at its target. Whether the fish is 3 or 30 lb, the overall effect is one of a sheer basic thrill. I returned to the Deadwaters in 1980 with Mike Prichard after a break of over ten years. The pike were still there, waiting . . . as if on cue!

food for the predators, and suitable cover from which they can ambush their prey. Smaller fish are attracted into the shallows where the warmth of the sun's rays encourages weed growth and sustains the complex food chain necessary for the successful balance of the environmental ecology. The predator is an important factor in this system.

Spinning from the shore

The angler who searches for his fish from the bank of either a river or lake, will have to contend with two major difficulties. The very reeds and weed beds which will give cover to the perch and pike fishermen seek make casting and retrieving a bait back to the bank extremely difficult. Where the margins are shallow, a certain amount of wading may be necessary or at least desirable, always remembering though that reeds have a fondness for growing in soft mud, and *soft mud* can often be not only soft, but very deep. If wading is possible, always search the margins first with several short casts, working in a fan shape so that all of the area within reach of the angler is carefully covered *before* entering the water.

Jetties and timber piers can act as useful casting platforms, but again, fish carefully along the structure from the bank, as fish will often lie close in or underneath in the shadows, waiting for unsuspecting fry to come too close. Look for bays which will give cover, or draw small shoal fish into the shallows. The deeper points either side of such bays are also worthy of attention, especially for big pike, providing there is a reasonable amount of cover.

On a river look for lies close in under the banks, on the quieter insides of bends and near any weed beds. If you see small shoal fish in any numbers at all, the predators shouldn't be too far away. Keep an eye out, too, for erratic movement of fry; scattering minnows or small fish on the surface is almost always an indication of a feeding pike or shoal of bigger perch.

Spinning from a boat

This method can often be far more rewarding than simply trolling a lure back and forward along a river or lake, in the hope that it passes close enough for a fish to take an interest. The boat can be stationary, drifting with the wind or current, or under power, either with oars or an outboard motor. For shallow work, an electric outboard will give the angler a better chance than with the noisier internal combustion engine, which produces far more underwater noise and vibration. To cover main lies as the boat moves along the margins where most spinning will take place, really requires two anglers, one spinning, and one operating the engine; even then, the boat may be travelling too fast to cover all the lies. With one angler on the oars, it is possible to fish more thoroughly, with each angler fishing in different directions. All the small bays and likely-looking lies can be covered efficiently, and then a few strokes on the oar can put the anglers over new water containing feeding fish. In a strong wind, it may be necessary for one angler to remain on the oars all the time, while the other casts, taking it in turn to fish the lies. The alternative is to anchor the boat off the holding water, at both ends if

Top right: Alan Hill puts a bend into his rod and stretches a lively pike into action. Alan moved from Scotland to the Province of Saskatchewan where he enjoys his favourite sport amongst the 'Northerns'.

Right: 5 lb line, a lure meant for perch, and a 10 lb Loch Lomond pike make for delicate handling by Shepley.

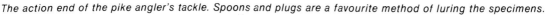

The action end of the pike angler's tackle. Spoons and plugs are a favourite method of luring the specimens.

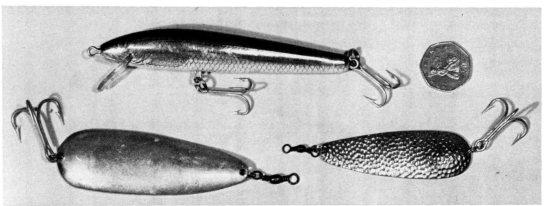

154

necessary, so that more than one rod can be operational at the same time.

Trolling

Many big fish have been taken trolling, but it is a method which can be laborious and often monotonous. In a big lake, it can be a means of covering a lot of ground, but the angler has to know at what depth to expect the fish, and where the best runs are. On a water where the depth varies a great deal over short distances, and where troughs and ledges can hold fish which might be undetected by a regular troll, a small depth-finder is a definite advantage.

The angler can also adjust the depth and speed of retrieve by varying the course of the boat in a zig-zag pattern, which will also help to cover a greater area of water over the chosen path. When trolling on a wide river, a technique called 'harling', can be adopted. This is a traditional Scottish method of salmon fishing where the boat's engine is adjusted to hold the craft against the current, and two or sometimes three baits are trolled behind the boat, the current keeping the action of the lures going. The boat is then angled

Predatory bream . . .!

Bream to me have always been something of an enigma. Often when fishing for them, I have failed to draw them into the swim, or get them feeding; and yet, two of my biggest fish came when least expected, both on a visit to the Lakeland Region of Ireland and County Clare while producing a film about Ken Giles and Clive Smith.

The first film shoot locality was at Lanesborough, on the warm water outfall at the power station. Ken had found rudd feeding to the far bank, and Clive had chosen a swim much closer to the outfall, where the bream were shoaling . . . and feeding. Clive's keepnet was soon bulging with bream averaging a good 5 lb, and in between shoots, I had some sport myself. Then Ken complained that the rudd had gone quiet, and that perhaps there was a pike in the swim. Out went a spoon on the 9 ft spinning rod and multiplier, and I promptly connected with a fish . . . not a pike but a bream of 6½ lb, neatly lip-hooked on the Toby! Bream aren't noted for either aggression or fish feeding, but will nevertheless take a lure occasionally, especially in the period shortly after spawning.

The second, even bigger bream came from a lake near Corofin in County Clare, and was hooked at 6 am while trolling for pike. Again, the fish was lip-hooked and put up a tremendous struggle, and it was several minutes before I realised that I hadn't hooked a large, stubborn pike. Although the bream had taken a plug bait only a foot or so below the surface, the depth was nearer six, and the bream made full use of it by playing deep and almost successfully snagging my line in some underwater weed bed. This bream went close to 10 lb, but not anticipating such a specimen, and only looking for a big pike with a view to photographing, not weighing it, I cannot record here the exact weight, but the short film sequence gives a fair indication to bream enthusiasts what a fine specimen it was. I am still waiting for such a fish on the right tackle; now, what a prize that would be!

A disappearing act . . .!

On a late April visit to Loch Lomond in 1981, pike proved virtually impossible to catch, and in spite of a dozen or more specimen hunters of considerable experience, only a handful of pike were taken. There were no doubt several reasons for this:

The loch was extremely low, making access to some of the better known lies, such as Cromar Bay, very difficult without disturbing the few fish which were there. After a relatively mild winter, and near summer conditions in early April, the area suffered a return to snow and frost just prior to the visit, which may have sent a large percentage of the pike back into the deeper water.

The River Endrick seemed devoid of shoal fish, apart from one or two very small perch, and although there was evidence of pike spawn, no activity could be seen from pike of any weight to the baits. The size of some of the spawn indicated that there were very large pike about on the spawning shallows.

Winter, and the pike will be lying close in under the bank, resting in the shadows of underwater debris, ready for the tearing, fin-thrashing rush of the perfect ambush.

Even small pike, like this tiny jack, can devour the biggest lures, and can be a nuisance when the angler is after the thrilling and protracted fight of bigger game.

Left: Timing is all important when casting with a big bait — and a multiplier.

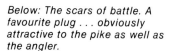

Right: The angler is spinning a plug to nearby reedbeds, in the hope of drawing a big pike over the waiting deadbaits.

Below: The scars of battle. A favourite plug . . . obviously attractive to the pike as well as the angler.

across the current, and worked from one side of the river to the other, gradually dropping back downstream until the whole pool is covered. This method would only be successful in those larger streams where there is sufficient draw to work the lures effectively, although a similar trolling technique could be adopted, with the boat working slowly upstream instead of down as in the case of harling.

Providing the angler doesn't just choose an arbitrary direction trolling his lures in a straight line at constant speed, the method can be effective; but it is only as successful as the thought given the method by the fisherman. Trolling without thought is no substitute for casting and for thinking how the bait is appearing to the fish. Throttle back, accelerate at times, change course. For, by altering the course and easing on the engine or oars, the bait will flutter, drop in the water, and change direction. It is often at that point fish will strike, and it is no accident either, as the lure will have looked far more natural and vulnerable than spinning or wobbling on a straight course. Within reason therefore, changes in direction, no matter how small together with change of pace, will bring its rewards in far more strikes from fish . . . and there will be a better chance of fooling the specimen which has seen far too many monotonous pieces of ironmongery, jointed wood and plastic to be impressed.

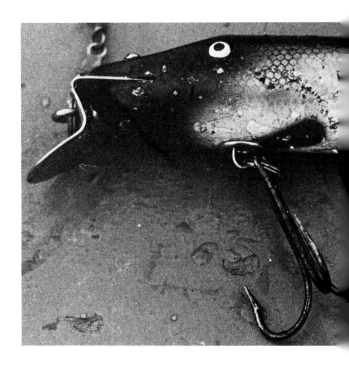

Pike which are regularly fished for, caught and returned to the water, inevitably become very wary of anglers and fishing tackle. Conservation amongst pike specimen hunters in recent years has meant that the bigger fish have become very shy in areas of concentrated fishing, and tactics have had to be adjusted to highly sophisticated levels to maintain success. This seems not only to apply to those fish already caught, but pike in general, where there is a higher than average activity with boats, natural baits and lures.

Deadbaiting

Deadbaiting, which is one of the most effective forms of angling for specimen-sized pike, normally requires a rig formed with two treble hooks to suit the size of bait being used. A few years ago fairly large deadbaits mounted on big trebles to match would have been acceptable to both angler and pike. However, now the tendency is for smaller baits, and equally small trebles, down to a pair of No 8s. A slimmer, easily taken

159

mouthful, such as a 4-oz dace, is preferred to an 8-oz perch or roach. Fresh herring tail is equally successful.

Fishing in shallow water amongst the reed beds where the largest hen fish congregate prior to spawning, means a sensitive use of tackle combined with equally careful use of boat or bank wading. If pike are established as feeding at regular times during the day, ensure that your arrival matches that period. Get the bait positioned early with as little noise as possible. This means using oars and not an outboard engine.

Pike habitat

Pike love weed beds, either in lakes or slower moving rivers. On the faster rivers, pike will restrict themselves to the eddies, backwaters and slower glides. As such, they are much more likely to be present in the slower meandering sections of the Bream Zone or Esturial Zone of rivers. As the river moves onto a lower plain, where it becomes wider and slower, the flatter topography and land structure, with its build up of silt, often creates a situation called 'ox-bow lakes'. These are long, curving ponds, which represent former meanders of the river bed that have become detached from the main river, due to the coursing of the water changing over the years through flooding or other displacement. The resulting environment of stillwater, rich meadowland and muddy reedbeds is ideal for the pike and here they can thrive and grow fat on other smaller species trapped with them, often roach, perch and bream.

Trees and shrubs are generally found along the banks of such ox-bow lakes; but due to the changing water tables, it is just as likely that some of these trees die and in time fall into the water, making even more likely lies for the pike and big perch. This isn't easy

Above: A small roach makes an ideal deadbait for pike, and can also be fished sink and draw.

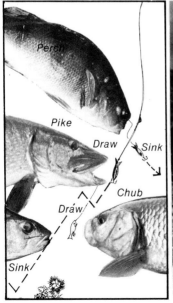

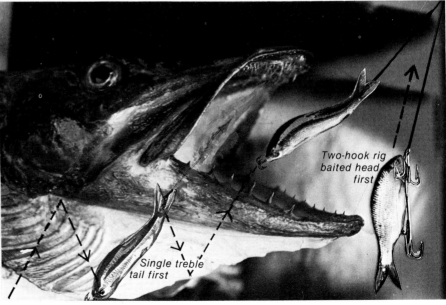

fishing, but characterises all that is exciting in fishing for pike. Even a modest fish of 6 or 7 lb, darting out from under a fallen bough to grab your well placed lure, sends a thrill of excitement up the spine which is hard to match. Of course, the pike misses first time, and then you wonder where he's going to strike next; pike seldom give up without at least two or three attempts at hitting the bait.

If you are working a deadbait sink and draw, you have much more chance of success. Even if on the first lunge the pike doesn't make contact, the next movement requires little action from the angler. Allow the fish all the time it wants. As it strikes, allow your senses to relax just enough to prevent the reflex action of a strike . . . the pike will have time to hit the bait, then turn and pick it up at leisure, and eventually move off. Now is the time to strike! Do not allow the fish to run too long with the bait, especially a small bait, otherwise it may be a difficult job removing the hooks. Few anglers nowadays treat pike with contempt; they prefer not to allow a fish too long a run because of the danger of a gorged bait and the difficulty of extracting deeply embedded hooks.

Attitudes

It has taken many years in Scotland, for anglers to become aware of the value of pike. In the sixties through the seventies many of the fish were killed, for no other reason than because they were pike and would be ' . . . better out of the water!' Left to rot on the bank, they were a sad reflection on the average Scot's attitude to pike. Nowadays, while pike are still culled on major trout fisheries, those anglers who do fish for them treat pike as a truly sporting fish which, at the end of the struggle, deserves its freedom and a quick release safely back into the water. Big ones *are* still killed, but on the major pike waters such as Loch Lomond, the dedicated band of specimen hunters have an unwritten code which has slowly spread to the casual angler.

Loch Lomond

This huge expanse of water is not only the home of monster pike, but holds large shoals of roach and perch, as well as salmon, sea-trout and brown trout. The powan, one of the whitefish, also shoals in the shallows of the loch and has been found in the stomach contents of many pike. In such a mixed ecology, the pike is predator but so, too, is the trout and to a lesser extent, the perch. If the whole spectrum of fish life is looked at, the pike is not really the arch villain but part of Nature's balance. Trout tend to be solitary. Browns at any rate will prefer either to feed individually or in small groups and being fast they are a difficult target for the pike. Perch and roach, on the other hand, offer the hungry pike a ready mouthful.

Treble versus single hooks

It was inevitable that somebody should look at the mortality rate for pike caught on rod and line, but it takes a special type of research unit to undertake the work. The necessary confinement of the fish, in order that they can be re-captured after a further period at liberty, puts close inspection beyond the resources of the keenest angling study group. Recently, I was fortunate to visit the fish farm owned by the Organisatie ter Verbetering van de Binnenvisserij (Inland Fisheries Trust) at Lelystad, Holland. They have looked into the problem of pike mortality, as a result of sport fishing, with particular attention to the type of hook used when the fish were captured.

The researched sample of pike were fished for with baits mounted on both single and treble hooks. Of 200 pike caught, 40 of the 63 fish taken on single hooks and 37 of the 87 treble hook-caught pike were found to be deeply hooked. The hooks could not be cleanly removed so the line was cut as close to the hook as possible.

Six months after the fish were caught and released to the holding water, they were again caught by draining the environment which ensured that no fish could escape recapture. Mortality among the deep-hooked fish, during the period at liberty proved to be 13%, although fish hooked in the mouth had returned a mortality of only 2%. There appeared to be no difference in the mortality rate for fish hooked on either single or treble hooks! Natural mortality among fish after their six-month period in the research holding water was nil.

The pike were then released to spend another four months at liberty during which time no further deaths occurred. Dissection of the pike showed that nearly 60% of the hooks (singles: 62%, trebles: 54%) had disappeared. They had become hidden within body tissues, apparently causing the fish little harm as the growth rate of the closely-inspected fish had in no way been affected.

This research work, by an organization financially supported by anglers with results reported to them, certainly upsets much of what has been published about the angler's use of treble hooks. There appears to be no valid reason for not using them. What did emerge from this carefully conducted research is that a deeply hooked fish is likely to die. It seems that the way in which we fish, the timing of the strike after a fish takes the bait and the length of run allowed to it are all critical factors in ensuring that our sporting predators are hooked properly . . . in the jaw!

Top left: More than 20 lb of pike makes a hefty armful; a superb specimen from Loch Lomond.

Above: A boat is invaluable in a reedy situation like this lake, where the pike will lie close into the weed banks.

Right: A specimen sized lure for a specimen sized fish.

Left: A livebait rig for pike. This method is banned in places, and the preference now amongst specimen hunters is to fish deadbaits.

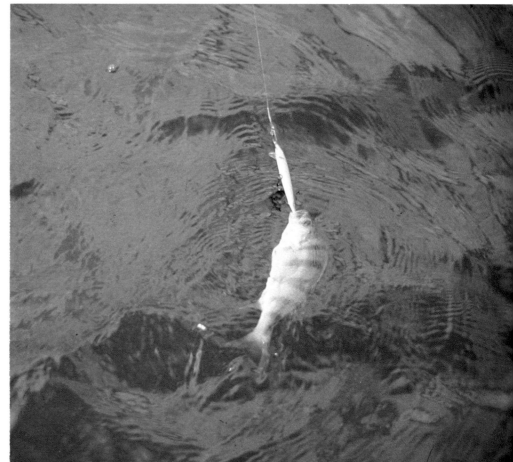

Pike after spawning

It is said that one should not fish for pike when they are gravid, but of course it's probably the only time that the bulk of anglers can get access to or even find the haunts of large pike.

In the fifties and sixties, the consensus of opinion regarding pike fishing was that this was a winter sport fish, and totally wrong for anglers to fish for pike in the summer, the suggestion being that pike take a long time to recover the energies expended during spawning activity. We now know this to be untrue, because the hardest fight from a pike is obtained in the sum-mer time. There is some evidence to indicate that cooler temperatures do in fact make certain species more lethargic when hooked. Sudden changes in water temperature have the same effect. Spring salmon entering a river in the early part of the year often play poorly, not because they have necessarily run hard in from the sea, but because of the relative temperature change between the cold, snow water in the river and the warmer saltwater. The licensing regulations for the English Water Authority Areas often prevent anglers from fishing for pike before 30 September in any year. The fighting qualities of pike also relate to the depth of water. Very often, the big pike come in

Above: Trolling through the shadows of dusk, an ideal time for big pike.

Right: How not to hold a pike; this sort of thing can damage gill rakers. At least the spoon is not deeply embedded, and should mean a quick release.

Left: Every comfort, including an admiring audience. Note the jack pike deadbait.

March and April, when fish have moved into shallow water for spawning. Here, the fish spend a lot of time jumping out of the water during the fight, but this could be because they have no place to escape to; they are then on spawning grounds with little more than a couple of feet of possible floodwater over grass meadow.

Performance

The largest pike concentration in the South of England was in the Norfolk Broads system and there, very little evidence was ever seen of pike except as the result of activity from the water birds that were being preyed on. When hooked, pike did not jump, and being prevented in the summer from fishing for the Broadland pike, it is speculation as to what performance might have been expected at that time of year. The quality of the fight of pike in the waters of the South and Midland regions of the British Isles is often based on the size of the average fish in the water. If there is a degree of competition in the feeding of a 'shoal' of pike of around 8 lb, the quality of the fight will be much better than where there are very few pike. On some of the East Anglian drains, where fish can range from 18 to 30 lb, they appear to fight no harder than the smaller fish.

Top left: Casting a deadbait means progressive power and good tackle.

Right: One of the best. Clive Loveland with his 39-pounder from Knipton Reservoir.

Left: Fun and games as a double-figure Irish pike takes to the air.

Below: One of the smallest; an ideal bait for bigger pike.

Fishing from boats

On a big water like Loch Lomond, a good boat and reliable
engine are a must.

Coarse fishing from boats is confined to the large lakes where distance to fish-holding ground is considerable. Boat fishing also enables the angler to take fish in areas denied to either the float or leger angler. There are a number of rivers where anglers moor up across the stream to present baits to fish that are migrating up from the sea.

In the first instance the angler uses his boat as an aid to stalking fish, searching out those likely haunts of shoal fish and specimens. The river angler, however, tends to locate his boat in an ambush position. Either way, the problems can be similar. The correct boat hull conformation must be chosen to give the angler satisfactory contact with the tackle and provide a stable fishing platform.

In a very still water, unaffected by high winds or the distance that the boat has to travel, the conventional flat-bottomed punt is probably the best of all craft. Although extremely slow to row or pole along, the punt can be a steady craft that has both the room to move around and the stability needed when one is forced to stand up. Fighting fish can be a hectic process and even the disciplined fisher will rise to his feet!

Larger waters mean that wind has a considerable effect on both the expanse of water and the boats that go out on it. A seaworthy hull can be as much desired by the coarse angler as by his counterpart that goes to sea. Places like Loch Lomond, the huge Irish loughs and

English Lake District are notorious for weather conditions that can be dangerous if disregarded by the fisherman. Traditionally, lake boats were made of wood. Clinker-laid planks on a stout frame produce a heavy boat, that sits neatly in the wave patterns and is unaffected by the gusting breezes when used on the drift. Both trout anglers and pike fishermen use this method of fishing where the boat is laid across the wind to drift down before the wind. These boats were, and still are, fine for the job they were made for. If they have a drawback, it is their inherent heaviness which means that the boats are hard to row. Being displacement hulls they can only be used with fairly small horsepower outboard engines.

Fibreglass hulls came next, and although they tend to blow about a little, are more easily managed which means that anglers can buy them, keep them at home and trail them to different fishing venues. Slightly different hull shapes give a boat that can go faster, yet sits happily in moderate wave patterns. Recently we have seen the arrival, from America, of the true sportfisherman's boat. Made from aluminium, semi-planing in hull shape, these boats are designed around the concept that the angler should have the maximum mobility to fish, with seated positions that allow him to cover the water available to the rod. The stability necessary is gained by extending the beam. The 'Ali' boat will go further and faster, on the same amount of fuel, than either wooden or fibreglass hulls! Little maintenance, if any, is needed and that must be a plus for anglers who aren't given to keeping their boats in good trim.

Left: By tethering the boat adjacent to reed beds, it is possible to groundbait close in and draw fish from the reeds, overcasting and drawing the hookbait back to the feeding shoal.

Right: Prebaiting a swim; a tidy angler wastes nothing, and the swill from the bait mixing bag produces a slick that would attract a shark!

Below: Now, if I tether my boat this side, and cast into the area marked private — am I poaching? Useful things boats!

One for the bows; a fine perch fell for this spinning outfit and a blade spinner.

The Orkney Longliner, a sturdy boat made in fibreglass—light but strong. Although intended for sea anglers, this boat has been adopted as a sailing club safety craft and heavy duty fishing dinghy for the large Irish and Scottish fly fishing waters.

Aids to finding fish

Nothing replaces local knowledge of any water, but there are ways in which the angler can 'read a water' quickly. The depth and the underwater contours are vital facts when searching any lake for big fish. When the lake is reasonably shallow, a plumb line can be brought into use to build up a picture of where the shallows are, where holes are located and that most necessary of all pieces of angling information: where the drop-off into deep water occurs. For it's along the line of shelves and sunken cliffs that fish tend to congregate, either for the food availability, or the currents brought about by the movement of warm and cold water.

In an electronic age, it is not surprising that the angling world has produced a market for depth sounders and fish-finding equipment. There have been tremendous advances in portability of the sounders which means that we do not over-burden ourselves with this equipment. In use, the sounder will do two things, with accuracy: find the actual depth and give an indication of the type of lakebed that the transducer is passing over. There are two types of instrument; one with a blinking neon light that moves around a dial graduated in feet or metres, and a more sophisticated sounder that has a paper roll giving a continual map-like readout of the bottom and any fish shoals that are swimming above it. Here is the value of the quality instrument in that it can show a body of fish and pinpoint their depth above the lakebed. Current drain is reasonable, using either dry batteries or, better from

an economy point of view, an old, 12 volt car battery, which can be used to provide the sort of voltage needed for a day's continuous running.

Not all forms of coarse fishing are possible from a boat. Certainly, float fishing is the only permissible style when fishing for shoal species. Legering is very difficult because of the difficulties of keeping both boat and body perfectly still. Spinning techniques are all suitable as are the various fly fishing methods that come into the realm of coarse angling. To hold a boat still one naturally has to anchor.

Above: A fine pike of more than twenty pounds is returned safely to the water.

Below: An important piece of equipment for the angler who wants to troll or find the shallows — an echo sounder

One safely in the net. Note the keepnet clamp, attached to the gunwhale away from the fishing action. Used this way, there is little likelihood of a fish becoming tangled on its way to the landing net.

A superb specimen roach to Mike Prichard's rod, from Loch Lomond the home of large fish of many species. Boat fishing in shallow water calls for an efficient anchoring system, especially when the wind blows across a huge water.

With no tide or serious current flow to worry about, the freshwater angler doesn't need the sophisticated anchoring systems that have been developed by sea anglers. Most situations can be handled with simple weights lowered to the lakebed. These can be made at home by pouring concrete into empty 2½ litre paint tins. A heavy wire ring can be embedded within the concrete to attach the rope. The handle of paint tins is not strong enough to cope with the constant use and it is inevitable that the tin will rot after a while. Make two anchoring weights, for one is needed at either end of the boat to stop the swing before the wind. Ideally, the boat should sit neatly across the breeze, steady as a rock, letting the boat's occupants fish downwind.

Long experience has shown that keepnets need a correctly designed bracket to fix them onto the gunwhales of various shaped hulls. One made with a thumb screw and G cramp, with at least a 5-in jaw, will fit on most lake boats. The top frame of the keepnet can be adjusted to suit a horizontal or near vertical stance. It is a good idea to invest in a wide net, one with at least 24-in rings, as the net will restrict fish far more than a net laid out in a lake or river. Hanging downward, with little water movement, means that fish attempt to get down into the bottom of the net where they pack tight causing distress to the smaller occupants.

Safety first

The rest of the boat's tack should be concerned with personal safety and comfort. That means lifejackets for everybody, to be worn on those occasions when an open water passage may have to be made in tricky conditions. Although most lake boats incorporate buoyancy tanks well able to support the craft and its occupants, there are always times when things are a little difficult: hauling the anchor weights in a gusting wind can be a moment when somebody has to go to the bow and take both hands to the job! Make certain that there is an adequate bailer or better still a pump. Keep all ropes tidy and stowed where they cannot wrap around anybody's feet at a moment when quick movement is called for.

Boats that are powered by an outboard engine must have a toolkit, with the basic tools aboard to change a plug or replace a drive pin. Spare fuel, with the correct oil mixed in *before* the boat leaves the lakeside, is a must. Spare rowlocks, even if the boat is engined, should be carried and the rowlocks ought to be tied into their seats as a safety factor. One last aid to angling is a map or chart of the water, especially if it is not known to the angler. On many lakes in the British Isles, there are sub-surface rocks that are a hazard to the newcomer. Always talk to the locals before venturing out onto a new fishery; they will be eager to advise, especially when it comes to displaying their angling knowledge!

The concentration of a World Champion. Dave Thomas on his way to victory.

Matchmen's attitudes

The smile of a champion, Dave Thomas; the World Individual title returns to England at Luddington on the Avon.

Matchmen, unlike pleasure fishermen, are rarely able to choose the piece of water that they would like to fish on. They will have favourite rivers and even favourite swims on some rivers, but it is conceivable that anglers in many matches will never have seen the water before. The organising committee provide a stretch of water, the draw for peg positions is made and off the competitors go.

Questions which have to be answered quickly, flash through the mind of the match angler as he struggles, tackle laden, to his peg: what is the depth of the water, how fast does the current flow and what sort of bed does the river or canal have? How much feed should have been brought? How many pounds of fish will be needed to get into the frame?

But, is match fishing so different from the styles and basic methods used by the pleasure angler? The answer must surely be that there are very few real differences . . . if any. What alters is the attitude to

fishing the water on that day. Matchmen have refined the various fishing styles to suit just about anything that can confront them. They approach the match after carefully adjusting experiences gained in earlier outings to similar waters. A searching look in a matchman's basket will indicate, clearly, the amount of tackle needed to keep among the action that happens on the regular circuit. Of course, not all matchmen are interested in the rigours of the big match scene. Most so-called matchmen are club anglers who will engage, at some time during the season, in a number of competitions. Their drive is not so much to win money, as to measure themselves, tactically, alongside known experts.

It is always a mistake to assume that the average matchman is only interested in small fish or that his tactics are only capable of handling tiddlers! The match circuit has parallels to the motor race track. Without the trials and hard fishing of our match colleagues, there would be little tackle development or

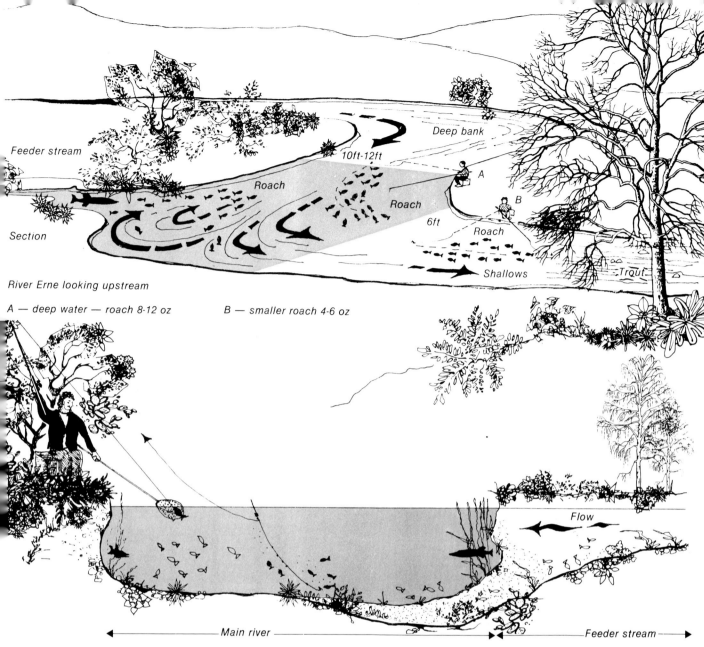

Feeder stream

Roach

10ft-12ft

Deep bank

Roach

A

B

6ft

Roach

Section

Shallows

Trout

River Erne looking upstream

A — deep water — roach 8-12 oz   B — smaller roach 4-6 oz

Flow

Main river

Feeder stream

The upper River Erne — an ideal match water.

experimentation in the production of baits and groundbait. The matchman has to be a master of the art of fine fishing, coupled with psychological ability, to cope with the pressures of a few hours' intense concentration. There is little conviviality during a match as the contestants are too busy reading the conditions. They may miss some of the pleasures of a day's fishing, but there is a pleasure in winning!

Reading the water

The important decision, on arrival at the waterside, is how to approach the fishing; whether to tackle up with float or leger gear and how to feed for effect. Match fishing is far more than attempting to catch fish that happen to be in front of the angler. He concentrates on developing a rhythm of feeding the swim, fishing it through and reaction to what the fish are doing.

Activity on any water, particularly when a large number of people have walked along the match stretch

to their pegs, will drive fish off to distance and probably dull their instinct to feed. Within a few minutes of the start of any match, feeding the water has to take place on several counts. First the fish have to be brought onto the feed once more. Bringing them within easy fishing range is desirable *and* the feeding effect of groundbait from anglers either side of the peg has to be counteracted. Having brought fish within range of efficient angling tactics . . . they've got to be held there!

It is easy to see that haphazard feeding, especially if it is done in great dollops of stiff feed, will fill the swim in, producing the reverse effect to that desired. The programme of feeding ought to be used as little as possible to keep fish interested and the swim worked up. Watching men like Ivan Marks and Ray Mumford, one gets a true indication of how the swim ought to be fed. They hook, land the fish, rebait and throw loose feed in what appears to be a continuous flowing action. Rhythm again!

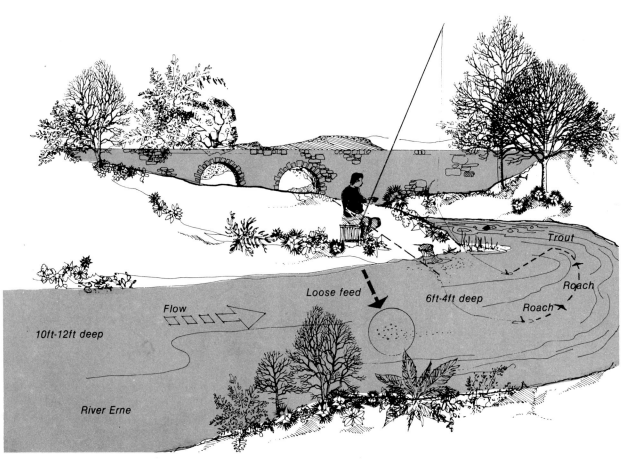

Trout

Roach

Roach

Loose feed

Flow

6ft-4ft deep

10ft-12ft deep

River Erne

For the deeper water (12 ft) in the adjacent swim upstream, flattened 'balls' of groundbait proved effective. Instead of dropping straight through the water, the pendulum effect causes pieces of groundbait and maggots to flake off, feeding the roach at all depths of the swim.

The match angler's tackle

Carbon fibre almost dominates the match angler's rod holdall. The rod's lightness, incredible tip speed and thin diameter blanks are hard to beat for function. If a rod has to be held in the hand for five hours, it is vital that its weight should be kept to a minimum. New moves in the production of glassfibre can match both the action and weight of most carbon rods. What the glass rod cannot do is give the speed through the air on a cast. Any windy day will soon show the difference between rods, where the blank has to cut into the breeze. For a few years now the closed faced fixed-spool reel has enjoyed a unique position on the match circuit. In trotting, it gives the clean run-off of line for so long associated with the centrepin, and is almost instantaneous in pick-up of nylon with the valuable facility that the reel can lift and rewind slack line that billows in front of the angler after a fishless strike. The skirted, open faced reel has been a considerable improvement over the early reels. It gives far better control over the slipping drag than the closed faced version but, of course, playing fish off the drag is losing favour with anglers. It is becoming common practice to use the backwind facility.

Fishing the pole

It is a remarkable thing that a fishing system, developed by the British angler, should have found such favour on the Continent. Now it's back in a big way among our matchmen. Its re-introduction has brought about a massive upsurge in tackle production specific to this style of fishing. Floats, sinkers and the associated bits and pieces are part of every tackle shop's display.

There was a time when England's lack of success in World Championship competition was attributed to our lack of understanding of pole fishing. That may have been partially true, but great strides have been made by the younger match element to learn the skills of pole fishing. We have even beaten some of our European neighbours at their own game, with a couple of British anglers taking the system into France — and winning! Pole fishing is truly a match fishing technique; admirable for tight lining under the rod tip, to snatch small fish out at speed. Its only limitations are the ability of the angler to handle lengths up to 10 m and the larger fish that happen along during the course of a contest.

181

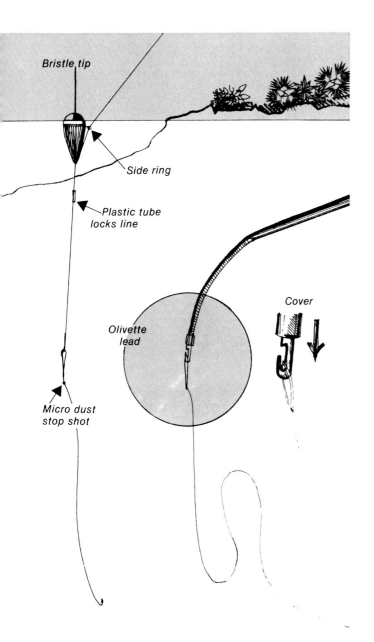

Bristle tip

Side ring

Plastic tube
locks line

Olivette
lead

Cover

Micro dust
stop shot

The World Championships
— the ultimate match

In 1981, the World Championships returned to England in September, fished on the River Avon at Luddington, just a mile or two below Stratford-upon-Avon. One of Birmingham's top match anglers, Clive Smith, was selected to fish in the English Team. The following comments were made in interview during a pre-competition fishing session at Edgbaston, and some months before the World Championships. They give an interesting insight into the match angler's attitudes to his sport, and the thinking that goes before any important competition.

The location of the interview: Edgbaston Reservoir, centre of Birmingham, in bright sunshine, during an early afternoon session prior to an evening match. Clive Smith was catching roach steadily . . .

The pole rig — left — is ideal for fishing slow moving rivers and canals, where fish will feed close under the pole tip.

Left: A good bream water; the Prosperous Canal during the Woolworth/Prosperous Angling Gala Week.

Anglers make ready for the start of the Benson and Hedges Competition; held at Enniskillen on the River Erne.

C.S. 'This evening, I'll probably use a bit of ground-bait with a few casters, and fish over the groundbait using single maggot, waggler style. The fish are quite shy here, so fine pound bottom to 2 lb reel line and No 18 hook will probably do.

Big fish here are a bonus, and are also rather unlikely just now as the water is not fishing well. I'd expect mainly roach, with odd perch and gudgeon; but roach will be the predominant species. There are odd tench in the water, but the reservoir would have to be fishing better I feel for them to show.

Everything is a bit early this year; another four weeks would probably make all the difference. In 'The National' recently in north Lincolnshire, the low weights could well have been as a result of the late spawning. Catches were very poor. Ken Giles had 1 oz and I had 2 oz, hardly what you would call productive. As in all bream competitions, however, there is always a shoal willing to feed and the top weights were 21 lb, 19 lb and 17 lb, but these three top weights were no reflection on the match. You had to be dead on the right peg. I was drawn next but one to the runner-up with 19 lb, against my 2 oz! That just goes to show how tightly packed the fish can be on a match stretch.

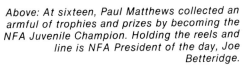

Above: At sixteen, Paul Matthews collected an armful of trophies and prizes by becoming the NFA Juvenile Champion. Holding the reels and line is NFA President of the day, Joe Betteridge.

Top right: Balderton youngster, at fourteen, is already a crack angler as this splendid net of fish reveals.

Left: Youngsters are joined in increasing numbers by the ladies in competition. This catch by Leicester's Erika Clewlow from Norfolk's Great Ouse gave her the Ladies Championship.

The World Championships are at Luddington on the Avon, a good match river. I'm a little bit worried, however, about the bombardment of groundbait, especially from the Continentals. Chub are the predominant species there and could be affected initially by too much groundbait going in. It's not the excessive groundbait that will disturb the fish, but the noise which I'm sure they associate with anglers. The fish shoals on this stretch of the Avon are of course well used to boats moving up and downstream; that doesn't bother them! But, in being bombarded with orange-sized balls of groundbait, they could well be upset and put off the feed.

As a team, the English squad have not as yet looked at tactics for the big match. I would suspect, however, that this will be a maggot match. I don't know whether we would groundbait or not, but I'd have a guess that loose feed, far bank tactics, and single maggot fished waggler style could well be the answer. The opposition could come from almost any team. If the fish do become upset by groundbait bombardment, then the Continental pole and bloodworm combination could win. If not, then the competition could come much more locally, perhaps from the Welsh team, followed by the Irish.'

'Clive, what tips would you give the up and coming match angler?'

C.S. 'There are so many well organised matches nowadays, that the up and coming match angler can do no better than go along to one of these matches and watch the better anglers in action. Competitions are well publicised and well sponsored. Watch the top matchmen in action, just the same as in professional golf, and follow their techniques. It's the best way to pick up the initial stages of match angling anyway. As far as tackle is concerned, try and choose the best you can afford. Don't save money on cheaper rods, as if you really get into the sport, you'll soon become keen enough to want to sort out the best possible tackle you can buy, even if it means waiting an extra month or two to get exactly what you want. If interested in match fishing, try to find a tackle dealer who is also a match angler. If game fishing is your interest, then that's the chap you should see to purchase your tackle. There are, of course, tackle dealers who have no connection with the sport whatsoever; although their tackle and prices can be just as good, it's hard to get any really helpful technical advice and fishing hints from them if you are a newcomer to the sport.

Always seek the advice that is genuine, and above all, keep your eyes open and watch the top anglers in action. You'll soon spot the difference! My satisfaction in matchfishing is that I always aim to do my best. There are some big sponsored matches nowadays, and I'd like to match some of my previous wins again in the future. Of course, in some of the big competitions such as 'The Embassy', fished for the last couple of years in Ireland on bream waters, you have to be right on top of the fish to win, and there's a very big element of luck in the draw.

Match fishing has never had the sort of money that the golfing circuit can produce, but things are slowly improving. With better television coverage and someone from inside the sport to help the TV networks improve their angling reporting techniques, the spectator awareness and therefore sponsorship potential could vastly increase.

The top prize this year is £10 000, but you would have to be very lucky to make that sort of money on the match fishing circuit. I doubt if anyone as yet could afford to go fully professional. A top match angler should be able to make up to £3000 with a couple of lucky breaks. The taxman has referred to these winnings so far as a 'grey area', but I think he could be in for a surprise; it's a very expensive game, match fishing. At the end of the day, nett winnings are not substantial; they help subsidise your fishing.

I certainly fish matches to win, and even in practice it's the development of a rhythm, fishing under the disciplined pressures of competitive match angling, that give me my enjoyment of the sport.'

185

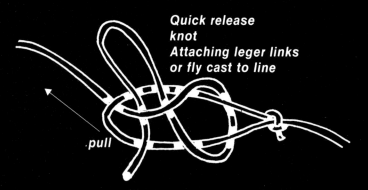

Quick release knot
Attaching leger links or fly cast to line

pull

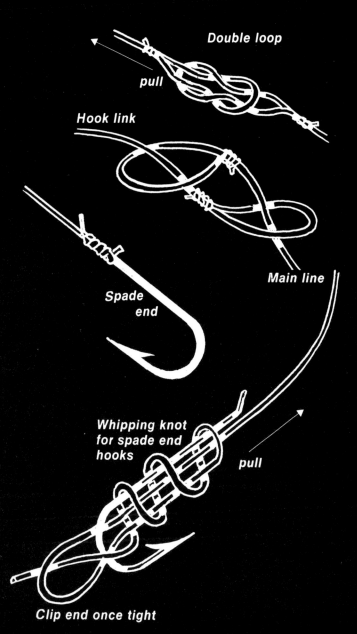

Double loop

pull

Hook link

Main line

Spade end

Whipping knot for spade end hooks

pull

Clip end once tight

or nylon

Two turn turl knot

Tucked
half blood knot

Alternative
Blood loop

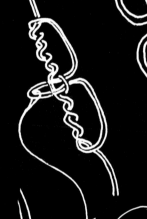

Blood knot
for tying
two lengths
of nylon
together

Used for
dropper

Double overhand
loop

Fishing upstream dry fly to rising roach on the East Lothian River Tyne below the village of East Linton.

Coarse fishing
with a fly rod

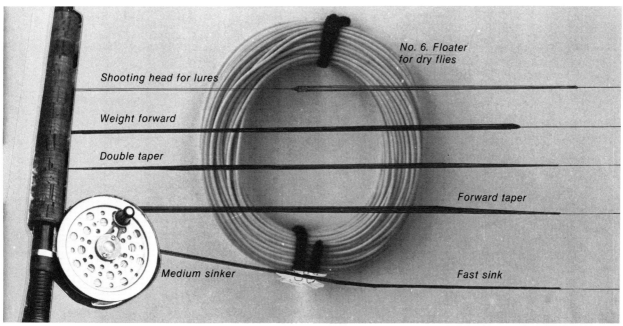

The angler has a bewildering choice of fly lines to choose from. Which does he choose?

Labels on image: Shooting head for lures · Weight forward · Double taper · Medium sinker · No. 6. Floater for dry flies · Forward taper · Fast sink

Fly fishing for coarse species is becoming increasingly popular, but is still very much a secondary technique for the coarse angler. The growing interest stems from the number of Midland and London based coarse anglers who, during the coarse fishing closed season, have taken advantage of the largely improved and readily available reservoir trout fishing close to the major conurbations.

A modest fly fishing outfit is within most anglers' pocket and need only consist of one rod, a basic fly reel and line, some nylon for casts, and a few flies. The rod, which should be capable of handling most fish including pike, will be about 9-10 ft long, and hollow glass best amongst the materials available.

Rod choice

Split or built cane rods are getting scarcer on the market, are expensive, and not really suited to the coarse fisherman. While possessing the beautiful, classical action so beloved by the trout traditionalists, cane tends to be far too heavy a rod material for most coarse fishing situations.

Carbon fibre is light but expensive for what, as far as the coarse fisher is concerned, would be a secondary rod in the holdall. It is also less capable than hollow glass when it comes to handling the heavier and bulkier streamers and bucktail lures the pike angler

Left: A 1½ - lb grayling is slid to the waiting net. The fish fell to a small nymph fished upstream on a sinking tip. The grayling was 'lumping' to nymphs just below the arch of the bridge, at Bibury.

Right: A good fly reel should balance the rod, hold enough line if after big fish such as pike, and give good retrieve and rim control.

may want to try. Carbon rods will, of course, cast the larger lures, but it is doubtful if the angler will feel the right response from the rod. About the only successful way of fishing the bigger lures with such a rod is to use a shooting head, and this method is explained more fully under lines and casting techniques.

Fly reels

The angler has a large range of reels to choose from; all are basically centre-pin drum style with fixed or optional ratchet. Perforated drums lighten the reel, and help balance the fly rod. Materials range from plastic and nylon compositions to light alloys and carbon. The very light reels are designed for use with carbon and ultra-light glass rods.

A well-balanced outfit should be one where the rod balances around or slightly above the handle. The hand position on a fly rod is situated above the reel, when loaded with reel, fly line and backing. Some fly reels have the added advantage of gearing, which allows the angler to retrieve the line back onto the reel at a fast rate. This can be invaluable, especially when fishing for big pike or chub, which have a tendency to turn and run back towards the angler when hooked on a longish line. It is imperative that the line is kept taut at all times, just as in bait fishing, so that the fish is unable to get slack and throw the hook. Fly hooks in particular have a nasty habit of falling free at the slightest opportunity. Reels not only vary in diameter, but also in width. A 3½-in diameter fly reel with a 1-in wide drum can be loaded with a full fly line and adequate backing for use with pike and other specimens.

The ideal fly fishing line

What is a suitable fly line? The angler has a choice as varied as the fish he can catch, ranging from floaters to sinking tips, slow and fast sinkers and shooting heads. Lines can be level (of the same diameter throughout), forward or double taper. Since most species that are of interest to the coarse fly fisherman will either be surface feeding or near the surface in relatively shallow water, the best all round choice will be a forward or double taper with a sinking tip, with a weight to suit the action of the rod. Weight forward lines are available, but tend to be unwieldy, making it difficult for the angler to present the fly or flies quietly on the water.

Correct balance

A good tackle dealer will never rush you over the choice of rod, reel and line. He will be happy, if space permits, to assemble the outfit, including the correct line to balance the rod, and see if the action appeals to you. If inexperienced in casting with a fly rod, then he will explain as simply as possible the mechanics involved. Handling a fly fishing outfit is not all that difficult.

Casting techniques

Unlike a bait rod, where lead weights and the choice of terminal rig dictate the actual casting weight which propels the tackle from rod to water, the fly line's own weight causes the rod to flex during the casting action, and thus shoot the line and flies on the forward cast to their intended target. It is when this action is incorrectly executed with the wrong rhythm, problems occur, ranging from a sloppy delivery and tangled cast, to flicking the flies off with a whip-like crack.

The fly rod requires an adequate length of line in the air, before producing the right action to deliver the

Grayling . . . the worthy one

The Grayling is a salmonid, and as such appears in William B. Currie's *Guinness Guide to Game Fishing*. But the grayling is quite rightly classed along with the coarse fish as well, by definition of habit, location, spawning and distribution. It has been adopted by the coarse angler, and frequently disregarded as a sporting species by game fishers, although in Yorkshire and by many Scots anglers who fish throughout the winter months, the grayling is a truly worthy and sporting fish.

Unlike the Arctic grayling, our species *Thymallus thymallus* doesn't jump when hooked, but will use the current against its large sail-like dorsal fin, backing off down the stream in a display of strength which has fooled many a game fisher into thinking he had hooked something far larger.

In appearance the grayling is beautifully streamlined, the sides large scaled and silvery, the head pointed and the tail deeply forked. The unmistakable dorsal can be spotted and these carry over and down the flanks to a greater or lesser degree, depending on habitat and location. These fish tend to shoal, especially when small — 7-10in — and even large specimens seem to feed in small groups or shoals of a size. Once the grayling have been located the angler can, with care, continue his sport for as long as the shoal remains undisturbed. On hooking grayling, especially in fast, streamy water, they naturally back off downstream, using their flanks and dorsal side on against the current. At this stage, it is better for the angler to allow the fish some line, to bring it below any other grayling feeding in the vicinity, and then play the fish back into the river bank, with the minimum of fuss. Held too hard, the angler not only risks a breakage from a big fish, but the grayling will inevitably break surface, and its splashing disturb other fish which might have taken a bait.

Grayling can be taken on the fly and a variety of baits, perhaps the most popular being a small pink worm or the striped brandling found in the farmer's midden. The best method of presentation is by trotting the worm bait down the selected stream on float tackle.

Grayling favour rivers with plenty of current, and require good, pollution-free streams. In late spring, they spawn in the gravelly shallows towards the tails of broader pools, but otherwise are generally to be found on the edge of faster streams and eddies, behind obstructions such as boulders or fallen trees, or the inside of bends, where they can pick up surface insects and nymphs on the edge of the current. They will lie adjacent to weed beds, and a certain amount of scouting can be invaluable in searching out a good shoal. Often the bottom gravel beside a weedy run will suddenly give up its secret to the wary and watchful angler. When all that could be seen at first glance was seemingly every stone and pebble on the river bed, further attention often highlights the ghostly grey shapes of grayling moving gently with the current. If the weather is warm, grayling display a splashy rise when surface feeding, quite unlike the dimple or bulge made by trout; they are also likely to be rising in groups, another characteristic which tells the experienced angler that he is looking at grayling and not trout.

For the coarse fisherman without fly tackle, even rising grayling can be taken, using a 12 ft float rod, and freelining a small worm on a size 16 hook with the minimum of shotting to allow the angler to place his bait upstream and within reach of the fish. With as little resistance as possible, allow the bait to swim naturally down to the fish. If the cast is made a matter of feet above the feeding grayling (10 ft or so will let the fish see the bait without frightening them by the sudden splash) the fish will follow the bait down from the surface.

The angler's first indication that it has taken the bait will be a sudden draw across the current. A lift on the rod is generally all that is necessary to set the hook. Remember that grayling have very soft mouths, and an over-eager strike can pull the hook out rather than setting it. Their mouth is also small, and therefore a small, pink worm or brandling is going to give a better chance of hooking than too large a garden worm fished on an ineffectively small hook. Maggot, especially in slightly coloured spate water, can also do very well. The originally accepted British record grayling was reputedly taken from the River Meldrum in Perthshire, a tributary of the River Tay. Today, the newly established records have been coming thick and fast, and Scotland still appears to offer the best chance of specimen fish. Two pounders are common on both the River Tay and Tweed and their respective tributaries. Tay's major tributaries, the Tummel and lower down the Isla and Earn, which flows into the tidal Tay, all offer splendid grayling fishing. Much of it is controlled by local angling clubs, or riparian owners from whom one seeks permission to fish. Providing you don't descend unannounced by the bus load, few salmon tenants object to one or two grayling fishers, who don't disturb the main salmon lies. There is little conflict here. Unfortunately, much of the poor relationships has come about through the thoughtlessness of a few individuals and clubs. It is mainly trout fishermen who, out of season, use the grayling as an excuse for fishing trout illegally; or in season, by swamping salmon water with neither courtesy nor consideration, and with no intention of paying for their sport.

Recent legislation on Tweedside, which covers the Eye Water, and all major tributaries of the Tweed, makes it illegal to fish for trout or grayling without permission. For the angler prepared to pay a modest sum for his sport, and to follow a reasonable code of conduct, the arrangement is for the better, allowing good management and finance for stocking. While the grayling is not regarded as a major asset, many locals and visiting anglers fish the Tweed and its main tributary, the Teviot, for the splendid grayling.

The River Clyde is Scotland's top west coast grayling water. A decade ago, a bag of grayling would normally hold at least one two pounder. The average weight has dropped since then, but good catches of over 20 fish to a rod are still regularly taken, mainly during the winter months or in late autumn. Grayling anglers on the Clyde perfected a technique which is so effective (and destructive) as to be banned. Teams of fishers would wade down a stream, 'shuffling' as they went. This not only coloured the water downstream of them, but as well as dislodging various aquatic insects, also disturbed the trout redds. The action of the waders on the gravel was in effect producing a groundbaiting action, which drew the grayling shoals directly below the angler; and all he had to do was trot a worm on a short line below to the waiting fish, which could, once the feeding frenzy got under way, be taken in rapid succession. The damage to the trout redds, however, was disastrous. For many though, grayling fishing is synonymous with crisp frosts, and snow-lined banks. The last of the leaves have gone in the winter wind, and the river looks grey and uninviting. And yet, the mysterious grey backs lie in wait for your worm or maggot bait, and once located, can keep the adrenalin flowing even during the coldest days.

Once spawning is complete, grayling will move slowly back into the streams, where they can be taken on a number of natural baits as well as the worm. Grubs include wasp larvae and docken grubs, and at times these can be even more effective than the worm. A light leger tackle, trundled along the edges of the stream, will also take grayling, but by far the most successful method is with a small float. Grayling are not aggressive feeders and will seldom act in a predatory fashion. They do, however, just prior and after spawning in the spring tend to hit lures generally meant for salmon, ranging from natural sprat to devons and spoons. Every November on Tweed, large grayling upwards of 2 lb are regularly taken on big tube flies again intended for salmon. Why they choose to commit such felony is pure speculation, but it is doubtful that it has anything to do with feeding. The size of the lures relative to the grayling's feeding-capacity and size of mouth, suggests if anything a territorial aggression or perhaps even curiosity. After all, if a fish wishes to inspect anything unusual or stop something which it cannot identify, then it has to use either its tail or mouth . . . it doesn't have hands! This could also explain foul-hooked fish; they haven't necessarily intended to *eat* whatever the angler has offered, and may just be chasing and reacting to something alien to their environment.

line and flies to the feeding fish. The angler has to flex the rod back and forward several times, lengthening the line by drawing it off the reel, and allowing the rod to increase the line it handles progressively on back and forward casts. This is known as *false casting*, performed until the required amount of fly line is in the air. For close targets, the amount of line extended can be as little as 10-30 ft. At this range the rod will handle properly, and if then the angler requires to reach a target at, say, 20 yd or more, the additional amount of line is stripped from the reel. The fly line, already in the air, draws the additional line through the rings on the forward cast. The angler releases the loose line at the right time, so that it shoots out towards the target. It is this timing, rather than strength, which is critical in fly fishing.

If the angler finds that his flies are being cracked off, the main cause is not allowing sufficient time on the back cast for the line to straighten out before starting on the forward thrust. It is helpful if the beginner says: 'Back — pause — forward,' as the casting cycle progresses, deliberately stopping between back and forward movements of the rod. Although the angler's arm will be stationary, the rod will continue to flex backwards until the line is fully extended; this action sets the spring, as it were, which provides the forward power guided and assisted by the angler's follow through to complete the cast. By holding the fly rod handle like a hammer, with thumb on top of the rod and elbow to the side, the angler will prevent the rod going too far back on the back cast. Let the rod do the work for you. A heavy movement of the arm will only detract from the power of the rod.

The double taper line

This assists the angler in long casting, where a quiet delivery is preferred when using small flies, imitating natural insects. A single taper line will do the same job when casting to fish at closer range.

The weight forward line

This fly line will give you distance, although it handles rather heavily, and will not produce such a subtle delivery, tending to land the lure or flies with a plop . . . or worse! It is, however, a useful line when using bigger flies and lures, imitating small fish.

The shooting head

This generally consists of a short length of level line spliced to a light braided nylon backing or monofilament. The length of the shooting head is designed to be sufficient to create the correct casting action in the rod. Then on the forward cast, the backing is stripped to the required distance and shoots through the rings drawn by the main fly line, but without the resistance associated with a full length fly line.

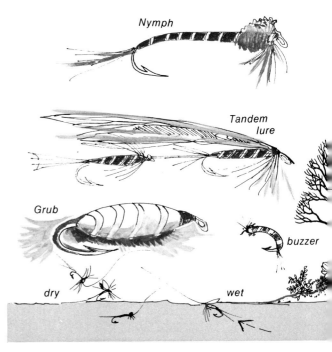

A selection of flies ranging from lures to take chub, perch and pike, to tiny dry flies for dace and roach.

Nymph

Tandem lure

Grub

buzzer

dry

wet

194

Developments of the shooting head have included nylon mono lines coated at the head with the fly line finish, the idea being to get a gradual taper and perfect continuity between shooting head and the backing, which in that case runs right through the shooting head. The method, however, has not reached perfection as the coating process tends to harden the nylon backing, making it less supple, more brittle and less suitable for shooting through the rings. A shooting head is ideal for fly rods, where larger lures and streamers are being used, and also allows the angler to get quickly down to the fish . . . especially for big perch and pike. The alternative for perch and pike fishing is to use a full sinking line, either slow or fast, depending on the type of water and depth you intend to fish. Ideally, of course, you can have more than one reel with a choice of lines to cover most situations.

Rudd — on the fly

Towards the summer, when water temperatures rise, rudd will begin to congregate in the upper layers of the lake. They will spend a lot of time just underneath the surface, in the top 2 ft or so. From here they will rise to take all manner of aquatic flies and insects, not just the ephemerids, but buzzers and gnats. During this surface activity, rudd will often make quite a commotion while feeding, and a reasonably presented dry fly, or wet fly cast will seldom disturb the fish. The take can vary from tiny plucks and pulls, especially evident when a large number of fish are working together . . . to a slow, deliberate gulp from the bigger individuals which feed in a more solitary manner.

A sinking tip or a slow sinker will work even better than a floating line. They allow the angler to cover those fish which may be surface feeding in the upper layers without actually breaking surface. The fly rod, with sinking tip line, is also an excellent method of presenting maggot or worm baits, although casting action will tend to throw off a bread flake bait. If you decide to fish an artificial, a finely dressed fly on size 18 hook to a tapered 9-ft cast and 2-lb breaking strain point will be right for most dry fly work. The Black Gnat or a Greenwell nymph will take rudd. For wet fly work, a cast of nymphs or some of the more attractive patterns with a touch of gold or silver in the body dressing do well.

Left: a fine roach for Shepley on the fly. Upstream spider patterns fished on a floating line will take river roach when surface feeding on insects and hatching flies.

Where to find rudd

Rudd love to work in amongst the reeds, an almost impossible place to catch them on the fly. They can be drawn out by use of loose feed, but then the angler will probably not choose thereafter to tempt them with the fly rod.

There are, fortunately, many other times when rudd shoals will move freely in the open, well into the lake, although their preference will be for shallower ground. They can also be approached *quietly* in open areas amongst the reeds, often an ideal place for ambush. Providing the angler watches his backcast, a good catch on the fly rod is possible.

Being shoal feeders rather than solitary fish, it is very easy to disturb rudd after a fish is hooked. They are surprisingly powerful fighters but can be led away from the main shoal by applying gentle pressure; then additional pressure will bring the rudd to the net without necessarily upsetting the rest of the shoal. With care the exercise can be repeated several times.

Upstream dry fly takes a Grayling this time.

Select your fish

When rudd are working the surface, it is often possible to see individual fish, select a good one, and cast specifically to the fish rather than at random. This is a very exciting alternative to fishing blind, where the fly cast sinks below the surface and you don't see the take. Beware striking too quickly if you see the fish take. You'll miss!

Chub on the fly

After emerging from winter hibernation, bees and wasps are very lethargic and often tend to fall from trees and overhanging bushes onto the water. Following the rigours of the new breeding period, these insects are drowsy and fall easy prey to the wily chub, which position themselves under the banks, in the shade of the bushes and trees which give them their food supply. Here, chub will rise to the falling wasps and bees as they tumble onto the surface, and get carried down with the current. Often, the first the angler sees is the blunt head of the chub breaking the surface, almost with an appearance of slow motion as its fleshy lips part to suck in the natural tit-bit.

For the fly angler, the chub represents a major challenge because of its location under the trees. This requires accurate casting, often using a sideways action, rather than an overhead loop. Bigger dressings than for rudd and dace are necessary, and to represent the wasps, bees and other big mouthfuls which come their way, bushy flies such as a Soldier Palmer or Zulu are most effective. Beetles form another important part of the staple diet of the chub, and again, a big fly such as the Black Pennell will draw the chub to the surface.

Chub are less inclined to take a wet fly cast, but will often do so when the cast includes one of the more fancy patterns.

Flies such as the butchers, Invicta, Alexandra and Hardy's Gold, where there is silver or gold in the dressing, will often be mistaken by the chub as small fry, rather than insects. They are particularly good when the river is running slightly coloured after rain, when a normal fly pattern might not show up quite so well.

Chub have a catholic taste, too, when it comes to the huge variety of baits on which they can be caught. As well as the artificial fly, chub will take a natural insect dapped on the surface, with the angler concealed in the undergrowth or in the overhanging trees above. This last position should always be achieved with caution. Check that the tree limbs are not rotten, and don't attempt this jungle warfare approach if a non-swimmer. A ducking into a cold, deep river can sometimes mean more than a disturbed swim.

The chub, unfairly perhaps in the Scottish waters which it inhabits, often has the reputation of being a poor fighter. This is normally the result of trout and sea trout anglers catching the chub in June and July, shortly after they have spawned.

Fly fishing for dace

The dace, while relatively small, makes up for its lack of size by its speed and sporting fight on light tackle, and the angler can do no better than try this silvery acrobat with the fly rod. The average fish on most waters will be less than ½ lb and therefore small flies will do best. Size 16-18 are ideal. Small dry and wet spider patterns and nymphs will all attract dace, and the somewhat unorthodox method of fishing a team of two or three dry-hackled spiders across and downstream in fast, broken water will often have the dace snatching at the flies every cast.

The dace is as fast as lightning, and the angler's reaction has to be just as quick. A 2-3 lb breaking strain cast is sufficient, and although this possibly sounds heavy to the normal bait fisher, the sudden take in fast water can break lighter nylon. If the dace are shoaling, the use of more than one fly on the cast often produces a double take, or even three fish at once, and that can lead to antics indeed. On slower reaches inhabited by dace, a single dry fly presented upstream to rising fish will often be more effective. Dace also like a little colour, so try some of the brighter patterns such as the butchers as well as the imitative dressings. In these slower stretches, the fly rod can also produce roach and perch, although the latter tend to go for sunk flies.

Perch on the fly

The obliging perch is no less keen when it comes to the fly rod. While they will sometimes move to surface fly, they are much more likely to take a cast of three wet flies, fished well below the surface. It wouldn't be the first time that a trout angler has put his rod down momentarily, with the line behind the drifting boat, and three perch have taken his flies simultaneously.

As well as the wet fly cast, an equally effective method is a single lure, imitating a small fish, used in conjunc-

196

tion with a slow or fast sinker to get down to the perch. This method, stripping the lure back towards the angler, is deadly, especially in the autumn, when last year's fry reach a similar size. Perch will hit their own fry, and one of the best imitative patterns is the Alexandra, with its red 'ibis' streak, and dark green peacock herl. A lure often takes the better perch, compared to straightforward wet fly or nymph patterns. To get right down to the bigger perch in deeper water, a shot nipped just above the fly will help. Fish with a steady draw, and at the first sign of a pluck, increase the retrieve rate, and wait for a firm take. Perch aren't the greatest fighters on a fly rod, especially from deeper water, but a 1-lb plus fish on a light fly rod, will give you a lot of fun.

Roach

Unlike the perch, roach will be found surface feeding, and will readily take a dry fly, especially towards last light during the summer months. The take is delicate, often little more than a dimple and a slight draw on the line. The roach, however, can move quickly, and reject the fly with lightning speed, so a fast, firm but gentle reaction is required from the angler. Feeding roach will not be solitary, and if a small shoal of fish are your target, try and draw a hooked fish away as quietly as possible, allowing the fish to keep well under the surface until clear of the other roach.

Pike

A stiffer rod and additional length help when handling the bigger lures needed for pike. A minimum of 14-lb nylon is required to prevent abrasive, needle sharp teeth from parting your line and company with the pike. Salmon tube flies and reservoir lures are ideal for pike; in the case of home tied patterns, strong doubles or trebles should be used in preference to the lighter gauge trout hooks on reservoir lures because of the bony nature of the pike's jaws. Fished sink and draw along the edges of reed beds and over weedy bottom cover these attractors can soon produce the desired response, not only from jacks, but bigger fish into double figures.

Grayling

The grayling, so like the trout in its feeding habits, is no doubt the most sought after of our fly fished species. The grayling will fall to wet fly, nymph and dry fly. Grayling often feed in small groups of up to a dozen fish, barely breaking the surface of the stream; the rises are delicate as the feeding fish take duns, or bulge at nymphs below the surface. The angler's reaction to the strike should be immediate and firm. The grayling has a small and delicate mouth, however, and the fisherman should not be over-strong on setting the hook. At times, grayling will rise and miss the fly, especially in very streamy water, but providing the angler has done nothing to alarm the fish, they will often rise several times to the artificial, until eventually hooked and landed successfully.

While grayling do not display the same wild antics of the brown trout when hooked, they nevertheless put up a powerful show, often backing off downstream characteristically, using their large sail-like dorsal against the current . . . and it can be a long way back to the net, leaving the angler to follow downstream to net his prize.

Top left: A selection of palmer-tied flies. The Soldier Palmer, Red Tag and Zulu will all take chub.

Top: Two chub, rising to surface, flies under the trees are circled. Can you spot the others?

Right: The Loch Lomond powan, which has been deleted from the current British record list.

Fishing afar . . .

Canadian Geese flight into the sunset, on
Holland's Sneekermeer, home of slab-sided bream
that run into double figures.

Anglers have always through their inquiring nature
been something of the explorer . . . the adventurer,
prepared not only to experiment in search of bigger
and better fish, but to travel as well, to visit new locations, new waters, and to try different styles and
techniques.

We are fortunate in having within the British Isles
such a wide spectrum of opportunities for the keen
angler, whether he be a coarse fisherman, sea angler,
or with a preference for other game — enough, one
would think, for any keen exponent of the rod.

Leisure and Travel

As leisure time increases, and travel opportunities ex-
pand, anglers have been quick to grasp the chances of
fishing abroad. It is now as cheap to travel across the
Atlantic to North America and Canada, as to fly to
many European destinations. Ferry crossings, hover-
ports and hydrofoils, coupled with road, rail and air
links, offer a bewildering choice for the modern angling tourist. Capacity at present still copes comfortably
with demand, and there are plenty of bargains to be
found for the careful researcher. Carrier attitudes

200

towards the angler and his equipment vary considerably. All too often, the flying fisherman finds an excess baggage charge for his rod holdall, while the golfing enthusiast, sitting in the next seat, has preferential consideration for his 'tackle' bag. Anglers on the road tend to have their own style of vehicle, often towing a boat. Bait in such a situation can go off in a big way, and maggots need constant supervision. Some shipping services, such as DFDS on the Esbjerg run, offer anglers with a bait problem refrigeration facilities, much appreciated especially during the summer months. Bait on the Continent and in Ireland is not always readily available nor does it always suit the angler's particular needs, and therefore many travellers carry their own supplies.

Tackle

Although there are plenty of tackle dealers in the main towns of Holland, Denmark and France, European preferences differ considerably from our own, and although the pole fisher is well catered for, the British angler would do well to ensure a healthy and well stocked tackle box before setting off abroad. Ireland, like Scotland, has a native preference for game fish, and this is generally reflected in the range of fishing tackle found in the shops, so that the coarse fishing enthusiast should again make sure he has most of what he wants with him; don't rely too much on finding a wide selection of floats, hooks, line or other terminal gear. Major items such as rods, reels and nets are also fairly restricted, although the choice will be reasonable.

Costs

With the exchange rate of the pound eddying and fluctuating like a west coast spate river, kroner, guilders, francs and punts will yoyo like a carp on the end of a continental pole. In general terms though, prices, and the cost of living, have stabilised and are very similar to our own. Twenty years ago, a visit to any of the major European countries was enough to chase you off the river bank and into the other to recharge the wallet. Today, many things are cheaper than at home, with perhaps the exception of clothes and hotel drinks.

Ireland

The locals have a distinct preference for salmon, trout and a black velvety liquid which embellishes many a story of fish lost and won. Ireland, with its vast limestone lakeland region, mighty river systems, streams, loughs and canals, welcomes the coarse angler; and a constant programme of development and management ensures easy access to much of the best fishing, but with ample scope for the modern explorer to find his own sport.

The Erne and Shannon watersheds alone give visiting coarse fishermen a lifetime of possibilities. Roach continue to spread their weight, and offer magnificent sport, while bream, too big for a fishmonger's slab, roll cheekily in lakes and the slower rivers. Nowhere is there conflict between game fisher and coarse angler. The salmon and trout prefer the relatively short spate rivers that tumble seaward, while the sedate inland waterways satisfy the other species as they flow silently, but strongly, through bog and lush meadow. Where game and coarse meet, neither fish nor fishermen get excited. Blackwater roach and dace prefer the slower, eddying glides and pools; the salmon, brown trout and sea-trout choose the runs, steams and broken water. Game fisher and coarse angler meet often, but these friendly encounters are more likely in the pub than on the river bank or lough.

Fishing for coarse species in Ireland is generally free, with exceptions on the few privately-owned stretches. There is no coarse fishing closed season. Waters are carefully stocked, and a continuing development programme of fishery management, improved access and waterside car parking, all go to making a coarse angling holiday in this beautiful country a worthwhile experience for the visitor.

Species are more limited than in England; carp, dace and tench tend to be localised. Roach have spread rapidly over the last decade, and some superb catches can be taken, particularly from the River Erne. Rudd are prolific and huge, and the Irish bream waters can match the best in Europe. Rudd-bream hybrids appear in many canal stretches and in the slower rivers, running to over 5 lb in weight. Through continental enthusiasm and a seemingly insatiable Germanic desire to eat Irish-flavoured pike, the famous *Esox* of the great loughs like Mask, Corrib and Conn have followed the depletion in even the smaller lakes. The predation of organised trout fisheries has also taken its toll on the pike loughs which have been systematically cleared of their pike, big and large. Such interference with Nature rarely improves a fishery, and attitudes are changing quickly. Not so long ago, visiting anglers

were actually encouraged to remove the pike they caught; now, pike, especially big specimens — if you can find them — should be returned to the water, and the authorities encourage anglers to do so. Livebaiting for pike, especially effective during the colder months, is now banned by law, and in 1975 a bylaw was introduced, forbidding the transfer of live roach from one fishery to another. The bream, tench and rudd all fish best during the summer months as in this country, with roach and pike offering a splendid reason to pack the rods for a winter break.

A well stocked tackle box is a must for the travelling angler. Fred Taylor's array of spinning lures is intended to cope with anything . . . and everything.

Above: Typical mountain lough in Ireland's rugged west. Species will include pike, perch, and trout.

Right: Anglers' cottages above Lough Inchiquin at Corofin; once famed for its large pike, but now regularly stocked with brown trout.

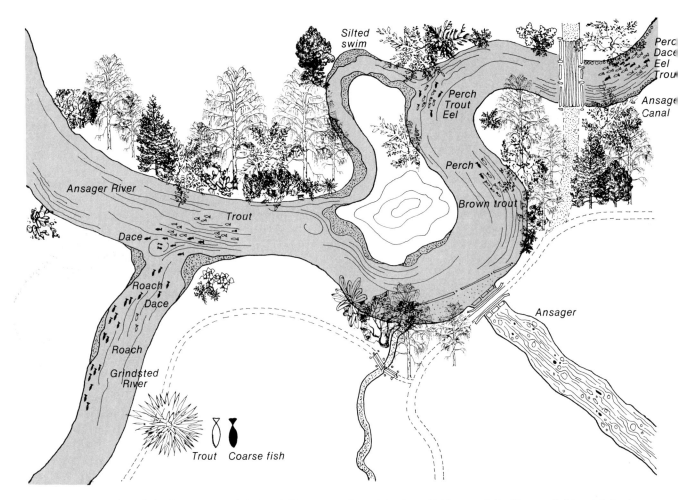

Silted
swim

Perch
Trout
Eel

Perc
Dace
Eel
Trou

Ansage
Canal

Ansager River

Perch

Trout

Brown trout

Dace

Roach
Dace

Ansager

Roach

Grindsted
River

Trout   Coarse fish

The junction of the Ansager and Grindsted Rivers — a short drive from Esbjerg and the Newcastle/Harwich ferries.

Denmark

If Ireland has a competitor in wooing the interests of the English coarse angler, it has to be Denmark. What a wonderful country, lush, green and very windy! Jutland is the largest and most accessible chunk of that friendly nation, and fortunately for us, holds some of the exciting rivers and lakes teeming with coarse fish to make the mind boggle. The country suffers from bouts of depression, and like Ireland and Scotland, it can be wet and windy; but these are necessary ingredients for successful angling which ensure that the rivers are well oxygenated, and the fish worthy opponents.

Denmark has a remarkable variety of fishing, and all is readily available to the tourist. Local fishing associations are well organised, licences easily acquired, and help readily offered to visitors.

Getting there

Jutland is accessible via Copenhagen by air, but this is time consuming and expensive. DFDS sail regularly from Newcastle and Harwich, and the journey to Esbjerg is entertaining and delightful. The Danish cold table on board is a feast, only dulled when the North Sea chooses to be particularly nasty, a not uncommon occurrence. There are a number of excellent free brochures and angling notes on coarse fishing in Jutland available from the Danish Tourist Board.

Where to go

Once you arrive in Esbjerg, you needn't travel more than a few miles before sampling excellent coarse fishing. The Varde, Sneum, Kongeaand Ribe and Holsted rivers are all within casting distance and offer superb sport. Many of Denmark's rivers are swift flowing, and the visitor quickly discovers that from diminutive dace and roach to broad-flanked bream, the fighting qualities of the fish are superb. Jutland, it very soon becomes apparent, is not large; roads are good, straight, flat . . . and by our standards, empty. Driving on the right creates little or no problem.

An hour or two in the fresh air, and you very rapidly become aware of the bird song. In fact, the cuckoos will literally 'drive you cuckoo!' It is quite rare to spot the nest-hopping cuckoo normally, but in Jutland you

can see two and three in the air at the same time. When they start nattering to each other from one side of a valley to the other, you start missing the bites. *Kros* are not Danish rooks, but inns, invariably sited on the river bank, and adjacent to the main tourist routes. Accommodation is superb, service and food wonderful, and prices have come very much into line with the UK. Varde, Grindsted, Silkeborg, Skive and Thisted are all excellent coarse fishing centres. The famed Gudenä at Silkeborg and the nearby lakes offer massive bream, roach and zander. The Resenbro Kro on the banks of the River Guden is within five miles of the swim which produced a world record bream catch in 1981. Grindsted is an excellent centre for the famed roach of the Ansager and Grindsted rivers; Hovborg Kro on the Holme is a short drive from the best fishing in this area.

Skive is at the mouth of the famed Karup River, which receives runs of outsized sea-trout. Coarse fishing on the lower reaches is excellent, although roach and perch are small. From there northward to Thisted there is a bewildering choice of fishing. The lake Skanderborg is more like a shallow, coloured sea, and indeed it nestles directly under the sand dunes which separate it from saltwater and the strong prevailing winds. Zander grow huge here, and the perch average over 1 lb in weight.

Licences and season

The closed season varies for different species and by region, so it is best to check locally. Most visiting coarse anglers are recommended to bring their own bait. Maggots are not available in Denmark, but meal-worms are generally obtainable from tackle shops in main angling areas.

If, as a coarse angler, there was one single criticism to offer objectively to our Danish friends, it is that there are far too many rainbow trout in many of the rivers, particularly around Grindsted. Mind you, the rainbows and wild brown trout make an interesting change. Our 'best' was over eighty in a day. Put them back, as they don't survive well in a keepnet. Persevere, and you can, eventually, get through them to the coarse species. Bang a couple on the head; they make a nice change grilled for breakfast!

Top left: Quality roach from Jutland's Ansager River. Several fish topped the two pounds mark.

Right: Another fine roach in the net. This swim, finished nearly ten years ago, proved to be silted up when Prichard and Shepley revisited the area in June 1981.

Left: Allen Edwards set up these two superb Ansager roach. They now swim in the Tourist Office, Grindsted.

Left: Superb quality from the junction of the Ansager and Grindsted Rivers in Jutland.

Above: The Ansager Canal holds specimen dace, but you have to get through the shoals of rainbow trout first!

Right: Perch and rainbow trout taken on consecutive casts from the Ansager. The trout seem to have pushed the specimen roach into quieter water.

Right: A Canarian tackle forum at Presa de Soria on Gran Canaria.

Bottom right: The results of fishing the Soria reservoir — splendid silvery small-mouth bass.

Below: Fishing on a crystal-clear stream near Chablis. Main species again is chub.

Spain

The Basque country offers the holiday angler the best coarse fishing, and the whole of this region also supplies much of Spain's game fishing: trout in the hills and salmon in the main rivers. As with the South of France, summer is to be avoided for serious angling pursuits. April through May offers the best of the sport, and also allows the angler peace from the main tourist season which follows on.

Spain has more than 46,000 miles of rivers and streams, as well as numerous dams, reservoirs and lakes throughout the country offering a bewildering choice of angling opportunities. CONA — the *Instituto Nacional para la Conservación de la Naturaleza* — leases and conserves vast areas of spectacular countryside owned by the Ministry of Information and Tourism. Constant fishery management and related stocking policies have made the sportfishing in these regions an unforgettable experience for anglers.

Species

The swift-flowing rivers which stream westwards in the north of the country into the Atlantic receive runs of salmon, while the headwaters of most mountain streams hold trout. These Spanish salmon streams are found throughout the Cantabrian Range and the coast of Galicia, with the River Mino marking the southernmost limit of *Salar* in Europe. As with Denmark, the rainbow trout is often present in greater quantities than the brown trout, and *Danube salmon* — Huchen — have also been successfully introduced. It is, however, in the middle and lower reaches of the rivers, and in stillwater locations, that the coarse angler will find most of his sport. Carp are particularly abundant. Spain also has two species of barbel, both of which grow to rod-bending size, and can be fished throughout the year. The black bass and pike are relative newcomers, but have established well in the richly vegetated Spanish water.

Licences

Permission to fish in Spain should be requested at the *Jefaturas Provinciales* of CONA, which covers the angler in waters subject to general regulations. A licence is required for all fisheries in Spain. A small percentage of private fisheries also exist, and fishing can at times be obtained by acquiring permission on payment to the owner.

There is no closed season for coarse fish in Spain, although the best times to fish are April, May and in the autumn. Crayfish abound in the streams, but there are local restrictions on the number which can be re-

211

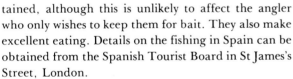

tained, although this is unlikely to affect the angler who only wishes to keep them for bait. They also make excellent eating. Details on the fishing in Spain can be obtained from the Spanish Tourist Board in St James's Street, London.

By chance, when visiting the Canary Islands (which belong to Spain) on a big game fishing survey, we came across some splendid black bass in the mountain reservoirs. That element of surprise is common to all countries likely to receive a visit from English anglers.

The Eastern Bloc holds vast stocks of coarse fish, some of them specimen-sized, and already surveys have been carried out to test the angling tourism potential in Russia. Germany seems to stand alone in its strict code of angling procedure, which more or less precludes involvement by the visiting angler.

From Sweden and Finnish Lapland, to Spain and the other Mediterranean countries, the choice and potential for the British coarse angler is vast and varied. It can certainly make a pleasant, if at times frustrating, change from the canal back home.

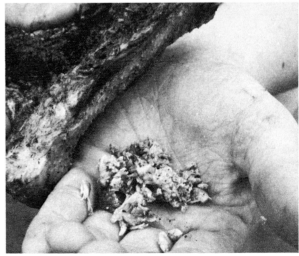

Fixed line

3ft

Loose feed

8ft

chub

Clean gravel

France

This is the home of the pole and tiny fish. That perhaps capsulates the average English coarse fisherman's opinion of France. To an extent it is true, but there is far more to see and catch. The rivers and canals are in *the grand manner*; broad, powerful sweeping watersheds, and lush, tree-lined streams. The water can range from the clearest pebble-bottomed stream to a rich, opaque olive green.

There are many kinds of roach, the slim nase being a regular inhabitant of many glides and streams; but it is the blunt-headed chub that offers perhaps the best river sport of all. They perhaps don't run large on average weight, but pounders abound, and light tackle with loosefeed tactics soon has them feeding. In France, the fishing improves with the wine. Chablis and its environs, famed for the quality of its white wine, has sparkling rivers teeming with chub. As you go south into Burgundy country, even the rivers take on a richness of colour, and the fish are deep and full-bodied. By the time you reach south of Lyon to the Mediterranean, wines again become lighter, and the attitudes of the angler have to match, otherwise fishing can be a frustrating experience. The rivers are warm, and many tourists spend the daylight hours sunning and bathing on the banks of the bigger rivers. Fishing is not for the serious-minded here; you can expect a snorkled swimmer to dive into your swim to inspect the underwater acrobatics of your hooked fish, or have your eye diverted from the waggler to similar naked movements, generally bronzed and in all shapes and sizes. This is fun fishing . . . and why not? Holidays, even angling ones, are light hearted affairs. If you want to be serious about your sport, fish early or late. You will soon discover, however, that the fish, even the bigger specimens, are so used to the sun and bathers, that they will seldom be frightened and put off the feed; although you may have to tempt them from under the bank or overhanging trees by loose feeding whatever was left over from the barbeque.

Top left: The tricky bit! Hand catching a lively chub can be difficult when you are eleven years old. The River Gardon in the Cevennes is well stocked with chub, although local anglers tend to concentrate on the nase.

Above: Trotting a small piece of chicken skin, loose feeding with chewed chicken drew nearly twenty chub from under the fallen tree, in spite of swimmers, canoes and inflatables.

Right: Success is a handful of chub. Chris and his younger brother took 16 — with the help of dad.

Left: Hook bait — and loose feed; chicken barbecued on the river bank proved just the thing for the river chub.

Holland

There cannot be many countries that have as much fishing water as Holland has when one considers the size of the country. Following centuries of land reclamation, the Dutch struck a balance between arable land and planned waterways. At one time the enclosed waters were brackish, but gradually they have lost their saltiness to become clean, pollution-free freshwater lakes. Constant draining, of this low-lying land mass, has provided a geometric pattern of canals, each with a thriving fish population.

Fish management, in Holland, is based on licence sales. The OVB operate on a national basis with a mandate for breeding coarse fish and trout. The fry are seeded into both private and public waters. Fish can be bought, from the breeding station each year and it is rare for OVB to fall short of their production schedules. One million pike were bred in 1980. The species is in constant demand in many European countries and they are sold as 5-cm fish at 4p each. Ten-centimetre perch cost 4½p a fish and carp fetch £2 per kilo to private purchasers (at 1982 prices). Angling societies and clubs pay about a third of those prices for their stockings.

Even the lowly eel has a massive demand with many millions of elvers being imported from Britain and France, each year, to support the eel fisheries of the Dutch lakeland. With no salmon, to confuse the access to water situation for anglers, almost any length of drain or enclosed water inevitably becomes a rod and line fishery. With over one million pounds, annual income from licences, OVB are able to provide superb fishery services to riparian owners and anglers alike.

The licence system, for the tourist angler, is very easily understood. All navigable waters, which includes rivers, canals and the large lakes, can be fished with a simple national licence (kleine viskaart) which allows the use of one rod with bread, maggot or worm baits. Using two rods, or fishing with livebaits, requires the possession of a special licence. In addition, waters controlled by a provincial angling federation or club will need an extra, but cheap, local licence. National licences are sold at all Post Offices, with tackle shops selling the special licences appropriate to their region.

Holland has most of the coarse fish found in Britain, together with some species common to Central Europe. The silver bream is very much in evidence, growing to bigger weights than we expect to catch in the East of England. The zander is a prized table fish that attains 20 lb or more in the lakes of Friesland, the lakeland area in the North of the country. Practically every water will hold common bream, rudd, roach, tench, carp, perch and pike in a group of lakes that resemble the Norfolk Broads. Holland has fishing

Above: This Friesland lake is noted for the excellent quality of its fine bream fishing.

Top right: Hoogeveense Vaart proved tricky to fish. Plenty of smaller fish, but bigger specimens conspicuous by their absence.

Above: Mike Prichard takes a fish-eye view of two captives from the Oranje Canal. Single maggot on size 18s and 20s to 1 lb bottom drew the fish.

Left: Loading a barge with cattle at Giethoorn. The fish were lying right under the barge.

camps, where a development of self-catering chalets is grouped alongside the best of fishing water. At Sneek, a small town above the Ijsselmeer known to us as the Zuiderzee, there is a unique coarse fishing centre. The angling guests live on a large boat which travels to the secluded parts of many lakes. The boat tows small angling craft to enable the fishermen to penetrate the far corners of each water. An accomplished angling guide accompanies the anglers throughout their holiday. This kind of enterprise introduces a safari element into angling tourism.

If one travels to the East of Holland, similarities to the Irish landscape emerge for this is the bogland area where the moors and minute fields· are laced with canals and small rivers. Each waterway will have its anglers, fishing the pole for shoal fish where the current flow slackens. On the bigger rivers, the English match rod appears, for it's in this part of the country, and over the border into Germany, where match angling holds sway. The canals are slightly deeper than would be expected, probably as many of them carry boat traffic the silt does not reduce the depth. With so many canals and slow-moving rivers, it is not surprising that Holland has a high proportion of hybrids, particularly the one between the silver and bronze bream, which causes confusion even among ichthyologists.

215

Goldeye carp

It seems a long way to go for river carp, but my first experience of river commons was in a creek off the Manitoba Red River, little more than an hour's drive from Winnipeg city centre.

The *End of Main*, as its name suggests, is the end of the road for travellers from the city's central Main Street. You just keep driving until the highway turns into a dusty track, and comes to a charming halt at Netley Creek beside the Red River. Here we met Ches Schofield, a big, cheery gentle man whose T-shirt proclaims: 'Where the Hell's the End of Main'.

Netley Creek, as Ches will tell you, is full of silver bass (freshwater drum), northerns (pike) and catfish; not the big, blue catfish common to the main river, but little bronze, tough-jawed nasties, which proved very difficult to get off the hook and release. I had met them before in the same creek, ice fishing, during a competition one February. An 8-in hole is made in the 3 ft of ice. As you drill through, the water pressure from below pushes a jet of freezing water up and out onto the ice. Our neighbour broke through, and out with the water came a catfish, which was promptly banged over the head with an ice shovel. His first fish of the competition! Nothing serious about the Canadians. . . their winter ice 'Derbies' are far more of a social get-together on ice than fishing competitions. In summer, the species include sauger and walleye (similar to the European zander), and just down from Netley was Goldeye Creek, joining a shallow, marshy lake with the Red River. It was here that the carp were. Local anglers discount the carp, not that they don't fight, but they prove far too difficult for them, compared to the free-biting saugers and drum. The carp turned out to be commons, averaging around 8 lb, and by the size of some of the fish patrolling up and down the creek, grew to well over 20 lb. These fish were in the creek itself, and were not really hook shy, providing you didn't parade in full view of the fish. Indeed a worm jig, and a leaded hook, baited with nightcrawlers (lob worms), bobbed up and down off the bottom caught a brace of fat, hard-fighting carp in only a couple of hours' fishing. I doubt, however, if 'bobbed lobs' will ever be popular in this country! My best, about 8-10 lb, was taken on a small jig hook, on a light 7-ft spinning rod and fixed-spool reel holding 4 lb b.s. line, and it took more than ten minutes to tame the carp and get it safely in the landing net.

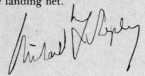

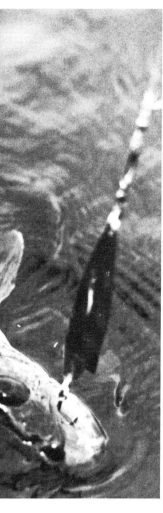

Canada

Top left: The fisherman's taxi in Canada — the Cessna 185 Skywagon, flies anglers into fish-rich waters full of pike, walleye, lake trout and bass.

Left: Unlike our zander, the Canadian walleye likes clear, deep water adjacent to rocky outcrops, and takes fly or spoon with wild abandon.

Below: Shore lunch on a Manitoba lake, is a tradition which the visitor has to experience. The Indian guide will cook walleye fillets, lake trout steaks or even pike; beautiful!

Bottom left: A moonscape in the middle of George Lake, a 15-minute air hop from the road end, little more than a couple of hours' drive from Winnipeg. Lake trout and bass are the main species here.

If Europe is increasingly easy to reach, you will excuse this short reference to North America and the Canadian Provinces. Crossing the Atlantic by air is, relatively, excellent value for money. A return trip direct from London to Winnipeg in Manitoba, by Air Canada, can cost little more than an oilman's visit from London by scheduled air services to Shetland and back.

Manitoba is one of the Prairie Provinces of Canada and is chosen as typical of the vast pine forests and lakeland regions which spread east and west for hundreds of miles. Rivers and lakes are crystal clear and teeming with fish. Giant Lake Winnipeg, an inland sea both shallow and treacherous, has the colour of silica sand. The lake, and the Red River which flows out of it, give accommodation to an endless variety of birds and fish; the pelicans, herons, gulls and North American Kingfisher feed on the bountiful supply of fish. In the creeks and bays, you can catch silver bass (drum), catfish, carp, sauger, walleye (like our zander) and pike. Yellow perch, smallmouth and largemouth bass also come to baits in many of the lakes. Whitefish and lake trout complete the exciting picture which is repeated nationwide. Sixty-three northern pike in one day from a North Saskatchewan lake, where Arctic grayling grabbed a fly in the mighty feeder rivers, is a red-letter day in anyone's book. The pike ranged from a five pounder to 23 lb, many of them on the fly. Try it some time!

Above: Mike Prichard plays a smallmouth bass on George Lake, Manitoba; alone with Nature and his sport.

Right: Carp and silver bass (freshwater drum) were the main catch from Goldeye Creek, an hour's drive from Winnipeg city centre.

Left: The collection of spoons and hairwing tube flies which accounted for more than sixty pike in a day's fishing. All but two — one for setting up, and the other for eating — were returned alive to the water.

The future

Sunrise over the beautiful Norfolk Broads symbolises the new hope. The pollution, increased boat-traffic and periodic salination have all taken their toll on this once prolific angling region. Does the future hold the key to a renaissance of clean waters and renewed angling enthusiasm?

Lelystad fish farm

Top left: An aerial view of one of the largest fish farms outside Soviet Russia. The O.V.B. farm at Lelystad in Holland, is over 2 miles long and a mile wide. Water, for the various rearing ponds, is drawn from the Ijsselmeer.

Above: Pike sac-fry hang from vegetation during the early days of their lives, using a sticky pad on the head. At this stage they are predated upon by larger fry but it isn't long before these tiny fish will be among the most voracious feeders in the freshwater environment.

Right: These are fertile trout eggs, showing the eyes and rudimentary structure of the fry through the thin but tough membrane of the ova.

Left: The trout fry, after hatching from the egg, retain a sac that hangs outside the stomach cavity. It is composed of food that gives the fish some nutrient during the early days of its life

A glance at the British rod-caught record list will confirm just how varied the fish stocks of our rivers, lakes and canals have become. Many have been introduced, although to our eyes they seem established residents which have swum quietly through timeless decades. They didn't just appear there. The monks were among the first fish farmers in our country, and an excellent job they did, too, in distribution and conservation. Food was their main reason, but sporting alternatives were not missed.

Conservation

As responsible anglers we have to ensure that our fish stocks continue to thrive; any natural or forced depletion therefore has to be counteracted by judicious seeding and management of our fisheries, to ensure continuity of sport, not just for ourselves, but for future generations of anglers. Breeding fish on a commercial scale varies greatly between Britain and mainland Europe. Here, we have to date concentrated almost exclusively on the rainbow trout, with browns and exotics such as the American brook trout, while on the Continent, emphasis is more on bream, pike, eels and other coarse fish. Coarse fish distribution and the development of coarse fisheries is, however, increasing dramatically. A number of men, like Walter Bower at Newark, have taken the natural environment — in Walter's case, the banks of the Trent — and systematically planned an improved fishery.

Through years of careful, steady feeding, fish have been drawn into this stretch of the Trent and remained there. The fish grew in numbers, size and variety. Gradually anglers took an interest, and subsequent groundbaiting by visitors has held the interest of the fish. In turn, the superb river carp, chub and other species attract an increasing number of enthusiasts to the river. In conjunction with this activity, Walter Bower has created a stillwater fishery consisting of a series of dug-out gravel pits. It is an ever-changing project, with one major pool, and another long, interesting stillwater, with enough island, weed beds and lily pads to excite the keenest specimen hunter, and further stillwater under ecological development. As the underwater environment matures, and is rich enough to support a good head of fish, so different species are gradually introduced, many of them coming originally from the nearby Trent itself.

Education

Anglers, true anglers, always respect the countryside. It is in our own interests to do so. Nobody likes to fish amongst a pile of rubbish or litter-strewn river banks. The finger has been pointed — with some substantial evidence — at the thoughtless

Rainbow trout are often stocked into a saltwater habitat in Holland. Here, at Lake Veere, the stockfish are being delivered by an O.V.B. vehicle equipped for the live carriage of trout and other species of fish.

One of the many rearing ponds at Lelystad, 12½ acres in size, being cleaned to accept a new season's stockfish.

somebody's private property, is a privilege, not a right, and should be appreciated as such. The education of youngsters keen to take up the sport, and the expansion of angling knowledge to the clubman, will ensure that respect of property, fish and our heritage safeguards the future for our children who want to go fishing.

The club

No matter how small your group of angling friends may be — you might only go fishing with one other angling mate — the friendship and companionship of fishing together, experiencing and witnessing success, is an important aspect of our sport. It is one we should share. Riverbanks and muddy reed beds are difficult for any angler, and doubly so for the disabled and blind. Much has been done to help, with special facilities in boats and shoreline or bankside improvements to assist those in need of our help. Here, the club can be invaluable in organising suitable visits, arranging transport and companionship and supervision where required.

Protecting the environment

Twenty years ago, the outlook for angling — and fishing waters in particular — was bleak. Now, well into the eighties the future looks surprisingly better. Pollution from industry, and water abstraction have gradually and steadily improved. This has been due to several factors. The new micro-technology is relatively pollution free, and has revolutionised our way of life. Manufacturing plants, such as paper mills, have closed and other water-based industry has either been relocated or become obsolete. Above all, there is a more conscious attempt by commerce and local authorities to meet higher standards of pollution control, although there still exists the anomaly that often the culprit wears the same hat as the legislator and the prosecutor. The Angler's Co-operative Association safeguards our angling heritage. It fights with all practical speed and legal expertise on our behalf any and every polluter who arrogantly defies or ignorantly evades the law and his responsibilities.

New fisheries are being created all the time, and access to existing waters, far from becoming more restricted, is being expanded in an attempt to accommodate the growing band of pleasure-seekers who head for the waterside. There have been pitfalls — fish introductions that have gone beyond initial intentions — and no doubt we shall make mistakes in the future. We can, however, with more than a degree of optimism, encourage and welcome the new generation of anglers. Who could keep such a rewarding and special sport from the enthusiastic newcomer?

carelessness of anglers discarding lead shot. Other tackle, hooks and nylon can have equally tragic results for bird life and small animals. It is not just the birds and animals who suffer from this carelessness, but the anglers themselves.

Access through farmland, or simply through

Keeping warm and dry . . .

Left: Snug as a bug in a rug. 'I'm glad I brought the umbrella, coat, and groundsheet.' Creature comforts!

Right: As well as keeping off rain, the tie-down brolly makes a useful windbreak.

Below: Quilted body warmers are justifiably popular. The thick, but loosely knitted Aran jumper helps retain body heat, causing warm air pockets between the angler and the waistcoat.

If you have to go fishing in inclement weather AND you want to keep dry and warm, then here are a few hints for you hardy anglers.

Mitts are to be preferred to gloves, as the latter prevent the proper *feel* of the rod, so necessary for continuity between the bait and the angler's reactions when a fish takes. Most coats now on the market offer an attached hood, or one which can clip on. Even where the angler wears a separate hat, a waterproof hood will help prevent those nasty drips from going down the back of the coat, and stop the draughts which can make an otherwise warm angler into a shivering contender for flu or worse.

A good stout pair of boots, with waterproof leggings or trousers, is to be preferred for mobility, unless the angler has to take to the water. Thigh and even breast waders should be avoided when fishing from a boat; they may be warm, but are less safe in the event of an emergency than overtrousers and a pair of ankle boots. For the bank or river angler who requires to wade, there are some excellent lightweight waders available, with or without brogues. It is again a personal choice whether the angler chooses waders with integral boots or not. What should be avoided in both cases is rubber soled boots, except in the safest of situations. Rarely, however, can an angler

foresee all the types of fishing location he is likely to meet, and rubber soles can be disastrous on slippery rock or an uneven surface. While on a gravelly lake bed, a slip might only result in a ducking, it can put an unsuspecting angler out of his depth and into fast, turbulent water on a river, especially during spate conditions, when the water is coloured. Boots attached to the waders or brogues should have studs, and if the angler intends using them regularly, then he should also check them regularly for wear and replace studs as necessary. Not only will they last a lot longer, they will keep him on a safe footing. Felt soles have their advocates, but even they can pick up slime and weed, which make them less effective.

The fishing umbrella

This is another necessary part of the regular coarse fisher's equipment, especially in our climate, and one item where it definitely doesn't pay to compromise or skimp on quality. The smaller umbrellas have 36-in ribs and will not fully protect you or your tackle. There is truth in the old saying that it is unlucky to open an umbrella inside. The angler who tests his new purchase in the tackle shop might be misled as to its size. A brolly with 42-in ribs is essential and the larger 45-in ribbed brollies allow the angler to sit in inclement weather comfortably

with tackle to hand. Rain is often associated with wind, and the larger umbrellas should be capable of being well pegged down. Seldom is the umbrella required in an upright position immediately above the angler, and that extra diameter makes all the difference in wet, blustery conditions.

Camping out

One of the most adventurous aspects of coarse fishing as a pleasure activity is spending a weekend or overnight stop at your favourite fishery, providing regulations allow for this. The pioneering feeling of the camp site, the stillness of the air, the animal sounds of the night, the welcome smell of a good hot brew, the sleeping bag becomes a way of life. Always respect the countryside though, always be aware of the dangers of lighting fires, and *don't* if in an area of woodland or when the weather has been particularly dry. Primus stoves and smaller apparatus are all very safe if used properly, and that means avoiding their use inside tents; don't be tempted just because it's windy or wet outside. That sort of activity is dangerous. Choose your camp site well, and leave everything as you found it . . . tidy and natural. If you can't burn or bury your rubbish, take it home with you!

Fishing records of the British Isles

A finely conditioned Loch Lomond pike from the Endrick Bank out from Balmaha, weighed, then safely returned alive to the water.

It is perhaps every angler's dream to catch, at least once during his angling career, a record fish and to have his name recorded for all time in the piscatorial history books. For any record catch to be of value, the authenticity has to be complete, beyond any doubt for those who follow on, even years hence. As soon as credibility is lost, even over one single record entry, then all others listed could be subject to question. This puts a tremendous onus on both captor and recorder, if integrity and authenticity are to prevail.

Recognition

The British Record (rod-caught) Fish Committee exists to recognise and record in a list published and updated regularly, all those species caught by fair angling methods in fresh and saltwater around England, Wales, Scotland, Northern Ireland and the Channel Islands. The Scottish Federation of Sea Anglers and the Welsh Record (rod-caught) Fish Committee are both members of the British Record (rod-caught) Fish

Committee. Scottish and Welsh records, which are also potential British records, are submitted by the respective organisation to which the initial claim is made. The Scottish Federation of Sea Anglers Fish Recorder has in recent seasons handed over the compilation and updating of Scottish freshwater claims to the Scottish Coarse Anglers' Federation. Claims for fish caught in Eire are dealt with by the Irish Specimen Fish Committee in Dublin. The Irish list of coarse fishing records is also published annually in the *Freshwater Coarse Angling Guide* by Bord Fáilte, the Irish Tourist Board.

Fish identification

One of the most controversial aspects of fish recording, and specimen fish in particular, is the requirement of the record committee to inspect the fish in its natural state, dead or alive, *not* to confirm its exact weight on capture. It is to identify beyond all doubt the species caught. While this must in many cases mean killing a

Scottish Freshwater Record Fish List ——————

SPECIES	LB	OZ	WEIGHT DM	KILOS	GM	DATE	CAPTOR & LOCATION
Bream	5	15	12 :	2	711	1973	H. Wood, Castle Loch, Dumfriesshire.
Carp	6	8	— :	2	944	1973	J. Nash, Kirkcowan, Wigtonshire.
Char	1	12	4 :	0	801	1974	C. Imperiale, Loch Insh, Invernesshire.
Dace	1	3	8 :	0	553	1979	G. Keech, R. Tweed, Coldstream.
Eel	4	6	— :	1	980	1979	S. Richmond, Loch Nr. Blairgowrie
Grayling	2	10	— :	—	—	1981	R.D. Hall
Perch	3	5	— :	1	499	1972	R. Southgate, R. Clyde, Hamilton.
Pike	35	8	— :	15	96	1981	C. Mason, Loch Lomond
Powan	1	7	— :	0	652	1972	J.M. Ryder, Loch Lomond
Roach	2	1	8 :	0	948	1972	G. Shuttleworth, R. Tay, Perth.
Salmon	64	—	— :	29	029*	1922	Miss G.W. Ballantyne, R. Tay, Caputh.
Tench	2	7	— :	1	102	1977	D.S. Keay, Loch Nr. Perth.
Trout Brown	19	9	4 :	8	880*	1978	J.A.F. Jackson, Loch Quoich, Invernesshire.

*Denotes British Record.

No Records exist for the following species but qualifying weights listed:

Crucian Carp – 2lb.
Chub   – 4lb.
Gudgeon   – 4oz.
Rudd   – 2lb.
Sea Trout   – 1lb.

For enquiries and claims for Scotland, contact the Keeper, Department of Natural History, Kelvingrove Art Gallery, Glasgow G3 8AG telephone 041-334-1134 who will advise, or send on a claim form or, if after 5 p.m. 'phone 041-649-3578 (Alastair Smith).

Any fish not required by its captor may be retained by Glasgow Museums to build up their collection of native Scottish freshwater fish.

potential record breaker, it is perhaps something which the specimen hunter has to accept as long as the rules governing claims require such action. One of the most controversial captures in recent seasons is Chris Yates' Redmore carp, 51 lb 8 oz, 36 in long with a girth of 34½ in, which was returned alive to the water; thus, unavailable for inspection by the record committee. Dick Walker's 44 lb Redmire carp remains the official record. The history of Yates' carp is well documented; it wasn't the first time that it had been on dry land, and no doubt, if caught again, may well be accepted if the correct procedure is followed. Surely, one single specimen, — no matter how large — can be accommodated safely, without injury in a keepnet or other suitable container; at least, long enough for correct identification and official weighing to take place in the presence of a committee representative. How often do we see photographs of several big carp taken in a single session, apparently with little or no harm to the fish. With smaller species, the difficulties of keeping a potential record breaker alive for 24 hours must become relatively easy.

The 'has beens'

Over the years, a number of controversial fish have been removed from the record list, notably three from Scotland: the Lomond pike, the Meldrum grayling and the Annan chub. Were they caught out of season? Scotland has no such closed season. Were the anglers concerned in those captures *really* after something else at the time? If so, why should this preclude their inclusion? Does a bream or barbel, hooked in the mouth on a spinning lure, not count? What about the disappearing fish — how many records have been eaten by their captors? Did Dr Cameron's huge Annan chub end its days as cat food? There are certainly chub to rock the current record still swimming in the River Annan.

. . . And the 'should they be'?

Fish farming nowadays has become an art as much as a science; fish, fattened like pigs, not only for the table but to offer instant specimen power to the casting elbow. Paunchy rainbows and bulbous brookies come dangerously close to such criticism as is directed by those who go in search of truly wild brown trout. What then if some unscrupulous piscator stuffed his pet gudgeon on Gulliver proportions of minced liver, and then claimed his fame . . . and record fish? Certain coarse species would lend themselves quite readily to such manipulation, even in relatively large fisheries. European fish farming methods have proved that by selective breeding and controlled feeding within a restricted environment, it is possible to *create* fish of enormous proportions . . . the prime example in Holland, Germany and the Eastern Bloc being the capacious carp!

How to go about it

For the angler with an eye on the record books, it is sensible to familiarise himself with the rules of procedure laid down by the committee *before* going for his chosen specimen. Since not all record fish come as a result of careful planning, it does no harm for any angler to know just what to do in the event he has been lucky enough to make contact with a record breaker. The following extract from the National Anglers' Council's *British Record (rod caught) Fish Committee Rules of Procedure* and current *British Record Freshwater Fish List*, together with the *Irish Specimen Fish Committee's Record Fish List*, should hopefully point the rod in the right direction.

RULES OF PROCEDURE

1. (a) The claimant should contact the Committee Secretary.

    (b) Advice will then be given concerning preservation, identification and claims procedure.

2. Claims must be made in writing to the Secretary stating —

    (i) the species of fish and the weight,

    (ii) the date and place of capture and the tackle used, and whether Shore or Boat caught in the case of sea fish, and

    (iii) the names and addresses of reliable witnesses both as to the capture by the claimant and the weight, who will be required to sign the forms supporting the claim.

    If no witnesses to the capture are available, the claimant must verify his claim by affidavit.

3. No claim will be accepted unless the Committee is satisfied as to species, method of capture and weight. The Committee reserves the right to reject any claim if not satisfied on any matter which the Committee may think in the particular circumstances to be material.

4. Identification of Species

    (a) To ensure correct identification, it is essential that claimants should retain the fish and immediately contact the Secretary of the Committee who will advise as to production of the fish for inspection on behalf of the Committee.

    (b) No claim will be considered unless the fish in its natural state dead or alive is available for inspection.

    (c) All carriage costs incurred in production of the fish for inspection by the Committee must be borne by the claimant.

5. Method of Capture

(a) Fish caught at sea will be eligible for consideration as records if the boat used has set out from a port in England, Wales, Scotland, Northern Ireland, the Isle of Man or the Channel Islands and returns to the same port without having called at any port outside the United Kingdom. Fish caught in the territorial waters of other countries will not be eligible.

(b) Claims can only be accepted in respect of fish which are caught by fair angling with rod and line. Fair angling is defined by the fish taking the baited hook or lure into its mouth.

(c) Shore fishing shall mean fishing from any land mass or fixed man-made structure. In cases of doubt the Committee will classify a claim on the information provided.

(d) Fish must be caught on rod and line with any legal hook or lure and hooked and played by one person only. Assistance to land the fish (i.e. gaffing, netting) is permitted provided the helper does not touch any part of the tackle other than the leader.

6. Weight

(a) The fish must be weighed on land using scales or steelyards which can be tested on behalf of the Committee. Where possible commercial or trade scales which are checked regularly by the Weights and Measures Department should be used. The sensitivity of the scales should be appropriate to the size of the fish, i.e. small fish should be weighed on finely graduated scales and the weight claimed for the fish should be to a division of weight (ounce, dram, gramme) not less than

The British Record (rod-caught) Fish Committee
British Record Freshwater Fish List

SPECIES & SCIENTIFIC NAME	LB	OZ	DM	KILOS	GM	DATE	CAPTOR & LOCATION
Barbel *Barbus barbus*	13	12	–	: 6	237	1962	J. Day, Royalty Fishery, Hants.
Bleak *Alburnus alburnus*	–	3	15	–	111	1971	D. Pollard, Staythorpe Pond, Nr. Newark, Notts
Bream (Common, Bronze) *Abramis brama*	13	8	–	: 6	123	1977	A.R. Heslop, private water, Staffs.
Bullhead (Miller's Thumb) *Cottus gobio*	–	–	10	: –	017	1978	E. Harrison, Leeds & Liverpool Canal, Leach Bridge.
Carp *Cyprinus carpio*	44	–	–	: 19	957	1952	R. Walker, Redmire Pool.
Carp, Crucian *Carassius carassius*	5	10	8	: 2	565	1976	G. Halls, at lakes Nr. King's Lynn, Norfolk.
Catfish (Wels) *Silurus glanis*	43	8	–	: 19	730	1970	R.J. Bray, Wilstone Reservoir, Tring, Herts.
Char *Salvelinus alpinus*	1	12	4	: –	801	1974	C. Imperiale, Loch Insh, Inverness-shire.
Chub *Leuciscus cephalus*	7	6	–	: 3	345	1957	W.L. Warren, Royalty Fishery, Hampshire, Avon.
Dace *Leuciscus leuciscus*	1	4	4	: –	574	1960	J.L. Gasson, Little Ouse, Thetford, Norfolk.
Eel *Anguilla anguilla*	11	2	–	: 5	046	1978	S. Terry, Kingfisher Lake, Nr. Ringwood, Hants.
Grayling *Thymallus thymallus*	2	13	–	: 1	275	1981	P.B. Goldsmith, River Test, Romsey, Hants.
Gudgeon *Gobio gobio*	–	4	4	: –	120	1977	M.J. Bowen, Fish Pond, Ebbw Vale, Gwent, Wales.
Minnow *Phoxinus phoxinus*	–	–	11	: –	020	1979	I.S. Collinge, River Calder, Padham, Lancs.
Orfe, Golden *Leuciscus idus*	4	3	–	: 1	899	1976	B.T. Mills, River Test, Hampshire.
Perch *Perca fluviatilis*	4	12	–	: 2	154	1962	S.F. Baker, Oulton Broad, Suffolk.
Pike *Esox lucius*	40	–	–	: 18	143	1967	P.D. Hancock, Horsey Mere, Norfolk.

the smallest division shown on the scales.

(b) A Weights and Measures Certificate must be produced certifying the accuracy of the scales used and indicating testing at the claimed weight.

(c) In the case of species weighing less than one pound the claimed weight must be submitted in grammes.

(d) The weight must be verified by two independent witnesses who, for example, should not be relations of the claimant or a member of his club or party.

7. Claims can be made for species not included in the Committee's Record Fish List.

8. The Committee will issue at least once a year its lists of British Record (rod-caught) Fish.

9. No fish caught out of season shall be accepted as a new record. For purposes of conservation, claims for the Burbot (Lota lota) will not be considered by the Committee for the time being.

10. A fish for which a record is claimed must be normal and not obviously suffering from any disease by which the weight could be enhanced.

IF YOU CATCH A RECORD FISH

Medium sized fish can be preserved for considerable periods by refrigeration (deep freeze) or immersed in a solution of one tablespoon of formalin (40 per cent solution of formaldehyde) to a pint of water. For despatch, the fish should be wrapped in a cloth wrung out in the solution, placed in a plastic bag sealed as far as possible, and wrapped in stout brown paper: please enclose the name and address of the sender and whether the fish should be returned — if so the postage. The fish should be weighed before being placed in preserving liquids.

Species	LBS	OZS	DMS	KILOS	GMS	Year	Captor
Pikeperch (Walleye) *Stizostedion vitreum*	11	12	—	5	329	1934	F. Adams, The Delph, Welney, Norfolk.
Pikeperch (Zander) *Stizostedion lucioperca*	17	4	—	7	824	1977	D. Litton, Great Ouse Relief Channel.
Pollan *Coregonus pollan*	Open						
Pumpkinseed *Lepomis gibbosus*	—	2	10	—	074	1977	A. Baverstock, G.L.C. Highgate Pond, London.
Roach *Rutilus rutilus*	4	1	—	1	842	1975	R.G. Jones, Notts. Gravel Pit.
Rudd *Scardinius throphthalmus*	4	8	—	2	041	1933	Rev. E.C. Alston, Thetford, Norfolk.
Ruffe *Gymnocephalus cernua*	—	5	4	—	148	1980	R.E. Jenkins, West View Farm, Cumbria.
Salmon *Salmo salar*	64	—	—	29	029	1922	Miss G.W. Ballantyne, River Tay, Scotland.
Schelly (Skelly) *Coregonus clupeoides*	1	10	—	—	737	1976	W. Wainwright, Ullswater, Cumbria.
Tench *Tinca tinca*	10	1	2	4	567	1975	L.W. Brown, Peterborough Brick Pit.
Trout, American Brook (Brook Charr) *Salvelinus fontinalis*	5	6	—	2	438	1979	A. Pearson, Avington Fishery, Hampshire.
Trout, Brown *Salmo trutta*	19	9	4	8	880	1978	J.A.F. Jackson, Loch Quoich, Inverness-shire, Scotland.
Trout, Rainbow *Salmo gairdneri*	19	8	—	8	844	1977	A. Pearson, Avington Fishery, Hants.
Vendace *Coregonus vandesius*	Open						

SPECIES OPEN FOR FRESHWATER CLAIMS	LBS	OZS	DMS	KILOS	GMS		
				MINIMUM QUALIFYING WEIGHT			
Sea Trout *Salmo trutta*	15	—	—	6	804		
Silver Bream *Blicca bjoernka*	1	—	—	—	454		

NOTE:- The above qualifying weights are subject to revision by the Committee if necessary.

Glossary

AAA Split shot size – refer to lead weight diagram for actual size, approximately 30 to the ounce and just over 3/16 in diameter.

ADIPOSE FIN A fleshy, rayless fin between dorsal and caudal fin, denoting a member of the salmon family.

ALASTICUM Trace wire, single strand; used mainly in pike fishing.

ANATTO Added to feed when breeding maggots to give butter colour.

ANTENNA Type of float where the body is below the surface, unaffected by wind, with a fine, slender tip above, acting as the bite indicator.

ANTI-KINK A lead weight placed above a spinning or wobbling lure, to prevent line twist; takes the form of a vane, moon-shape or keel.

ARLESEY BOMB Streamlined leger weight with swivel moulded in to top end.

BB Shot size, approximately 5/32 in diameter.

BACKING Monofilament or braided line spooled onto a fly reel prior to loading the fly line; normally spliced to main fly line to allow a big fish to take additional line from the reel and through rod rings during playing.

BACK SHOT Split shot fixed between float and rod adjacent to float, to sink line in windy conditions.

BALE-ARM The mechanism on a fixed-spool reel which lays the line on the drum. Hinged, so that line can be released for casting. The armature is normally stainless steel.

BANK STICK Used for fixing rod rest or keepnet, spiked at other end.

BARBULE Fleshy appendage on or near to the maxillary bone or chin of the fish.

BELLY Downstream or downwind curve in fishing line caused by the current moving the line faster than the bait or fly, resulting in drag at the hook.

BITE The take when a fish picks up the bait, recorded on the rod or line.

BLANK Basic glass or composite sections from which a rod is made.

BLOODWORMS Midge larvae, found in mud and decaying vegetation on canal beds and ponds.

BOB FLY The top dropper on a cast of three flies, nearest to the rod, which 'bobs' on the surface.

BOMB A lead weight shaped for distance, round cross section tapered towards the end.

BRANDLING Type of small worm, red with yellow rings, found in dung heaps.

BREAD FLAKE A bait pinched out from the soft inside of a new loaf.

BREAD PUNCH A small cutting tube in different diameters for producing uniform cylindrical pellets of bread for hook baits.

BREAKING STRAIN (BS) A line's strength, giving the pounds test pull at which the line breaks when dry. Some monofilament lines also quote wet breaking strain.

BUNG Large onion shaped float, generally used for pike live or dead baiting.

BUTT INDICATOR Bite indicator when legering, fixed near to the reel.

BUZZER Flat-winged flies, midges and gnats found in or hovering above the surface film. Also an audible bite indicator, used for night fishing and specimen carping.

CAPTA Pyramid-shaped leger weight, fitted with a swivel, and designed to remain static on the river or lake bottom.

CASTER A maggot at the chrysalis stage, used as loose feed (sinkers) and hook bait (floaters).

CASTING The act of putting a rod into compression to propel a bait towards the fish.

CENTRE-PIN A revolving drum reel with handles attached, on revolving drum 1:1 ratio.

CHECKING THE FLOAT In river fishing, to hold back the float by stopping the line with finger pressure, thus making the hook bait rise attractively in the water, and to ensure that the float does not over-run the bait, which should precede the float downstream.

CHRYSODINE Yellow-orange dye used for colouring maggots.

CLOSED-FACE Popular bait casting reel (fixed on top of rod) or for long trotting (under rod), where the fixed spool is enclosed in a sleeve which protects the line from wind influence during the cast.

CLOUD BAIT Fine groundbait which sinks slowly attracting fish at all levels of the swim.

COCKTAIL Mixture of more than one hook bait; eg worm tipped with maggot.

COFFIN Coffin-shaped lead, best fished on nylon sliding link.

CONTROLLER Float used to provide weight when casting a very light bait where the use of leads is undesirable.

CRIMP Light metal sleeves used to secure hooks and swivels on wire or heavy nylon traces; these ferrules are pinched with pliers to secure the trace wire, forming tight loops taking the accessories.

CRYSTAL Type of hook with sharp bend above the point.

CYPRINIDS Members of the carp family.

DAPPING Presenting a natural or artificial fly or bait on a silk line, blown by the wind ahead of a drifting boat, or by dropping the lure vertically from a concealed position above the fish, such as an overhanging tree, in a natural manner onto the water.

DEAD BAITING Presentation of a dead fish as bait to predators or scavenging species; the bait can be bought (mackerel, herring, rainbow trout) or freshly caught (roach, gudgeon, bleak, minnow).

DETRITUS Disintegrated matter, debris, silt or sand found on the bottom of ponds, lakes and slow-moving rivers and canals.

DEVON Metal, wooden or plastic lures which are free-spinning on a metal swivelled mount armed with a treble hook. Vanes which produce the spin are sometimes reversible to prevent line twist.

DISGORGER Metal tool for removing hooks from inside the fish's mouth.

DOUBLE RUBBER When float is fixed on the line both top and bottom with pieces of plastic or rubber tubing.

DOUBLE TAPER A fly line which tapers from a thicker middle section both forwards and to the back of the line, giving excellent casting properties.

DOUGH BOBBIN A bite indicator made from paste squeezed onto the line between reel and second rod ring.

DRAG The slipping clutch on most multiplying and fixed-spool reels. Also the effect of current produced by wind or stream on the line, causing the float or terminal tackle to move unnaturally.

DROPPER Link of nylon or wire fixed at right angles to the main line, and carrying the baited hook, or fly.

DRUM The spool of a reel, normally associated with a centrepin.

DRY FLY An artificial fly which is presented to surface feeding fish and floats on or in the surface film.

DUST SHOT Smallest sizes of lead shot, no 10-12.

EPILIMNION Warm water layer in a lake.

END RING The rod ring at the thin extremity of the rod furthest away from the reel.

EYED Type of hook with an eye on the end of the shank normally tied to the reel line.

FALSE CASTING In fly fishing, the method of increasing line length to the stage where the rod works efficiently and can propel the additional line held loosely by the angler. The to and fro action of the rod also dries the fly and line in dry fly fishing.

FEED Bait, other than hook bait, used to attract fish into the swim.

FIXED SPOOL A reel where the spool is at right angles to the rod axis, and line is wound on by means of a rotating bale arm. The spool moves against a ratchet to give line if a powerful fish is hooked.

FLASHERS Metal strip attractors, used in conjunction with lures or natural baits to attract predators, especially in poor visibility.

FLOATANTS Grease or silicone additive applied to fly lines or flies to improve their floating characteristics.

FLOAT RUBBERS Small piece of rubber or plastic for holding the float in position.

FOLD OVER LEAD Washer-shaped lead folded over the line and pressed in position. Adds weight and also acts as a keel or anti-kink device.

FREELINE The method of allowing a bait to move naturally with the current, without the addition of float or weights.

FRY Small young fish of most species.

GAFF Metal hook used for landing fish, especially large pike. The gaff should be inserted under the chin, where it will not cause permanent damage. Used less nowadays, with specimen hunters preferring to use a large net instead.

GEAR RATIO Refers to the relative number of turns of the spool of a reel, to the single turn of the reel handle. Most centre-pin and fly reels will have a 1:1 gear ratio.

GOZZER A large white grub, produced by the bluebottle — *Calliphora eryphrocephala* — and normally fed on wood pigeon. Excellent bait for bream.

GRAVID A ripe hen fish, full of mature eggs, and ready to spawn.

GROUND BAITING Feeding a selected area with cereal and hookbait mix, to attract and hold fish in the region of the angler's hook, done both before and during the fishing.

HACKLE A feather from the neck cape of a hen or cockerel, used in fly tying to represent the legs of the insect imitated. Cock hackles are stiffer and used for dry flies.

HARL Working a spinning or wobbling lure or natural sprat from a boat, back and forwards across a river, slowly working downstream, rather than trolling which tends to be in a straight line.

HATCH Transition from the nymph to fully winged insects rising to the surface, resulting in trout, grayling, roach and dace rising and feeding vigorously on the surface.

HEN Female fish

HERL Term used for strands taken from whole feathers which are in effect lengths of soft quill with very short fibres or 'flue' on them. Ostrich and peacock are amongst the most popular. Used for bodies and wings in artificial flies.

HOLT Lair or resting place; often used to describe a pike's haunt.

HOOK LENGTH The nylon length attached to spade end hooks, looped at the other end for rapid attachment to the reel line or terminal rig.

HYBRIDISATION The crossing of two different species to form a fish having the characteristics of both parents. Rudd-bream hybrids are amongst the most common examples, which normally occur in a canal or slow-moving river situation, or stillwaters.

HYPOLIMNION Cold water zone in a lake.

JACK Young pike

JAM To cause a knot to hold effectively by jamming coils, of line, together.

JARDINE A kind of spiral lead, often used also as an anti-kink device, where the line is wrapped in grooved around the weight.

KEEPNET A netting tube, spaced by rings, and closed at one end, secured to the bank or boat at the open end, used to keep fish alive without damage, until returned to the water.

KELT A spawned salmon or trout.

LARVAE A grub prior to the chrysalis or pupa stage.

LATERAL LINE The 'hearing' mechanism of fish; a canal of connected cells down each side of the fish which transmits vibrations, waterborne sounds and pressure waves back to the fish's brain.

LAYING ON Float fishing technique where the bait is fished hard on the bottom, with line tight from float to weights which also lie on the river or lake bed.

LEAD Weights to assist casting and sink hook bait and/or cock floats. Stainless steel and other metals are increasingly being used in preference to lead itself.

LEADER Nylon or wire terminal rig attached to the reel line, taking hook and any weights.

LEGERING Bait fishing on the bottom, with a running weight which tethers the bait, without being discernible to a feeding fish.

LIE Resting place of a fish, normally in a river situation.

LINE BITE A false bite caused by a fish rubbing against the line.

LINK Metal item used to join two pieces of tackle or line.

LOADED FLOAT Float with built-in weight; useful where the bait is fished 'on the drop'.

LOCHAN Small loch, normally associated with mountains, hills or glacial topography.

LOCK SHOT Split shot fixed either side of the float to determine the position of float relative to the bait.

LOOSE FEED Ground baiting with small quantitites of hook bait to attract and hold fish.

LURE Artificial bait, spoon, spinner, plug or fly.

MAGGOT Larval form of *Diptera* flies.

MAGGOT DROPPER Container for maggots, which is opened remotely by the angler, once the case is in the desired position.

MAXILLARY The small jaw bone which runs either side of a fish's mouth.

MENDING THE LINE Throwing a loop of line upstream in fly fishing to prevent line drag on the fly cast caused by the current. Also allows the fly to fish more slowly and deeper.

MULTIPLIER A centre-pin reel geared to produce a high rate of retrieve, with free spool action used for casting line direct from the revolving drum.

NYMPH The larva of the *Ephemeridae* family of flies; one of the best imitative patterns.

OPERCULAR BONES The bones that form the gill case or cover that protect the gill filaments or rakers.

OVER-RUN Inefficient casting control, excessive power and lack of rhythm during the cast cause the drum on a multiplier or centre-pin to revolve faster than the line leaving the spool, resulting in a 'bird's nest' of tangled line coils.

PALMERED FLY An imitative pattern where a hackle feather is wound the length of the body, representing either a bushy body or legs along the segmented body of the insect.

PARR Young salmon or trout.

PASTE Hookbait made from soaked bread, kneaded into a stiff dough.

PATERNOSTER Terminal rig, with weight fixed at the bottom and one or more hooks on droppers above the weight; fished on a tight line between lead and rod tip.
The term paternoster is believed to originate from the latin – our father – after the Paternoster Row, in the City of London, where rosaries were made. Fishing tackles resembled this stringing of beads onto fine wire or twine.

PATTERN The style of imitative fly dressing produced from a selection of fur and feather materials tied with silk and tinsel.

PECTORALS The paired fins behind the gill case of a fish.

PEG A pre-numbered position, drawn by a match angler during a competition.

PELVICS Paired fins placed low down behind the pectoral fins towards the tail of the fish; also known as the ventral fins.

PENNELL TACKLE Two hook tackle, normally used for worm fishing, with the hooks tied to nylon one behind the other.

PHARYNGEAL Muscular membrane linking mouth and nostrils.

PICK UP Bale arm on a fixed-spool reel.

PINKIE The grub or larva of the greenbottle fly (*Diptera*). Small, tough maggots with a pinkie hue, used as hookbait or loose feed.

PITCH The angler's chosen fishing position on the river or canal bank or lake side.

PLANKTON (ZOO AND PHYTO) Minute animal and vegetable life organisms, free-floating and found in both salt and freshwater.

PLUGS Artificial lures, normally of wood or plastic used to imitate sick or injured fish. Mainly used for pike. They dive, sink or float, and are hinged in larger sizes, often carrying more than one treble hook.

PLUMBING Method for finding the depth of the swim, by attaching a lead to the hook. The float is adjusted until the accurate depth is found.

POINT The tip of a fly cast; usually refers to a tapered nylon cast when dry fly fishing, or the tail fly on a three fly wet cast.

PRICKED When a fish feels the hook, but is not actually hooked by the angler. Fish pricked in this way will seldom take a second time.

QUIVER TIPS Bite indicator at the end of the rod, screwed into the rod tip, which vibrates when a fish touches the bait.

PRIEST A weighted cosh used to kill fish humanely – perform the last rites.

RATCHET Check on a reel, which gives an audible warning as a fish takes line from the reel, and also acts as a drag against a powerful run.

RIG The terminal set up of tackle, including hook, weights, swivels etc.

RIM CONTROL The exposed rim of fly reel or centre-pin, which allows an angler to check the pull of a fish, adapting pressure variations continuously during the fight.

RINGS Circular guides through which the line is fed along the rod, giving a progressive curve when the rod is stressed during the playing of a fish.

ROACH POLE Multi-sectioned ringless rod, to which the fixed line is attached.

ROD REST Metal support for fishing rod, normally used in pairs by the coarse angler, to keep the reel clear of the bank debris, and adjacent to the angler's hand.

ROLL CAST Method of rolling the fly line off the water where trees or other obstructions prevent the angler from using the normal back cast.

SACANDAS (SARKANDAS) A type of reed from which float stems are made.

SALMONOIDEI (SALMONIDAE) Members of the salmon family.

SEDGES Waterside plants or flies of the *Trichoptera* order. Also known as caddis flies, they are related to some of the moths and are nocturnal by instinct, hatching out on warm evenings around dusk.

SHOT LOAD Amount of lead weight required to cock a float to its correct position.

SINKING LINE Fly line denser than water, which causes it to sink. Used for fishing lures, nymphs and wet flies.

SKIMMER Small common bream; also name given to awkward downstream wind.

SLIDER Another name for a sliding float, used for fishing deep water. The float slides on the line, stopped by a stop knot which can pass easily through the rod rings.

SLURRY Liquid, residual deposits, which washed from areas of pig farming can cause serious water pollutions particularly through a build up of phosphates.

SMOLT Immature salmon and sea trout following the parr stage, when the silvery-scaled fish make their way back downstream to the sea.

SNAP TACKLE Wire trace with treble hooks, for presenting a live or dead bait for pike.

SNOOD Nylon loop to which the hook is attached, which can be quickly attached to the terminal rig by means of split ring or swivel.

SPAWNING PELAGE Colouration of fish prior and during spawning. The male fish often assumes the more colourful roll.

SPECIMEN A large fish, relative to its average size for a particular water.

SPIGOT Ferrule-less joint between two sections of hollow glass or carbon to form a rod.

SPINNERS Metal artificial lures imitating small injured or sick fish, where the main blade or body revolves regularly around the axial mount.

SPIRAL Lead weight, where the line is wound around the body of the lead.

SPLIT CANE Rod material, formed by glueing a number of cane segments together. Heavier than glass or carbon, but giving excellent action, valued by the fly fisherman.

SPOONS Metal lures of varying shapes that tend to wobble rather than spin. Bladed spoons however do spin.

SPRING TIPS Form of quiver tip, utilising a tensioned spring to indicate the bite; more sensitive than fibre glass.

SQUATT The grub of the common housefly. The larvae are tiny, yellow coloured, normally used in groundbait, or on tiny hooks when small fish might help in a match.

SSG Size of lead shot

STEW Pond where fish are fed artificially, before releasing to the water where anglers can fish for them. Stewed wheat, is excellent bait for trotting, especially for autumn roach.

STOP KNOT Used to stop a float at a particular depth. (See slider)

STREAMERS Artificial lures or flies which imitate small fry.

STRET-PEGGING Float fishing in stages down a river, where the float is checked, and the bait fished over depth, laying on, progressively working downstream.

STRIKE The upward or sideways movement of the rod to set the hook.

STRIPPING LINE The action of a fish taking line through the rod rings, or by the angler working a fly back towards the rod, pulling line back through the rod rings.

SWG Standard wire gauge.

SWIM The angler's choice of fishing location, where he thinks fish should be lying.

SWIM FEEDER Small container attached to the line adjacent to the hook bait on a leger rig, filled with maggots, to allow free samples of the hook bait to trickle out.

SWING TIPS An arm, pivoted at the rod tip, which acts as a bite indicator, whether dropping or lifting depending upon how a fish swims off with the bait, or moves towards the angler.

SWIVEL Metal link which prevents line twist, used mainly in spinning or legering in running water.

TACKLE Collective term for angler's gear or a definitive rig, or terminal make-up.

TAKING SHORT Where fish aren't hooking themselves, although tentatively mouthing the bait. Happens mostly with larger baits, worms, or artificials.

TAPER The rate of reduction from butt to rod tip, of the blank diameter.

TELLTALE Tiny shot, fixed close to the hook which gives sensitive bite indication at the float if the fish lifts the bait.

TEMPER Quality of metal used in hook manufacture. Too highly tempered causes brittleness, while the opposite can result in soft hooks which straighten.

TERMINAL RIG The tackle make-up at the end of the reel line, which delivers and presents the bait to the fish.

TEST CURVE The amount of pull on a line which will curve a rod so that the tip and butt section are at right angles; used also to express the breaking strain suited to the rod.

THERMOCLINE Water layer subject to rapid temperature change.

TRACE Nylon or wire terminal tackle, attached to the reel line by link or swivel, and normally associated with spinning or deadbaiting.

TRAIL Hook length between leger weight or split shot, and hookbait which normally rests on the bottom.

TREBLE Three hooks on the same shank, normally used with lures, plugs and spinning lures, or when fishing dead or livebait. Also used for tube flies.

TROLL A lure or bait, spun behind a boat at varying depths and speeds.

TROT Working a bait, normally on float tackle, downstream at the pace of the current.

WEEDLESS SPOON A lure where the hooks are protected by a lightweight wire spring, which prevents snagging on underwater weed and reeds, but deflects when a fish strikes the bait, so that the hooks can penetrate.

WET FLY Artificial fly pattern, which fishes below the surface film, at varying depths.

WINGS Artificially formed wings on a fly pattern, made by matching paired segments from the wing feathers of various birds to represent the insect being imitated.

ZOOMER Antenna type float with built-in weight for long and accurate casting.

INDEX

bodied waggler, *50*, 51, 66
needle float, *50*, 51
stick float, *48*, 48-9, 64, 66
waggler, *50*, 51, 65, *69*
floats (slow-running water),
dart, 52
inert waggler, 52-3
onion, 52
straight antennae, 53
zoomer, 52
floats (stillwater),
antennae, *54*, 54-5
quill, 54, *54*
floatfishing,
carp, 130
from boat, 173
match rod, 42-3
roach pole, 43
tench, 136
trotting rod, 42
floatfishing (rivers and streams),
dace, 71
float paternostering, 68, 69, *70-71*
holding back, 68
laying on, 66, 68
perch, *70-71*
stret-pegging, 68
swimming, 64-6
trotting, 62-4
floatfishing (stillwater),
floating bait, 110
float paternostering, 110
laying on, 106, 110
lift float, 104-5
over-shotted float, 105
rudd, 137
sliding float, 112
slow-sinking bait, 105-6
weed problems, 110
wind action, 106
float paternostering,
perch, 69
rig, *70-71*
river, 68
stillwater, 110
flounder, 21, *22*, *98*
fly,
Alexandra, 196, 197
Black Gnat, 195
Black Pennell, 196
bucktail lure, 191
butcher, 196
buzzer, *194*, 195
Greenwell nymph, 195
grub, *194*
hairwing tube, *218*
Hardy's Gold, 196
Invicta, 196
nymph, *190*, *194*, 196, 197
Red Tag, *196*
reservoir lure, 197
salmon tube, 197
Soldier Palmer, 196, *196*
spider patterns, 196
tandem lure, *194*
Zulu, 196, *196*
flyfishing, *188-90*, 191-7
from boat, 173
fossil, fish, *10-11*

Foster, David, *13*
France, 201, 213, *210*, *212-13*
Franck, Robert, 13
free-lining, 79, 88
Freshwater Fishing (Falkus and Buller),
36
Friesland, 214, *214*

gaff, 87-8
Gardon, R., *212-13*
Garradice, Lough, *see* Lough
Garradice,
George Lake, *216*, *218*
Germany, 10, 212
Giethoorn, *214*
Giles, Ken, 65, 156, 183, *201*
Gjovik, 11
Grand Canal, *23*, *28*, 107
grasshopper, 100
grayling, 19, 34, *34*, 192-3
bait, 99, 100
Canada, 217
flyfishing, *190*, *195*, 197
record, 230, 231, 232
spinning, 82, 88-90
Grayling Zone, *18*, 19, 20, *21*
Grindsted, R., *204*, 206, *208*
groundbait, 27, 100
bream, 143
fishing from boat, *170*
lake, 113
legering, 77-8
match fishing, 179, *181*, 183, 185
rudd, 137
trotting, 63, *63*
grubs,
caddis, 100
docken, 99-100, 193
wasp, 99, 193
Guden, R., 206
gudgeon, 19, *34*, 35
record, 232
Guinness Guide to Coarse Fishing
(Currie), 192

'harling', 155, 158
hearing, fish sense of, 26
Hightae, 13
Hill, Alan, *155*
holding back (float fishing), 68
Holland, *198-9*, 201, 214-15
Lelystad Fish Farm, *222-5*
Holme Pierrepont, *23*
Holme, R., 206
Holsted, R., 205
Hoogeveense Vaart, *215*
hook, fish, 55-6, *55*, *56*
carp, 129
development of, 10-13, *12*
eyed hook, 55, *55*
faults, 56
flyfishing, 192
hook to nylon, 55, *55*
legering, 120
Mustad crystal, *55*
shapes, 56
spade end, 55, *55*
tench, 136
treble, 161

hookbait,
bait additives, 97
berries, 100
caddis grub, 100
crayfish, 100, *101*
daddy-long-legs, 100
docken grub, 99-100, 193
freshwater mussel, 100, *101*
freshwater shrimp, 100
grasshopper, 100
snail, 100
wasp grub, 99, 193
worm, 98-9
Houghton, The Rev., 109
hydro-electric plant, 18

ide, 19
Ireland, 14-15, 202, *202-3*
bait, 201
bream, 29, 108, *120-21*, 156
canal fishing, 107
carp, 135
dace, 33
highland lake, 22
roach, 36
rudd, 111
Irish Coarse Fishing Championship,
108
Irish Inland Fisheries Trust, 137
Isla, R., 193

Japan, 10
jigging, 86-7
Jutland, *148-9*, 205, *208*, see also
Denmark

Karup, R., 206
keepnet, *58*, 59
boat clamp, *174-5*, 175
King, Trevor, 108-9, *145*
kingfisher, *128*
Kirby, Charles, 13
Knipton Reservoir, *167*
knots, *186-7*
Kongeaand Ribe, 205

lake, fenland, 113
lake, highland, 22
lake, lowland, 22
Lake Mjosa, 12
lake, park, 23
lamprey, 26
landing net, 57, *57*, 59, 111, 141
bream, *140*
spinning, 87-8
Lanesborough, *60*, 65, 156
laying-on, 43
bream, 144
rivers, 66, 68
stillwaters, 106, 110
tench, 136
lead weights,
legering weights, 47
mouse droppings, 46, *46*
olivette, *46*, 46-7
rolling leads, 47
spinning leads, 47
split shot, 46, *46*, 225
static leads, 47

237

Index by Anna Pavord.

Conversion tables

These tables were devised by the Angling Trade Association with the Metrication Board, as an aid to retailers wishing to describe fishing tackle in metric measurement. The conversions are to the nearest convenient measure.

MONOFILAMENT LINES

conversions to nearest 50g:

½lb	0.25kg
¾lb	0.35kg
1lb	0.45kg
1¼lb	0.55kg
1½lb	0.70kg
2lb	0.90kg
3lb	1.35kg
4lb	1.80kg
5lb	2.25kg
6lb	2.70kg

conversions to nearest 500g:

7lb	3.00kg
8lb	3.50kg
9lb	4.00kg
10lb	4.50kg
11lb	5.00kg
12lb	5.50kg
14lb	6.50kg

conversions to nearest kg:

16lb	7kg
18lb	8kg
20lb	9kg
22lb	10kg
24lb	11kg
26lb	12kg
28lb	13kg
30lb	14kg
35lb	16kg
40lb	18kg
45lb	20kg
50lb	23kg
55lb	25kg
60lb	27kg
65lb	30kg
70lb	32kg
75lb	34kg
80lb	36kg
90lb	41kg
100lb	45kg

KEEPNETS

4ft 11in (5ft)	150cm
6ft 6in (6½ft)	200cm
8ft 2in (8ft)	250cm
9ft 10in (10ft)	300cm
11ft 6in (11½ft)	350cm
13ft 1in (13ft)	400cm

DIAMETERS OF NETS AND FRAMES

13¾in (14in)	35cm
15¾in (16in)	40cm
17¾in (18in)	45cm
19½in (20in)	50cm
21½in (21in)	55cm
23½in (24in)	60cm

LANDING NET LENGTHS

10in	25cm
12in	30cm
15¾in (16in)	40cm
19½in (20in)	50cm
21½in (22in)	55cm
23½in (24in)	60cm
25½in (26in)	65cm
27½in (28in)	70cm
29½in (30in)	75cm
35½in (36in)	90cm

LEAD WEIGHTS

⅛oz	3g	2½oz	70g
¼oz	7g	3oz	90g
⅜oz	10g	4oz	120g
½oz	15g	5oz	150g
¾oz	22g	6oz	180g
1oz	30g	7oz	210g
1¼oz	35g	8oz	240g
1½oz	40g	9oz	260g
1¾oz	50g	10oz	290g
2oz	60g		

RODS

conversions to the nearest 5cm:

5ft	150cm	10½ft	320cm
5½ft	170cm	11ft	335cm
6ft	185cm	11½ft	350cm
6½ft	200cm	12ft	365cm
7ft	215cm	12½ft	380cm
7½ft	230cm	13ft	395cm
8ft	245cm	13½ft	410cm
8½ft	260cm	14ft	425cm
9ft	275cm	14½ft	440cm
9ft 3in	280cm	15ft	455cm
9½ft	290cm	15½ft	470cm
9ft 9in	295cm	16ft	490cm
10ft	305cm	16½ft	505cm

ROD RINGS

Quoted by internal dimension in mm